Earnings
Interrupted

Ahmed Riahi-Belkaoui

ISBN: 1463621493
ISBN-13: 9781463621490

Introduction

The major threat to the quality of information is the phenomenon of earnings opacity. It is a measure that reflects how little information there is in a firm's earnings number about its true, but unobservable, economic performance. The questions which arises are: a) how prevalent is earnings opacity internationally, and b) what are the main causes of earnings opacity.

This books provides answers to both questions by showing that earnings opacity is prevalent internationally , has definite antecedents and consequences, and is due to fraud, slack behavior, income smoothing, and earnings management.

Chapter 1:

Antecedents and Consequences of earnings Opacity: Toward an International Contingency Theory

1. Introduction

The quantity and quality of accounting information is crucial to economic and human development internationally (Belkaoui and Maksy, 1985; La Porta et al., 1999a; Riahi- Belkaoui, 1995, 1996, 1998, 1999). The major threat to the quality of information is the phenomenon of earnings opacity. This may be easily defined as the measure that reflects how little information there is in a firm's earnings number about its true, but unobservable, economic performance (Bhattacharya et al., 2002). The variations in earnings opacity internationally suggest the presence of local factors that act as major determinants of its level and change, as well as the potential of affecting local economic, market, and governmental conditions that define the well-being of a country.

This paper posits that the level of earnings opacity internationally is not only the result of legal, religious, political, economic, social and accounting antecedents but also the determinant of consequences for the quality of the government, the productivity of nations, corporate valuation, and economic growth. To validate these relationships, the paper presents empirical evidence on the interactions between earnings opacity and a set of antecedents and consequences as a first step toward the development of an international contingency theory of earnings opacity.

In what follows, section 1 defines the concept and measurement of earnings opacity. The antecedents and consequences of earnings opacity are introduced in section 2. Empirical evidence on antecedents and consequences is presented respectively in sections 4 and 5. Section 6 presents a summary and conclusions.

2. Earnings Opacity: Concept and Measurement

The quality of accounting in a given country is measured by three dimensions of earnings opacity—*earnings aggressiveness, loss avoidance, and earnings smoothing*—where opacity is viewed as a complex interaction between the three factors of managerial motivation, accounting standards, and the enforcement of accounting standards (audit quality) (Bhattacharya et al. 2002). The level of earnings is opaque because: (a) the motivation of managers to manipulate earnings, (b) the accounting standards are either loose or just bad, and (c) the enforcement is lax. The three measures of earnings opacity derived from the study by Bhattacharya et al. (2002) are explained and measured as follows:

a. Earnings Aggressiveness: The opposite of accounting conservatism, earnings aggressiveness results from the tendency of managers to increase reported earnings numbers (to understand these managerial motivations, see, for example Teoh et al. (1998), Healy (1985)). Earnings aggressiveness is expected to be positively related to earnings opacity, as it may delay the realization of losses and speed the realization of gains. It is measured at a point in time as the median for country i, year t, of accruals divided by lagged assets.

Scaled accruals are defined as

$$ACC^{kt} = (\Delta CA^{kt} - \Delta CL^{kt} - \Delta CASH^{kt} + \Delta STD^{kt} - DEP^{kt} + \Delta TP^{kt}) / TA^{kt} \quad (1)$$

Where

ACC_{kt} = Scaled accruals for firm k, year t

ΔCA_{kt} = Change in total current assets for firm k, year t

ΔCL_{kt} = Change in total current liabilities for firm k, year t

$\Delta CASH_{kt}$ = Change in cash for firm k, year t

ΔSTD_{kt} = Change in current portion of long-term debt included in total current liabilities for firm k, year t

DEP_{kt} = Depreciation and amortization expense for firm k, year t

ΔTP_{kt} = Change in income taxes payable for firm k, year t

Ta_{kt} = Total assets for firm k, year t-1

The higher the median observation of scaled accruals of country i in year t, the higher is the earnings aggressiveness in country i, year t.

a. **Loss Avoidance Behavior:** It is the second measure of earnings opacity following evidence that U.S. firms engage in earnings management to avoid reporting negative earnings. Loss avoidance is measured by the ratio of the number of firms with small positive earnings minus the number of firms with small negative earnings, divided by their sum. The higher this ratio for country i in year t, the higher is the loss avoidance in country i, year t.

b. **Earnings Smoothing:** It is the third measure of earnings opacity as artificially smoothed earnings fail to depict the swings in underlying firm performance and increase earnings opacity. It is measured by the cross-sectional correlation between the change in accruals and the change in cash flows, both scaled by lagged total assets, in country i, for year t. The lower this correlation in country i in year t, the higher are the earnings smoothing in country i, for year t.

c. Battacharya et al. (2002) computed these three measures of earnings opacity for a sample of 36 countries for the years 1985 through 1998. An average of the three measures is used in this study as a measure of the earnings opacity and accounting quality for each country.

3. Antecedents and Consequences of Earnings Opacity

Earnings opacity is a pervasive phenomenon internationally. Although it is mainly an accounting phenomenon, it does not necessarily happen in a vacuum and is not without consequences. Basically, what is essentially viewed as an accounting phenomenon, is in fact the product of environmental causal factors or antecedents and is certainly the cause for many environmental situations or consequences. That is the essence of a contingency theory of earnings opacity, as the accounting phenomenon is assumed to be the result of specific causes and the reason or motivation for specific consequences.

Figure 1 depicts this assumed situation about earnings opacity internationally. These relationships of antecedents to earnings opacity and of earnings opacity to consequences are examined empirically as a first step to the validation of the contingency theory.

The antecedents to be tested are:

a. Law and Religiosity (Riahi-Belkaoui, 2004b),

b. Political Connectedness (Riahi-Belkaoui, 2004b),

c. Corruption (Riahi-Belkaoui, 2004), and,

d. Elements of social, economic, and accounting order (Riahi-Belkaoui and AlNajjar, 2006)

The consequences to be tested are:

a. Quality of Government (Riahi-Belkaoui, 2004),

b. Stock Market Wealth Effect and Economic Growth (Riahi-Belkaoui, 2005),

c. Productivity of Nations (Riahi-Belkaoui, 2004), and,

d. Investor Protection and Corporate Valuation (Riahi-Belkaoui, 2004),

The measurement of the antecedents, consequences, control variables and the list of countries examined are shown respectively in Tables 1-4.

4. Antecedents of Earnings Opacity Internationally

4.1 Law and Religiosity as Moral Values Earnings Opacity may be viewed as an international misreporting of the true economic earnings, and as such may be perceived as a less than acceptable practice. As it deviates from the truth, earnings opacity is likely to be viewed as unethical from the legal and religious viewpoints. One may argue that the degree of law enforcement and aspects of religiosity are likely to act as a deterrent to earnings opacity.

A. Earnings Opacity Model

Accounting is a function of its environment (Saudagaran and Meek, 1997; Wallace and Gernon, 1991). This suggests that the technical and social aspects of accounting are intricately linked and that the technical aspects cannot be studied by neglecting the social (Gernon and Wallace, 1995). The technical aspect is expressed by earnings opacity. A particular focus is that the social context is related to the law and religiosity components of the environment. This emphasis can be argued by referring to earnings opacity as a far from correct business behavior and outcome that can only be tempered by the pressures brought by both law and religion. In a sense, it can be argued that fear and/or guilt induced by law or religion lead to a lesser reliance on earnings opacity.

Earnings opacity reflects accounting and business cultures that are shaped by the legal and religious environment. Figure 2 indicates the relationships between earnings opacity and the main characteristics of the law and religiosity environment. That environment is depicted by both church attendance and belief in heaven. The legal environment is measured by the degree of law enforcement.

Each of these relationships is described as follows:

i. Religiosity:

The model posits a negative relationship between earnings opacity and religiosity as expressed by church attendance and belief in heaven. Religiosity means any shared set of beliefs, activities and institutions premised upon faith in supernatural forces (Iannaccone, 1998). Religiosity differs from culture as it bases its beliefs, activities and institutions on faith while culture bases them on habits and rituals. Religiosity acts as a club, a molder of behavior and a key component of systems of beliefs (Greif, 1994).

Religious people commonly strive to be truthful. It follows that if earnings management can be framed as a less than truthful outcome of the financial performance, we would expect earnings opacity to be negatively related to aspects of religiosity.

However, most theorists have attempted to explain religiosity by the secularization hypothesis (Weber, 1930). According to this hypothesis, economic development causes people to become less religious, as measured by church attendance and certain religious beliefs, and causes organized religion to play a lesser role in political decision making and in social and legal processes (Barro and McCleary, 2003). It follows from the secularization hypothesis that earnings management would not be affected by religiosity.

This study's suggested hypothesis of a negative relationship between earnings opacity and religiosity as expressed by church attendance and belief in heaven is an attempt to reject the secularization hypothesis. Church attendance and belief in heaven are chosen as aspects of religiosity as the first is considered an input of religion and the second is considered an output of religion.

ii. Law Enforcement:

- The model posits a negative relationship between earnings opacity and the degree of law enforcement. The rule of law was first seen as comprising three fundamental characteristics:

- the supremacy of law as opposed to arbitrary power, i.e., the rule of law, not men

- equality before the law of all persons and classes, including government officials

- The incorporation of constitutional law as a binding part of the law of the land (Dicey, 1915).

- The rule of law is assumed to have the beneficial consequence of producing both individual freedom and economic prosperity and to place inherent limitations on the size and scope of government intrusiveness in the economy and civil society. The rule of law requires that individuals be able to practically conform their behavior to the laws. In most countries the rule of law translates into a degree of law enforcement. In the context of a strong degree of law enforcement, managers feel more pressure to present information that is truthful, and therefore, resort to less opportunistic choices of accounting techniques, resulting in lower levels of earnings opacity. We predict that the degree of law enforcement predisposes to a lower level of earnings opacity.

B. Results and Discussion

To examine the determinants of earnings opacity, the following regression equation was used:

$$OEO^i = \alpha_1 + \alpha \ LPCGNP^i + \alpha \ MCA + \alpha \ BIH + \alpha \ DLE + \mu^i \quad (2)$$

Where:

OEO i = Overall earnings opacity measure for country i

LPCGNP = Log per capita GNP for country i

MCA = Monthly church attendance

BIH = Belief in heaven

DLE = Degree of law enforcement

Table 5 presents results regarding the impact of the selected variables on earnings opacity. The results and discussions are presented as follows:

i. Law Enforcement:

The degree of law enforcement is negative and significant ($t = -2.77$, $p = 0.001$). This finding conforms to the thesis that the high degree of law enforcement and the resulting increase in legal monitoring makes it necessary to follow the rule of law, thereby decreasing insiders' incentives to hide their rent-seeking activities and henceforth the level of earnings opacity. Thus, the higher the degree of law enforcement, the lower the earnings opacity in a given country. The major input of law—the degree of law enforcement—acts as a deterrent to the opportunistic use of accounting techniques in earnings management internationally.

11

ii. Church Attendance:

- The level of church attendance is negative and significant (t = -2.732, p = 0.05). This finding conforms to the thesis that church attendance, as an aspect of religiosity, may lead individuals to be more truthful in their behavior and actions, thereby decreasing insiders' incentives to hide their rent-seeking activities and henceforth the level of earnings opacity. Thus, the higher the church attendance, the lower the earnings opacity in a given country. This major input of religiosity—church attendance—also acts as a deterrent of the opportunistic use of accounting techniques in earnings management. It appears that the act of belonging, as expressed by church attendance, reduces the level of earnings opacity internationally.

iii. Belief in Heaven:

- Belief in heaven is positive but insignificant. This is not in conformity with the thesis that belief in heaven as an aspect of religiosity may reduce earnings opacity. It appears that the act of believing has no impact on earnings opacity. The act of *belonging* rather than the act of *believing* acts as a deterrent of earnings opacity. The results on both church attendance and belief in heaven can also be used to reject the secularization hypothesis.

4.2 Political Connectedness

While earnings opacity may just be viewed as a technical accounting matter, its excesses may be connected by the enforcement of laws. This calls for two possibilities:

(1) Where the enforcement of laws may not work effectively, as in the case of "political connectedness" of firms—i.e. Firms that benefit from government-created rents and protection. In this case of political connectedness, management may feel more empowered to be aggressive in their choices of accounting methods leading to a higher level of earnings opacity.

(2) Where the enforcement of laws may work even with instances of political connectedness as in the presence of market discipline. Where the percentage of market capitalization of connected firms is high, a lower level of earnings opacity may be expected, as better accounting quality may be required by market participants.

1. Earnings Opacity Model Based on Political Connectedness The political analyses of accounting [e.g. Miller, 1990; Arnold, 1991] argue that the technical aspects and political aspects of accounting are intricately linked in the sense that the technical cannot be studied by neglecting the political (Burchell et.al. 1980; Stulz and Williamson, 2001). In the context of this study,

the technical aspect is expressed by earnings opacity and it can only be studied in the total political context. It stems from a contingency theory of accounting that argues that accounting and its phenomenon are a function of its environment in general and the political environment in particular. (Gernon and Wallace, 1995, 1995; Wallace and Gernon, 1991). Applied to the context of this study, earnings opacity arises essentially from the political culture and environment in a particular country. Figure 3 indicates the hypothesized relationships between earnings opacity and the main characteristics of the political environment. The political environment is depicted by a) the percentage of politically connected firms, b) the connected firms as percentage of market capitalization, and c) the degree of law enforcement. Each of these relationships is describes as follows:

A. Percentage of Politically Connected Firms: The model posits a positive relationship between earnings opacity and the percentage of politically connected firms in a given country. Political connectedness of a firm is generally defined by the fact that a large shareholder (holding at least 10% of the votes) or top managers (i.e., CEO, president, vice- president or secretary) is a member of parliament, a minister (including the prime minister), or the Chief of the State (i.e., dictator, president, King or Queen), or is "closely-related" to a top politician. (Faccio, et. al 2002). The situation, known as "crony capitalism", implies that the dominant political leaders use their power to the advantages of their families and friends, individuals or firms, who benefit from government-created rents. It amounts to a form of capitalism in which politicians channel resources toward favored and connected firms, distorting incentives, misallocating investments, and increasing the extent of corruption (Scleifer and Vishny, 1994). The significance of the benefits extracted by connected firms is supported both in the U.S. (i.e., Agrawal and Knoeber, 2001; Ang and Boyer, 2000; Knozner and Stratmann, 1998; Roberts, 1990) and abroad (Fishman, 2001; Hellman, Jones and Kaufmann, 2000; Johnson and Milton, 2002). Faccio et al. (2002) finds that connected companies enjoy easier access to debt financing, lower taxation and stronger market power. However, in spite of these significant benefits, Faccio et al. (2002) finds that connected firms under perform their peers on an ex-ante basis. The end result of this situation is the potential for more aggressive opportunism from managers of politically connected firms in the form of shirking and sharking (Orts, 1958), and managerial rent- seeking (Edlin and Stiglitz, 1997; Shauer, 2000). The increase in opportunism also has important economic consequences (Gallabero and Hammon, 1998). To camouflage their bad performance and feeling empowered by their political connectedness, managers will likely resort to more alternations of firms' reported economic performance leading to an increase in earnings opacity.

B. Market Capitalization: The model posits a negative relationship between the connected firms as a percentage of market capitalization and the level of earnings opacity. The principal-agent conflict between the firm's insiders and its outside investors suggests that insiders are more inclined to mask firm performance to minimize outsider and/or legal intervention and/or to present a financial picture that can be deemed as financially attractive by outsiders. This "camouflage" activity is at the essence of the concepts and techniques of earnings opacity. The main private gain is the weakening of outsiders' ability to monitor and discipline insiders as a result of information asymmetries between insiders and outsiders created by earnings opacity. The only resources left to outsiders are to: (a) write contracts that confer them rights to discipline insiders (e.g. to replace managers), and/or (b) to vote with their feet and reinvest their capital on less earnings management prone firms. Both actions are more likely to depend on the level of market capitalization. Firms in general, and politically connected firms in particular, are more likely to be scrutinized by outsiders on all aspects of their activities, including the level of accounting quality they provide. One may argue that earnings opacity will be more widespread in countries where the politically connected firms have a low market capitalization.

C. Law Enforcement: The model posits a negative relationship between the degree of law enforcement and earnings opacity. The degree of law enforcement was first seen as comprising three fundamental characteristics: (a) the supremacy of regular law as opposed to arbitrary power, i.e., the rule of law, not men; (b) equality before the law of all persons and classes, including government officials; and (c) the incorporation of constitutional law as a binding part of the ordinary law of the land (Dicey, 1915). [1]Law enforcement requires that individuals and firms be able to practically conform their behavior to the laws. Therefore, managers of firms, including politically connected firms, feel the legal pressure to present information compatible with the law and degree of law enforcement. The higher the degree of law enforcement, the less likely managers will resort to opportunistic choices of accounting techniques, resulting in lower levels of earnings opacity. The prediction in this study is that the degree of law enforcement predisposes to a lower level of earnings opacity. [2]

2. Results and Discussion

To determine the impact of political connectedness, market capitalization of connected firms, and degree of law enforcement on earnings opacity internationally, the following regression was used:

$$OEO^i = \alpha_2 + \alpha\ PCLF + \alpha\ CFMC + \alpha\ DLE + U^i \qquad (3)$$

Where:

OEO i   = Overall earnings opacity measure for country i

PCLF I = Percentage of politically connected listed firms

CFMC I = Connected firms as percentage of market capitalization

DLE i   = Degree of law enforcement

Table 6, column 1, presents results on the impact of the selected variables on earnings opacity. The results and discussions are as follows:

A. Percentage of Connected Listed Firms: The impact of the percentage of connected listed firms is positive and significant level. ($t = 2.01$, $p = 0.05$). This is in conformity with our thesis that the high level of political connectedness leads to more managerial opportunism in general and an increase in earnings opacity. Managers of politically connected firms feel more empowered to hide their rent-seeking activities and henceforth the level of earnings opacity.

B. **Market Capitalization:** The impact of the connected firms as a percentage of total market capitalization is negative and significant ($t = -0.037$, $p = 0.05$). This conforms to a "diversion" thesis whereby insiders are more inclined to provide better quality accounting and less earnings opacity as the likelihood of outsiders scrutinizing their activities is higher with high market capitalization of the connected firms.

C. **Law Enforcement:** The impact of the degree of law enforcement is negative and significant ($t = -4.96$; $p = 0.01$). This very much conforms with the thesis that the higher degree of law enforcement and the implied penalties for failing to meet the legal requirements predispose to a lower level of earnings opacity.

The model is also expanded to investigate the potential impact of accounting order. The accounting order is measured by the following three variables

(1) **Auditing:** The relative number of auditors as a proxy for the demand for auditing discipline

(2) **Disclosure:** The amount of financial disclosure in a country as a proxy for accounting transparency

(3) **Accounting Standard:** The adoption of International Accounting Standards (IAS) as a proxy for demand for international accounting harmonization.

The model is also expanded by adding a dummy variable for the legal system (common law 1; civil law 0), and economic growth, measured by the real growth of GDP for 10 years.

The results of the expanded model in column 2 of Table 6 show that all the new variables added were insignificant and did not contribute to the original model. It seems that the manifestation of opportunistic use of accounting techniques– resulting in the level of earnings opacity observed– is independent of the quality of accounting order, the nature of the legal system and the economic growth rate.

4.3 **Corruption** The major premise of this section is that the level of corruption existing in a particular country is a major determinant of the level of earnings opacity since the illegal rents created by corruption need to be at most "camouflaged"; that is most feasible with earnings management. Accordingly, this section investigates whether the level of corruption in a given country affects earnings opacity in general or its components, namely, earnings aggressiveness, loss avoidance, and income smoothing.

A. Earnings Opacity and Corruption

Corruption exists in all societies and has a definite negative influence on investment, growth and the political behavior of citizens (Easterly & Levine, 1997; Ehrlich & Lui, 1999; Kaufman et al., 1999a; Knack & Keefer, 1995). It has been defined as the misuse of public or business office for private gain. The general consequences of corruption are the thwarting of growth and investment (Mauro, 1995), and the creation of a serious obstacle to attempts to consolidate democratic institutions and open market economies (Schleifer, 1997; Schleifer & Vishny, 1993).

One consequence largely ignored in the economic and accounting literature is the impact of corruption on the quality of accounting. One premise of this study is that the lack of corruption will decrease earnings opacity, used as a measure of the quality of accounting.

Two arguments may be used to justify this thesis of a negative relationship between the lack of corruption and earnings opacity as follows:

i. **Private Gains:** Corruption is the misuse of a public or business office for private gains. It involves transfer payments from bribe players to bureaucrats or business people. In a world in which the actions of a policy maker or bureaucrat (as well as their consequences) are only partly observable to citizens, the former have incentives to appropriate parts of the latter's income. This rent seeking behavior needs to be as "hidden" as possible and therefore needs a system of accountability flexible enough to "camouflage" the actions and consequences of corruption. It amounts to the need for a lower quality accounting to facilitate a higher level of corruption.

ii. **Unethical Atmosphere:** Corruption creates an unethical atmosphere that forces individuals to accept the appropriation of other people's income as acceptable. The low level of corporate ethics, resulting from corruption, extends easily to other activities involving the collection and dissemination of information in general and accounting information in particular. One would expect a low quality of accounting from a country that tolerates or fails to reduce corruption.

These two arguments imply that the level of accounting quality is a result of the level of corruption. One obvious manifestation of a low level of accounting quality is the high level of earnings opacity (Bhattacharya et al., 2002). Earnings opacity, like earnings management, may be defined as the alteration or design of a firm's reported economic performance by insiders to either "mislead some stakeholders" or "to influence contractual outcome" (Healy & Wahlen, 1999). It is conditional on the level of corruption prevailing in a particular country. Accordingly, to estimate the causes of variations in earnings opacity, we use the following regression model:

Earnings Opacity Index = $\alpha 0$ + $\alpha 1$ Lack of Corruption Index+ $\alpha 3$ Control Variables + $\varepsilon 1$ (4)

The model assumes a negative relationship between the level of earnings opacity and the level of the lack of corruption in a given country.

The following set of control variables is introduced to test the robustness of our measures:

i. "Economic Development," measured through the log of gross national product.

ii. "Human Development," measured by the U.N. Human Development Index (HDI) for 1998.

iii. "Size of Government,"

iv. "Economic Freedom." [3] The regression model in Eq. (1) was used to develop the following five models for estimating earnings opacity:

Earnings Opacity Index$_{EAG}$ = $B 0+ B 1$CORR   (4a)

Earnings Opacity Index$_{LA}$ = $B 0+ B 1$CORR   (4b)

$$\text{Earnings Opacity Index}_{ES} = B_0 + B_1 CORR \quad (4c)$$

$$\text{Earnings Opacity Index}_{AVR} = B_0 + B_1 CORR \quad (4d)$$

Where: EAG = earnings opacity as measured by Earnings Aggressiveness;

LA = earnings opacity as measured by Loss Avoidance;

ES = earnings opacity as measured by Earnings Smoothing;

AVR = average of EAG, LA, and ES;

CORR = indicator of subjective perceptions of Public Corruption.

$$\text{Earnings Opacity Index} = B_0 + B_1 CORR + B_2 logGNP + B_3 HDI + B_4 EFI + B_5 \frac{GE}{GDP} \quad (4e)$$

Where: log GNP = measure of economic development;

HDI = United Nations Human Development Index;

EFI = Economic Freedom Index;

GE/GDP = size of government as measured by government expenditures/GDP.

The first four models were used to test individual measures of earnings opacity based on earnings aggressiveness (EAG), loss avoidance (LA), earnings smoothing (ES), and the average of EAG, LA, and ES (AVR). The fifth model was used to test an overall measure of earnings opacity adding the control variables log GNP, HDI, EFI, and GE/GDP to CORR as dependent variables.

4 Results and Discussion

The results for model 1 through 4 are shown in Table 7. These results show that the individual earnings opacity measures based on earnings aggressiveness (EAG), loss avoidance (LA), earnings smoothing (ES), and average earnings opacity (AVR), have a significant negative relationship with the lack of corruption variable with an R^2 ranging from a low 12.8% in the case of loss avoidance, to a high of 27.8% in the case of the average earnings opacity. As hypothesized, the earnings opacity is negatively related to the lack of corruption in a given country.

Model 5 (equation 4e) introduces the four control variables to assess the robustness of the previous results. Economic development, as measured by log GNP, economic freedom, as measured by an index of economic freedom, and size of government, as measured by the level of government expenditures/GDP have a negative and statistically significant relationship with earnings opacity. These results suggest that the quality of accounting is increasing with the size of the economy, the level of economic freedom, and the size of the government. However, human development as measured by the UN Human Development Index has a positive and significant relationship, indicating that the quality of accounting is decreasing with human development. Model 5 registers a high ^{2} of 40.98%. The F statistics for the five models range from a low of 6.12 to a high of 14.89. The RESET (regression specification error list) as suggested by Ramsey (1969) and Thursby (1981,1985), and the Hausman test as suggested by Hausman (1978), were also used as specification tests. The results of the RESET test, used to check for omitted variables, incorrect functional form, and non-independence of regressors, show that the model used in this study was not mis-specified.

4.4   Elements of Social, Economic and Accounting Order

A.   Earnings Opacity Model

The socio-cultural and organizational analyzes of international accounting [e.g. Burchell et al., 1980;] argue that the technical and social aspects of accounting are intricately linked in the sense that the technical cannot be studied by neglecting the social

(Gernon and Wallace, 1995, p.58). In the context of this study, the technical is expressed by earnings opacity and it can only be studied in the total social context.

The contingency theory approach offers a systematic approach toward the conceptualization of the economic, social and accounting variables that may have a significant bearing on the differences in earnings opacity internationally. This relationship stems from the general theory that accounting and its phenomena are a function of its environment (Saudagaran and Meek, 1997; Wallace and Gernon, 1991).

Applied to the context of this study, earnings opacity arises from the accounting and business cultures that are shaped by the economic, social and accounting environment in a particular country. Figure 4 indicates the relationships between earnings opacity and the main characteristics of the economic, social and accounting environment. The economic environment is depicted by the economic growth and the economic freedom variables. The social world is depicted by the rule of law, the level of corruption and the quality of life variables. Finally, the accounting world is depicted by the level of reporting disclosure, the number of auditors and the adoption of international accounting standards. Each of these relationships is described as follows:

i. **Economic Order:** The model posits a positive relationship between earnings opacity and economic order as expressed by economic growth and economic freedom variables.

   a. **Economic Growth:** Economic growth creates not only opportunities for firms with good investment opportunity sets but also more competition. The increase in competition raises the probability of liquidation, may reduce the firm's profits and could make high managerial effort less attractive (Schmidt, 1997; Hermalin, 1992; Scharfstein, 1998). The end result is the potential for more opportunism from managers in the form of shirking and sharking (Orts, 1998), managerial rent- seeking (Edlin and Stiglitz, 1997; Shauer, 2000), and demands for golden parachutes. The increase in opportunism has not only important economic consequences (Gaballero and Hammom, 1998) but also specific effects on the cash compensation of executives (Matolcsy, 1999). It will likely lead to more alteration of firms' reported economic performance by insiders and an increase in earnings opacity.

   b. **Economic Freedom:** The model posits a potential relationship between economic freedom and the level of earnings opacity. The principal-agent conflict between a firm's insiders and its outside investors suggests that insiders are more inclined to mask firm performance to minimize outsider and/or legal intervention and /or to present a financial picture that can be deemed as financially attractive by outsiders. This "camouflage" activity is at the essence of the concepts and techniques of earnings opacity. The main private gain is the weakening of outsiders' ability to monitor and discipline insiders as a result of information asymmetries between insiders and outsiders created by earnings opacity. The only resources left to outsiders are to: (a) write contracts that confer them rights to discipline insiders (e.g. to replace managers), and/or (b) to vote with their feet and reinvest their capital on other less earnings management prone firms. Both actions are more likely to depend on the level of economic freedom. The level of economic freedom is found to cause economic growth and to facilitate the exercise of human and economic rights (Ali, 1977; Farr and Wolfernberger, 1988). Therefore, earnings opacity activities in the context of economic freedom call for two competing hypotheses as follows:

1. **Diversion Hypothesis:** One may argue that earnings opacity will be more widespread in countries with a low level of economic freedom. This "diversion" hypothesis is based on the thesis that insiders are more inclined to mask firm performance as the likelihood of outsiders exercising their economic rights is low.

2. **Penalty Hypothesis:** Similarly, one may argue that earnings opacity will be more widespread in countries with a high level of economic freedom where greater expected penalties are possible. This "penalty"

hypothesis is based on the thesis that the higher penalties existing in countries with a high level of economic freedom motivate insiders to hide their rent seeking activities.

Social Environment: The model posits a potential relationship between earnings opacity and the social environment as expressed by the rule of law, the level of corruption and the quality of life variables.

Rule of Law: The rule of law was first seen as comprising three fundamental characteristics: (1) the supremacy of regular law as opposed to arbitrary power, i.e., the rule of law, not men; (2) equality before the law of all persons and classes, including government officials; and (3) the incorporation of constitutional law as a binding part of the ordinary law of the land (Dicey, 1915). The rule of law is assumed to have the beneficial consequence of producing both individual freedom and economic prosperity and to place inherent limitations on the size and scope of government intrusiveness in the economy and civil society. The rule of law requires that individuals should be able to practically conform their behavior to the laws. However, in most countries the laws enacted for economic regulation of businesses create unnecessary burdens and accentuate the difficulty of doing business within the law (De Soto, 2000). In these contexts, managers feel more pressure to present information compatible with the excessive laws, and therefore, resort to opportunistic choices of accounting techniques, resulting in higher levels of earnings opacity. The prediction in this study is that the rule of law predisposes to a higher level of earnings opacity.

Corruption: The main result of ineffectiveness of government is the existence of corruption. Corruption is the misuse of the public offices for private gain. It involves transfer payments from bribe players to bureaucrats. In a world in which the actions of a policy maker or bureaucrat (as well as their consequences) are only partly observable to citizens, the former have incentives to appropriate parts of the latter's income (Adsera and Boise 2001). This rent seeking behavior made possible by and/or calls for "manipulating" the accountability measures used to evaluate the bureaucrat. Corruption appears as the result of a low level of accountability and accounting quality maintained in a particular country. Earnings opacity, a result of earnings management process, implies a low level of accountability and accounting quality. As a result, both managers in private firms and bureaucrats in public office benefit from the low accountability situation and the lack of transparency to engage in rent seeking behavior. Basically, insiders (i.e., managers and controlling stakeholders) engage in earnings management to mask their diversion and rent seeking activities from outsiders (Leuz, Nanda and Wysocki, 2001).

Consumption Goods vs. Public Goods: Accounting quality in general and earnings opacity in particular is a "good" created by the firm with the intent of influencing investor market and societal behavior. This question needs to be answered: "Is the quality of accounting an ordinary consumption good which managers should be free to select at will, or is it in some important sense a true 'public good'?" This study posits that the quality of accounting is both a consumption good for investors and a public good for everyone else. The society as a whole has an interest in ensuring the quality of accounting because everyone experiences the impact on their affairs and henceforth on their quality of life. Thus, having chosen a certain level of quality of life, a society will demand an appropriate level of accounting quality. This study advances the thesis that quality of life is negatively related to earnings opacity. The higher is the level of earnings opacity, the lower is the level of quality of life.

3. Accounting Order: The model posits a potential relationship between earnings opacity and accounting order. The accounting order is expressed by three variables: (a) the amount of public financial disclosure in a country as a proxy for accounting transparency, (b) the relative number of auditors as a proxy for the demand for auditing discipline, and (c) the adoption of international accounting standards (IAS) as a proxy for demand for international accounting harmonization. Briefly, the model uses the empirical findings of related research to posit that earnings opacity will be decreasing in disclosure level, number of auditors and adoption of IAS (Saudagaran and Meek, 1997; Wallace and Gernon, 1991; Gernon and Wallace 1995).

B   Quality of Life

Three known approaches are used to construct a composite index of the quality of life: (a) the Borda rules, (b) the Copeland rules and (c) the Paul Rues (Borda, 1785; Copeland, 1951; Paul, 1988; 2002). They are as follows:

i.   The Borda score of country i is given by

$$S_i = \sum_{k=1}^{m} S_k^i = \sum_{k=1}^{m} (n - a_i^k) \quad (5)$$

Where a_i is rank order of country i in respect of attribute k. A country performing best is given a rank of 1 and the one with worst performance is given a rank of n. On each attribute k a country which is performing best gets a score of n-1, performing second best gets a score of n-2, and so on until the worst performing country gets a score of zero. The scores are summed for all the attributes resulting in a Borda score for each country. These scores are then ranked to lead to a measure of quality of life based on the Borda rules. (Sen, 1981; Dasgupta and Weale, 1992).

ii. The Copeland rule ranks countries by their Copeland scores based on the majority criterion. If for a majority of attributes, the country i performs better then j, i is given a score of 1. If for majority of attributes, the country j performs better than i, i is given a score of -1. A tie leads to a score of zero. The sum of all the scores when i has compared with every j (J ≠ i) results in the Copeland score for i, i.e.

$$S_i = \sum_{j \neq 1} S_{ij} \quad (6)$$

Where

S_{ij} = 1 if $a^k_i < a^k_j$ for a majority of k

= -1 if $a^k_i > a^k_j$ for a majority of k

= 0 if a tie occurs.

iii. The Paul rule (1998; 2002) uses the following scoring function:[6]

$$S^k_{ij}(a^k_i, a^k_j) = a^k_j - a^k_i \text{ if } a^k_i < a^k_i \qquad j$$

$$= 0 \text{ if } a^k_i \geq a^k_j$$

Summing over all j gives the score of country i in respect of attribute k, and summing over all the attributes gives the total score of country i:

$$S_i = \sum_{k=1}^{n} S^k_i (a^k_i) = \sum_{k=1}^{m}\sum_{j=1}^{n} S^k_{ij}(a^k_i, a^k_j) \quad (7)$$

The countries are then ranked on the basis of their final score with the highest score ranking first. The three rules are used by Paul (2002) for an international comparison of the quality of life of 109 countries based on 9 important attributes of well being: (a) per capita GDP, (b) life expectancy in birth (years), (c) adult literacy rate (percentage), (d) infant mortality rate (per 1000), (e) number of people per doctor, (f) radios and televisions per 100 people, (g) telephones per 100 people, (h) index of political liberties and (i) index of civil liberties. The rankings provided by Paul (2002) are used in this study as alternative measures of quality of life.

C.   Results and Discussion

To examine the determinants of earnings opacity, the following regression equation was used:

$$OEO_i = \alpha_8 + \alpha_i ROL_i + \alpha_7 AU_i + \alpha_2 DISC_i + \alpha IAS_i + \alpha EF_i + \alpha_5 EG_i + \alpha_i Qualityoflife + M_i$$

Where:

OEO i = Overall Earnings Opacity measure for country i

ROL i = Rule of Law score for country i

AU i = Auditors per 100,000 population

DISC i = Disclosure Level from the Center for International Financial Analysis and Research

IAS i = Dummy variable for IAS use by a country i.

EF i = Economic Freedom score for country i

EG i = Average Annual Growth of GDP Per Capita over the 1985-1998 period

Quality of Life i = Quality of Life for country i measured as

(a) PR, using the Paul rules

(b) BR, using the Borda Rules, and

(c) CR, using the Copeland rules

Table 8 presents results regarding the impact of the selected variables on earnings opacity. The results do not differ between model 1, 2, and 3 where quality of life is measured either by the Paul rules, the Borda rules or the Copeland rules. The results will be discussed using the statistics provided in column 1 of table 7. The results and discussion are as follows:

i. **Rules of Law:** The impact of the rule of law is positive and significant ($t = 3.58$, $p = 0.01$). This is in conformity with our thesis that the high level of the rule of law and the resulting increase in regulation make it difficult to conduct business, to innovate and to meet profit targets. As a result insiders' incentives to hide their rent-seeking activities, and henceforth the level of earnings opacity are increased (De Soto, 2000).

ii. **Accounting Order:** The impact of the accounting order is positive but insignificant when measured by the number of auditors ($t = 1.06$), the level of disclosure ($t = 0.11$), and the adoption of IAS ($t = 0.87$). It seems that the manifestation of opportunistic use of accounting techniques, resulting in the level of earnings opacity observed, is independent of the quality of accounting order in terms of (a) the amount of public financial disclosure as a proxy of accounting transparency, (b) the number of auditors as a proxy for demand for auditing, and (c) the adoption of IAS as a measure of accounting harmonization with the rest of the world.

iii. **Economic Freedom:** The impact of economic freedom is negative and significant ($t = 3.85$, $p = 0.01$). Given that economic freedom is higher with higher scores, the results indicate that earnings opacity is more widespread in countries with a low level of economic freedom. This finding supports the "diversion" hypothesis whereby insiders are more inclined to mask firm performance as the likelihood of outsiders exercising their economic rights is low.

iv. **Economic Growth:** The impact of economic growth is positive and significant ($t = 1.99$, $p = 0.10$). These results conform to the thesis that the opportunism created by a more competitive environment, results in more alteration of firms' reported economic performance by insiders and an increase in earnings opacity.

v. **Quality of Life:** The impact of the quality of life is negative and significant ($t = 2.10$, $p = 0.05$). Given that the quality of life is rank ordered, these results are consisted with thesis that the higher level of accounting quality attained in a country, the higher is the demand for accounting quality and thus the lower is the earning opacity. As such accounting quality is a public good that is sought by countries seeking to preserve a given quality of life.

vi. **Corruption:** The impact of corruption is negative and significant (t = 2.19, p = 0.05). Given that the measure used reflects lack of corruption, the results are in line with thesis that the higher the level of corruption in a country, the higher is the level of earnings opacity. Basically, management benefits from the low accountability created by earnings opacity to engage in rent seeking behavior and corruption.

The results of Table 8 rely on White's (1980) adjusted standard error estimates to deal with heteroscedasticity. The Wald test for joint significance is reported in the Table. In addition, for the three regressions used, there is no evidence of serious multicollinearity among the independent variables. The RESET (regression specification error test) as suggested by Ramsey (1969) and Thursby (1981, 1985) and the Hausman test (1978), as suggested by Wu (1973) and Hausman (1978), were used as specification tests. The results of the RESET test–used to check for omitted variables, incorrect functional form, and nonindependence of regressors–how that the

models used in this study are not misspecified
(see diagnostic check statistics in Table 8).

5. Consequences of Earnings Opacity Internationally

5.1 Quality of Government The quality of government
refers to good government performance. Government
performance can be measured using, for example, measures of government intervention, public sector efficiency, public good provision, size of government, and
political freedom as in La Porta, et al. (1999), or using
measures of political accountability as in Adsera, et al.
(2001). Whatever measures used, there is strong evidence
of different government performances among countries
calling for research on the possible determinants of the
quality of government. Previous research relied on three
theories of determinants of institutional and more specifically government performance: economic, political,
and cultural (La Porta et al., 1999). Each of these theories can provide theoretical and empirical validation for
the choice of the determinants of the quality of government (North, 1990; Landes, 1998;). A variable that may
serve as a basis for the success of the cultural, political
and economic determinants is the quality of information in general and the quality of earnings in particular.
Briefly, an accounting order generating quality earnings
information is essential to the cultural, political and economic order and therefore may play a pivotal role in the
setting of government quality.

Accounting may provide a clear determinant of the quality of government through the salient role of the quality of earnings generated by economic firms in a particular country. To investigate this accounting relativism to the quality of government, we investigate the relationship between various measures of government effectiveness and the level of earnings opacity internationally.

A. Quality of Government: An Earnings Opacity Model

Theories of institutional development in general and quality of government in particular fall in three broad categories: economic, political and cultural. (La Porta et al., 1999). The focus is on social efficiency needs in the case of economic theories, redistribution towards powerful groups in the case of political theories, and social beliefs in the case of cultural theories. The main argument of the accounting relativism is that the three theories implicitly assume the positive role of accounting in general and the quality of earnings in particular. The thesis can be argued as follows:

i. **Economic Theory of Institution:** The economic theory of institutions assumes that institutions are efficient (Demsetz, 1967; North, 1990) and contribute to the quality of government. The argument is valid as long as the efficiency of

41

institutions is defined by an accounting order, a high level of quality of accounting information, and an accounting monitoring process (Prakash and Rappaport, 1975). Inefficient institutions are reflected in the lack of quality of accounting information in general and earnings in particular. Therefore, earnings opacity leads to inefficient institutions and to "bad" government.

ii. **Political Theory of Institution:** The political theory of institutions argues in general that some group in society becomes powerful enough to shape policies to its own rather than social advantage. The quality of government is then shaped by the ability of these players in extracting rents (Delong and Shleifer, 1993). To be able to extract rents without affecting political order and create unrest, these players need to "camouflage" their activities. Offering a lower level quality of accounting information in general and earnings quality in particular creates a more favorable environment to the extraction of rents by influential players, leading to a lower level of quality of government.

iii. **Cultural Theory of Institution:** The cultural theory of institutions argue that good government may be the result of pervasive and persistent beliefs and ideas generally referred to as "culture" (Putman, 1993; Coleman, 1990; Fukuyama 1995; Landes, 1998). For example,

Putman's theory states that trust in strangers facilitates collective action and the provision of public goods, while Landes argues that cultures of intolerance, xenophobia, and close-mindedness may retard development. Accounting relativism may argue that the quality of accounting information and the practice of public and fair disclosure may create a "cultural" environment more conducive to high trust and tolerant societies. In short, the quality of government is a result of cultural factors shaped by the role, importance and quality of accounting information in general and the quality of earnings in particular.

Accordingly, the following hypothesis is proposed: *"The quality of government is negatively related to the level of earnings opacity in a particular country."*

The control variables used include measures for market performance, economic freedom, newspaper circulation, and emerging versus developed countries. These variables are expected to control for economic, political and cultural factors assumed to affect the level of the quality of government.

B. Results and Discussion

Tables 9 to 14 present the results of the regression analyses. Each of these tables includes five models and a two year analysis for each model corresponding to the measurement of the dependent variable in 2001 and 1998.

Model 1 in each of these tables examines the relation between one of the measures of the quality of government and the level of earnings opacity.

The results show a strong negative relation between the level of earnings opacity and each of the six measures of the quality of government. These results are in line with the accounting relativism thesis advocated in this paper in the sense that countries that have a high level of earnings opacity, implying a low level of accounting quality, will exhibit a low level of quality in each of six government performance measures used. Basically, countries with low level of earnings opacity and high quality of accounting have more efficient governments in the sense of high voice and accountability, high political stability, high government effectiveness, high regulatory quality, high rule of law and high control of corruption.

Models 2 to 5 include the control variables of market return, economic freedom, newspaper circulation/population and emerging developing countries. Without exception, all these variables introduced separately show a positive and significant impact on each of the six measures of government performances.

The negative effect of earnings opacity on the six measures of government performance persists after the inclusion of these control variables.

5.2 Stock Market Wealth Effect and Economic Growth

The marked difference in growth rates among countries raises the empirical question, "What determines the rate of economic growth?" The debate on the question, taking place mainly in the economic literature, produced a variety of explanations such as macroeconomic stability, openness to international trade, institutional development, economic freedom and ethnic diversity (c.f Al Najjar, 2002; Karras, 2002). Research has also considered the impact of the level of accounting disclosure (Ndubizu, 1992; Riahi-Belkaoui, 1995: Larson, 1992). The research to date has not considered the single or combined effect of stock market wealth and earnings opacity, where earnings opacity is a measure that reflects how littler information there is in a firm's earnings number about its true, but unobservable, economic performance (Battacharya, et al., 2001).

Economic research assumes either that stock market wealth effect and earnings opacity, as a measure of accounting quality, are given or that the impact of both variables is inconsequential or both (Talaga and Ndubizu, 1986; Vishwanath and Kaufamnn, 1999; Stiglitz, 1975; Demirguc-Kunt and Maksimovic, 1998). We are warranted in using both earnings opacity (as a measure of accounting quality) and stock market performance (as a measure of the wealth effect) because accounting quality affects both stock market performance and overall economic growth (Prakash and Rappaport, 1975; Vishwanath and Kaufamn, 1999). Accordingly, this issue is addressed by modeling and testing two related questions: (1) How does earnings opacity affect stock market wealth? (2) Is there then a casual link between stock market wealth and economic growth?

The results of this empirical study on data from 34 countries indicate that (a) earnings opacity is negatively related to stock market wealth, and (b) exogenous component of stock market wealth—the component defined by earnings opacity-is positively associated with economic growth. The direct effect of earnings opacity on economic growth was negative but insignificant.

A.   Growth Model

The quality of accounting information plays an important role in the workings and efficiency of the capital markets by determining the supply and demand of securities (Prakash and Rappaport, 1975). Figure 5 indicates the relationships between accounting quality, stock market performance and economic growth. Four links comprise the model. They are explained next:

i. Conventional   Growth   Determination:
The first link is between conventional growth

determinants and economic growth. Standard growth models and their economic representations typically model real per capita GDP growth, ECG, as a function of a number of growth determinants. These growth determinants universally include initial income and initial level of human development (or education) to capture conditional convergence and the importance of human capital and other relevant variables, such as government expenditures (Levine and Servos, 1998; Levine, 1999).

ii. Market Wealth: The second link implies a positive effect of market wealth on economic growth. Various models emphasize that well-functioning financial intermediaries and markets ameliorate information and transaction costs and thereby foster efficient resource allocations, faster efficient resource allocation and hence faster long-run growth (Bencivenga and Smith, 1991; Bencivenga, et al., 1995;). This premise of a positive impact of banks and markets on economic growth is widely and empirically supported (Levine and Zervos, 1998; Arestis Demetriades and Lwintel, 2000; Rousseau and Wachtel, 2000; Atje and Jovanovic, 1993; Harris, 1997; Levine, 2001; Bekaert, et al., 2002; Henry, 2000).

iii. Earnings Opacity: The third link implies a negative relationship between earnings opacity and economic growth. Earnings opacity, as a measure of the lack of accounting quality, is assumed to be an important negative determinant of economic growth. This hypothesis is based on the following arguments: (Riahi-Belkaoui, 1995)

a. Information quality produced by the accounting system serves the economy by allowing for increases in the efficiency of resource allocation among competing interests (Talaga and Ndubizu, 1986; Larson, 1992).

b. An important element of the efficient capital market is the existence of a sophisticated accounting infrastructure comprised of the facilities of quality information production, the framework of information monitoring, and contract enforcement (Lee, 1987).

c. Quality of accounting information disclosed stimulates economic growth through its beneficial effect on the efficient capital market allocations of scarce resources (Ndubizu, 1992)

d. Quality of accounting is vital to the planning, decision making, performance evaluation and data-structuring process of various economic institutions vital to economic growth (Prakash and Rappaport, 1975)

e. Three alternative perspectives on accounting method choice—the opportunistic behavior, efficient contracting, and information perspectives-may be relevant to the accounting information quality thesis (Holthausen, 1990; Healey, 1985). The efficient contracting hypothesis implies that accounting methods are chosen in order to minimize agency costs among the various parties to the firm, hence resulting in maximizing the value of the firm (Watts, 1977). According to the opportunistic behavior perspective, the same choice allows managers to behave opportunistically to transfer wealth (Watts and Zimmermann, 1978). Finally, the information perspective implies that the accounting methods are selected to provide information about the future cash flows of the firms but do not affect them directly (Holthausen and Leftwich, 1983). The opportunistic behavior and efficient contracting hypotheses link accounting to cash flows and wealth transfer implying that accounting ultimately affects economic growth. Thus, countries with higher accounting information adequacy in terms of quality may be expected to experience greater economic growth.

iv. **Stock Market Performance:** The fourth link implies a negative relationship between earnings opacity and the characteristics of stock market performance. Evidence on this relationship exists in the pricing of accruals literature (Bowen, et al., 1987; Dechow, 1994). In the pricing of specific discretionary items, DeAngelo, DeAngelo and Skinner (1993) and De Chow(1994) document that the exclusion of special items improves the ability of earnings to explain returns. An emerging literature also presents international evidence on the relationship between earnings opacity and characteristics of stock market performance. Bhattacharya et al. (2002) document that an increase in earnings opacity is linked to a decrease in trading in the stock market of that country. Bushman et al. (2001) state that the cross-country differences in earnings opacity can be linked meaningfully to the cross-country differences in economic efficiency and institutional factors. This study extends this research and posits that the negative effect of earnings opacity on stock market performance influences the positive effect of the latter on economic growth. In other words, the exogenous component of the stock market wealth effect—the component defined by earnings opacity—is positively associated with economic growth.

v. A standard growth equation is used in this study (Levine and Servos, 1998; Levine, 1999_). Standard growth models and their economic representations typically model real per capital GNP growth, ECG, as a function of a number of growth determinants. Similarly to other studies, the growth determinants used include initial income and the initial level of human development to capture conditional convergence and the importance of human capital. To control for macroeconomic stability, government expenditures are included as a growth determinant. These variables are measured as follows:

1   Initial income as measured by the log of 1998 per capita GNP.

2   Initial level of human development as measured by the log of 1998 U.N. Human Development Index. It is generally a more realistic measure of human development than mere GNP per head (Riahi-Belkaoui, 2000).

3   Government expenditures are measured by the proportion of government expenditures over gross national product for the 1998-01 period.

B.   Earnings Opacity as a Determinant of Market Effect

To examine the impact of earnings opacity (a measure of accounting quality) on the stock performance (a measure of wealth effect), the following regression equation was used:

$$LMMR_i = \alpha_1 + \alpha LPGNP + \alpha LDYDG + \alpha LODO + \mu_i \qquad \text{(a)}$$

Where

LMMRi   = Logarithm of one plus mean monthly returns scaled by the standard deviation of returns for country i for 1986-98.

LPGNPi = Logarithm of 1998 per capita GNP for country i

LDYDGi = Logarithm of one plus mean monthly dividend yield over dividend growth for country i for 1986-98.

LOEOi = Logarithm of overall earnings opacity measure for country i

Both LPGNP and LDYDG were included in equation (a) to control for both country size and dividend policies and are expected to be positively significant (Levine, 1999; Bhattacharya, 1979). Table 15 presents results regarding the empirical connections between earnings opacity and stock market performance. Consistent with our predictions, countries with higher earnings opacity tend to have lower stock market performance. The coefficient of earnings opacity is equal to -0.1474, has a t-value of -2.14, which is significant at a 0.05 level. The relative impact of earnings opacity is evident by the 8% increase in R^2 from model 1 to model 2. As predicted, both control variables (LPGNP and LDYDG) are positive and significant.

C. Causality: Earnings Opacity, Stock Market Effect and Economic Growth

This section examines the impact of earnings opacity on stock market performance by using the earnings opacity as an instrumental variable for stock market performance. We examine two research questions: (a) whether the exogenous component of stock market performance is positively associated with economic growth, and (b) whether earnings opacity also has a direct and negative association with economic growth.

i. Stock Market Effect and Economic Growth: The first research question is examined by running the following regression

$$ECG_i = \alpha_0 + \alpha_1 LGNP + \alpha LHDI_i + \alpha_3 \frac{LGC}{GDP_i} + \alpha_4 ELMMR_i + \mu_i \qquad (10)$$

Where

ECG_{ii}	= GNP growth for the 1998-01 period for country i
$LGNP_{ii}$	= Log of 1998 per capita GNP for country i
$LHDI_{ii}$	= Log of 1998 human development index for country i
LGC/GDP_{ii}	= Log of government expenditures over GDP for the 1998-01 period for country i

ELMMRii   = Estimated stock market performance
from equation (1) The choice of the
1998-01 period for the measurement of GNP growth is motivated
by the thesis that the impact of earnings opacity on economic growth
is lagged (Riahi-Belkaoui, 2002;
2003)

As shown in Table 16 the estimated stock market performance enters the growth regression significantly
at the 0.01 level. Thus, the data are consistent with
the view that the quality of accounting, as measured
by earnings opacity, induces improvements in the
stock market performance that accelerate economic
growth.

ii. **Direct Earnings Opactiy on Economic Growth:**
Equation (10) does not include the hypothesized
negative effect of earnings opacity on economic
growth. This possible relationship is examined by
an extension of equation (2) as follows:

$$ECG_i = \alpha_3 + \alpha\ LGNP + \alpha\ LHDI^2 + \alpha\ \frac{LGC}{GDP_i} + \alpha\ ELMMR + \alpha\ LOEO + \mu_i \quad (11)$$

Equation (11) extends equation (10) by including the
potential direct effect of earnings opacity on economic
growth. Table 16 presents results that confirm the
earlier findings, namely, that stock market effect has a

positive association with economic growth. However the coefficient of earnings opacity, although negative as expected, is not significant. The data rejects the hypothesis of a significant negative relationship between lack of accounting quality and economic growth. The regression was also run with alternative measures of the financial reporting en lieu of earnings opacity. The results were insignificant with the use of (a) the number of auditors per 100,000 population (Saudagaran and Diga, 1997), (b) a disclosure level variable (Center for International Financial Analysis and Research, 1995) and (c) the extent of compliance with international accounting standards (Choi, Frost and Meek, 1999).

D. Sensitivity Analysis

A first concern in this study is with the choice of a lagged relationship between economic growth and both wealth effect and earnings opacity. The regressions were run again with economic growth measured for the 1985-1998 period to correspond to the same period of measurement of stock market performance and earnings opacity. The results were insignificant in support of the lagged relationship. Similarly, a dummy variable used to distinguish between developed and emerging countries was found to be insignificant for all the regressions used in Tables 15 and 16.

The second concern in this cross-country analysis is with country fixed effects resulting from the omission of an important variable, which is actually driving the observed results. Following previous economic growth studies, we included the following explanatory variables to test the robustness to changes in the standard set of economic determinants: (a) economic freedom index from *Economic Freedom of the World* (Gwartney, Lawson and Block, 1995), (b) estimates of unofficial economy (Friedman, Johnson, Kaufman and Zoido-Lobatin, 2000) and (c) six basic governance concepts: voice and accountability, political instability and violence, governmental effectiveness, regulatory burden, rule of law and graft or corruption (Kaufman, Kray and Zoido-Lobatin, 1999). Each of these variables is used to examine the robustness of this study's results by controlling for: (a) lack of economic freedom, (b) level of unofficial economies, and (c) governmental effectiveness. Including these additional explanatory variables did not alter this study's findings that: (a) the exogenous component of stock market development as defined by earnings opacity is positively associated with economic growth, and (b) that the direct and negative effect of earnings opacity on economic growth is statistically insignificant. The results of both Tables 15 and 16 rely on White's (1980) adjusted standard error estimates to deal with heteroscedasticity. The Wald test for joint significance is reported in both tables. In addition, for all the regressions used, there is no evidence of serious multicollinearity among all the independent variables. The RESET (regression specification error test), as suggested by Ramsey (1969) and

Thursby (1981, 1985) and the Hausman test (1978), as suggested by Wu (1973) and Hausman (1978), were used as specification tests. The results of the RESET test, used to check for omitted variables, incorrect functional form, and nonindependence of regressors, show that the models used in this study are not misspecified (see diagnostic check statistics in both Tables 15 and 16).

5.3   Productivity of Nations

Productivity, in terms of output per worker, differs from one nation to another. One fundamental challenge of economic research is to explain the large differences in productivity internationally. Our hypothesis is that differences in output per worker are fundamentally related to differences in earnings opacity across countries. A low earnings opacity as a result of high accounting quality provides an environment that supports productive activities and encourages capital accumulation, skill acquisition, and technology transfer. What are the implications of earnings opacity? The results of this study make a case that the ability of accounting quality, resulting from a low earnings opacity, to correctly and fairly portray the output of individual productive units and to reduce opportunistic behavior by management, is important. Earnings opacity results from insiders (i.e., managers and controlling shareholders) engaging in earnings management to mask their diversion and rent- seeking activities from workers and outsiders. Accounting is assumed to protect against these activities of diversion, but it all too often constitutes the chief vehicle of diversion in the economy. Across 34 countries, we find negative association between output per worker and earnings opacity in a given country. Countries with low earnings opacity scores produce much more output per worker. Important insights into differences in output per worker can also be obtained by fitting a production function (Jones and Hall, 1997). The differences in output per worker among countries are attributed to differences in physical capital, human capital, and productivity. The impact of earnings opacity on capital intensity, human capital per worker and productivity was also significantly negative. Earnings opacity with the addition of control variables explains more than 58% of the variations in output per worker, more than 18% of capital intensity, more than 44% of human capital per worker, and more than 16% or productivity. The analysis of the determinants of differences in economic performance among countries can be summarized as follows:

Output per worker ← (Inputs, Productivity) → Earnings Opacity

A. Earnings Opacity Model The main danger to productive activities is predation or diversion. Where predation or diversion are prevalent, the individuals and/or the firms will spend more of their time protecting their assets rather than using them for productive activities. Where diversion is socially controlled, the main benefits are better rewards for producers and more resources devoted to production. The main assumption in the economic literature is that social action through government is essential to the promotion of output per worker (see example, Ohlson, 1965; 1982; Baumol, 1990; North, 1990; Grief and Kandel, 1995; and Weingast, 1995). Theoretical models of equilibrium assume protection against predation is incomplete and workers choose between production and diversion (See for example, Murphy, Shleifer and Vishny, 1991; Acemoglu, 1995; Schrag and Scotchmer, 1993; Ljungqvist and Sargent, 1995; Grossman and Kin, 1996). Poor equilibrium is possible with little payoff for production and high payoff for diversion if enforcement is ineffective.

Good equilibrium is possible for high payoff for production and little payoff for diversion if law enforcement is effective (Rapaczynski, 1987). To suppress diversion that takes place in the form of rent seeking, Jones and Hall (1997) advocate the creation of a good social infrastructure, meaning the institutions and government policies that constitute the economic environment within which individuals accumulate skills, and firms accumulate capital and produce output (Jones and Hall, 1997). Their empirical results show that a high- productivity country: (a) has institutions that favor production over inversion, (b) has a low rate of government consumption, (c) is open to international trade, (d) has at least some private ownership (e) speaks an international language, and (f) is located in a temperate latitude far from the equator. The essence of the argument is that a favorable social infrastructure helps a country both by stimulating the accumulation of human and physical capital and by raising total productivity. This study takes the view that accounting equality is an essential element of the social infrastructure. Basically where social actions by government may prove ineffective in dealing and suppressing diversion, accounting quality is paramount in providing the information needed to restore confidence and promote productive activities. Where managers of firms engage in the alteration of firms' reported economic performance to either mislead some stakeholders or to influence contractual outcomes (Healey and Wahlen, 1999), earnings opacity results. With earnings opacity, insiders can camouflage their diversion and rent-seeking activities, and in the process create conditions less favorable to production. Where workers may feel that they are not getting their just rewards as a result of earnings opacity, they may act in non-productive ways. Basically with earnings opacity, poor equilibrium is possible with little payoff for production and high payoff for diversion.

This section analyzes the relationship between economic performance and earnings opacity. The main expectation is of negative relationships between earnings opacity and each of the following measures of economic performance: (a) output per worker, (b) capital intensity, (c) human capital per worker and (d) productivity. Our analysis of the determinants of differences in economic performance among countries can be summarized as follows:

Output per worker (Inputs, Productivity) Earnings Opacity

Our analysis is based on a dataset of measures of output per worker, capital intensity, human capital per worker, productivity and control variables in 34 countries. The dependent variables were based on output per worker from the Summers and Heston data. The output per worker data was decomposed into inputs and productivity based on a Cobb-Douglas approach. The production function in terms of output per worker, Y/L is written as

$$Y/L = \left(\frac{K_i}{Y_i}\right)^{\alpha(1-\alpha)} h_i A_i \quad (12)$$

Where:

H	= H/L= human capital per worker
K_i	= the stock of physical capital
H_i	= the amount of human capital-augmented labor used in production
A_i	= labor-augmenting measure of productivity
$(K/Y)^{\alpha/1-\alpha}$	= Capital intensity

This study used Y/L, H/L, (K/Y) $^{a/1-a}$ and A as the dependent variables denoting respectively output per worker, human capital per worker, capital intensity and productivity.

For the main independent variable of earnings opacity, we rely on the data used by Bhattacharya et al. (2001). They computed three measures of earnings opacity for a sample of 34 countries for the years 1985 through 1988. These measures are as follows:

(a) **Earnings Aggressiveness** which results from the tendency of managers to increase reported earnings,

(b) **Loss Avoidance Behavior** following evidence that firms engage in earnings management to avoid reporting negative earnings, and

(c) **Earnings Smoothing** since artificially smoothed earnings fail to depict the savings in underlying firm performance and increase earnings opacity.

An average of these three measures is used in this study as a measure of earnings opacity. The control variables used include ethnic fractionalization and company law. These variables are expected to control for major aspects that can affect the social infrastructure of a country (La Porta et al., 1999; Jones and Hall, 1997).

C. Regression Results and Discussion Tables 17-20 present respectively the results of the regression analysis on the impact of earnings and selected control variables on output per worker, capital intensity, human capital per worker, and productivity. Each of the tables includes a column on the sample impact of earnings opacity and a second column that adds the impact of the control variables. As expected and in conformity with our thesis, the level of earnings opacity in a country has a significantly negative impact on output per worker, capital intensity, human capital per worker and productivity. It also explains more than 39% of the level of output per worker, more than 10% of capital intensity, more than 18% of human capital per worker, and more than 18% of productivity. (Tables 17 to 20 respectively) The impact of the control variables is mixed. In the case of the level of output per worker, the control variables of ethnic fractionalization and legal origin are significantly negative. Combined with earnings opacity, they explain 58% of the level of output per worker. (See Table 17) In the case of capital intensity, only the ethnic fractionalization is negatively significant. The control variables, combined with earnings opacity, explain more than 18% of capital intensity. (See Table 18) In the case of human capital per worker, both control variables are negatively significant. Combined with earnings opacity, they explain more than 44% of the level of human capital per worker. (See Table 19) In the case of productivity, the control variables are not significant. The negative impact is restricted to earnings opacity. The basic results as reported in Tables

17-20 support our hypothesis that a low earnings opacity is critical to economic success, whether it is measured by the output per worker, capital intensity, human capital per worker, or productivity. This economic success can be intensified by a reduced ethno linguistic fractionalization and the choice of a legal system more compatible with common law rather than civil law.

5.4   Investor Protection, Earnings Opacity and Corporate Valuation

Investor protection has been examined in the accounting and finance literature as either a determinant of corporate value and/or earnings opacity.

The finance literature presents results suggesting that the legal protection of outside investors is a key determinant of market development, capital and ownership structures, divided policies, and private control benefits around the world (for surveys see Schleifer and Vishny, 1997 and La Porta et al., 2000a). Of interest to this study is the evidence of a positive relationship between investor protection and corporate valuation. More specifically, La Porta et al., (2002) find evidence of higher valuation of firms in countries with better protection of minority shareholders and in firms with higher cash flow ownership by the controlling shareholder.

The accounting literature examined and found evidence on the relation between outside investor protection and earnings management (Leuz et al., 1999), accounting and auditing (Francis et al., 2001) and corporate transparency (Bushman et al., 2001).

Investor protection was expressed in terms of either the nature of legal systems, common versus civil law, and/ or in terms of specific measures used such as an index of anti-director rights. This section argues that earnings opacity is a function of the specific measures used to protect investors rather than of the nature of the legal system while corporate valuation is a function of both the nature of the legal system while corporate valuation is a function of both the nature of the legal system as a measure of investor protection and earnings opacity as a measure of accounting quality. We choose to address this argument by modeling and testing two related questions: (1) How does investor protection, as measured by an anti-director rights index, affect the level of earnings opacity? And (2) Is there then a causal link between earnings opacity and corporate valuation?

The results of this empirical study on data from 24 countries indicate that (a) anti-director rights is positively related to earnings opacity in line with a penalty hypothesis, and (b) the exogenous component of earnings opacity—the component defined by anti-director rights—is negatively related to corporate valuation. The direct effect of civil law on corporate valuation was also negative and significant.

A. Corporate Valuation Model Two factors are assumed to have an impact on corporate valuation: (a) investor protection, as measured by the nature of the legal system and an anti-director rights index, and, (b) accounting quality, as measured by earnings opacity.

Figure 5 indicates the potential relationships between investor protection, earnings opacity and corporate valuation. Three links comprise the model. They include:

i. **Legal System:** The first link is between corporate valuation and the nature of the legal system. This follows from the findings that systematic differences among countries in the structure of laws and their enforcement, such as the historical origin of their laws, account for the differences in financial development (La Porta et al. (1997, 1998). A law system geared to the protection of the rights of investors and the limitation of expropriation is bound to lead outside investors to pay more for financial assets such as equity and debt, raising in the process the price that such securities fetch in the marketplace. Consisting with this thesis, La Porta et al. (2002) find evidence of higher valuation of firms in countries with better protection of minority shareholders and in firms with higher cash flow ownership by the controlling shareholder. Given the evidence that countries with the common law legal origin have better protection of minority shareholders than do countries with civil law legal origin (La Porta et al. 1998), and better corporate valuation (La Porta et al. 2002), this study hypothesizes that corporate valuation will have a negative relationship with a variable depicting a civil law legal origin.

ii. **Corporate Valuation:** The second link implies a negative relationship between earnings opacity and corporate valuation. Evidence on this relationship exists in the pricing of accruals literature (Bowen, et al., 1987). In the pricing of specific discretionary items, DeAngelo, et al. (1993) and DeChow (1994) document that the exclusion of special items improves the ability of earnings to explain returns. An emerging literature also presents international evidence on the relationship between earnings opacity and characteristics of stock market performance. Bhattacharya et al. (2002) document that an increase in earnings opacity is linked to a decrease in trading in the stock market of that country. Bushman and Smith (2001) state that the cross-country differences in earnings opacity can be linked meaningfully to the cross-country differences in economic efficiency and institutional factors. This study extends this research and tests the negative effect of earnings opacity on corporate valuation.

iii. **Director Rights:** The third link is between anti-director rights, as a measure of investor protection and the level of earnings opacity. The principal-agent conflict between firm's insiders and outside investors suggests that insiders are more inclined to mask firm performance to minimize outsider and/or legal intervention, and/or present a financial picture that can be deemed as financially attractive by outsiders. This "camouflage" activity is at the essence of the concepts and techniques of earnings opacity. The main private gain is the weakening of outsiders' ability to monitor and discipline insiders as a result of information asymmetries between insiders and outsiders created by earning opacity. The only resources left to an outsider are (a) to write contracts that confer to them rights to discipline insiders (e.g. to replace managers), and/or (b) to vote with their feet and reinvest their capital in other less earnings opacity prone firms. Both actions are likely to depend on the level of investor protection in general and of anti-director rights in particular. The level of anti-director rights typifies the level of the quality of enforcement of investor protection that potentially affects insiders' incentive to manage accounting earnings. Therefore, earnings opacity activities in the context of anti-director rights call for two competing hypothesis as follows:

a. **Diversion Hypothesis:** One may argue that earnings opacity will be more widespread in countries with low level of anti-director rights. This "diversion" hypothesis is based on the thesis that insiders are more inclined to mask firm performance as the likelihood of outside investors exercising their protection rights is low.

b. **Penalty Hypothesis:** Similarly, one may argue that earnings opacity will be more widespread in countries with high level of anti-director rights. This "penalty" hypothesis is based on the thesis that the higher penalties existing in countries with a high level of anti-director rights motivate insiders to hide their rent seeking activities.

This study extends prior research on the relationship between investor protection and earnings opacity (Francis et al. 2001) by testing whether the positive or negative effect of anti-director rights on earnings opacity influences the negative effects of earnings opacity on corporate valuation. In other words, the exogenous component of the earnings opacity effect—the component defined by anti-director rights—is negatively associated with corporate valuation.

The dependent variable of corporate valuation is Tobin's q provided by La Porta et al. (2002) for their sample of 539 firms. Two variables were used for the measurement of investor protection, namely the nature of the legal system and an anti-director rights index (La Porta et al. 2002). The nature of the legal system was measured by a dummy variable equal to one if a country's company law or commercial code is of civil origin, and zero otherwise. Because of the small sample size, no distinction was made between French, German, and Scandinavian civil laws origin. The second measure of investor protection is the index of anti-director rights from La Porta et al. (1998 a) and La Porta et al. (2002).

The quality of accounting in a given country is measured by three dimensions of earnings opacity, earnings aggressiveness, loss avoidance, and earnings smoothing.

B.   Anti-director Rights as a Determinant of Earnings Opacity

To examine the impact of anti-director rights (as a measure of investor protection) or the level of earnings opacity (as a measure of accounting quality), the earnings opacity score was regressed against the anti-director rights score and the three control variables: (a) market share of world's capital, (b) number of auditors per 100,000 population, and (c) disclosure level. The three control variables were included in the regression based on the thesis that the larger the market capitalization compared to the world's market, the level of the auditing force and the level of disclosure adequacy, the lower will be the level of earnings opacity (Francis et al., 2001).

Table 21 presents results regarding the empirical connections between earnings opacity and anti-director rights. The results show a positive relation between anti-director rights and earnings opacity. The higher the control on directors, the higher the level of earnings opacity. This conforms with the penalty hypothesis whereby the higher penalties associated with higher anti-director rights moti-vate insiders to hide their rent seeking activities, resulting in higher levels of earnings opacity. As expected, the control variables of market share of world's capital, the number of auditors per 100,000 population and the disclosure level were negative and significant at the 0.05 level.

C. Causality: Corporate Valuation, Earnings Opacity, and Investor Protection

To examine the impact of earnings opacity and inves-tor protection on corporate valuation, two models were tested.

Model 1 regresses the dependent variable of Tobin's Q on (a) civil law, (b) estimated earnings opacity from the regression results presented in Table 21, and (c) the interaction between civil law and the estimated earnings opacity model. This model is used to test if both civil law and the exogenous component of earnings opacity—the component defined by anti-director rights—are negatively related to Tobin's Q.

Consistent with our predictions, Table 22 presents results indicating negative significant relations between Tobin's Q and both civil law and estimated earnings opacity at a 0.01 level. As expected, the interaction effect is positive and significant at 0.01 level. Thus, the results are consistent with the view that both the civil law origin and the level of earnings opacity have a negative effect on corporate valuation measured by Tobin's Q.

Model 2 adds the anti-director rights as an independent variable to test the incremental and direct impact of this variable. Column 2 of Table 22 presents results that confirm the earlier findings–namely, earnings opacity leads to lower valuation. However the coefficient of anti-director rights is not significant, rejecting the thesis of a potential direct impact on corporate valuation.

D. Sensitivity Analysis

The main concern in this cross-country analysis is with country fixed effects resulting from the omission of an important variable which is really driving the observed results. Following previous studies, this study included the following explanatory variables to test the robustness to changes in the standard set of economic determinants: (a) economic freedom index from *Economic Freedom of the World* (Gwartney, Lawson and Block, 1995), (b) estimates of unofficial economy (Friedman, Johnson, Kaufman and Zoido-Lobation, 2000) and (c) six basic governance concepts: voice and accountability, political instability and violence, governmental effectiveness, regulatory burden, rule of law and graft or corruption (Kaufman, Kray and Zoido-Lobation, 1999 a, b).

Each of these variables is used to examine the robustness of this study's results by controlling for (a) lack of economic freedom, (b) level of unofficial economies, and (c) governmental effectiveness. Including these additional explanatory variables did not alter this study's findings that (a) the exogenous component of earnings opacity as defined by anti-director rights is positively associated with corporate valuation (b) and that the direct and of anti-director rights in corporate valuation is statistically insignificant.

The results of Tables 21 and 22 rely on White's (1980) adjusted standard error estimates to deal with heteroscedasticity. The Wald test for joint significance is reported in both tables. In addition, for all the regressions used, there is no evidence of serious multicollinearity among the independent variables.

The RESET (regression specification error test) as suggested by Ramsey (1969) and Thursby (1981, 1985) and the Hausman test (1978), as suggested by Wu (1973) and Hausman (1978), were used as specification tests. The results of the RESET test, used to check for omitted variables, incorrect functional form, and nonindependence of regressors, show that the models used in this study are not misspecified (see diagnostic check statistics in both tables).

6. Summary and Conclusions

This paper views the empirical relations between earnings opacity and its antecedents and consequences as a first step towards the development of an international contingency theory of earnings opacity. The main findings and conclusions are shown in Figure 6 and explained as follows:

1. **Law and Religiosity:** It appears that the inputs of both law and religiosity-namely the degree of law enforcement and church attendance are negatively related to earnings opacity. Basically, the fear of the law and the act of belonging to a religion played a deterrent effect on earnings opacity internationally as a result of a decrease in insiders' incentives to hide their rent seeking activities. Belief in heaven, the output of religiosity, did not have a significant impact on earnings opacity pointing to a greater role of the act of belonging than the act of believing.

The main implication of the findings is that the moral and penalty constraints created by law and religiosity appear to be more conducive to the supply of more accountability and higher quality of earnings. The answer to the problem of the quality of earnings internationally rests more with creating the 'right' religious and legal imperatives in a society.

Future research could also extend our findings in a number of directions. One extension would be to use cultural variables in addition and in lieu of religiosity variables to sort out the differential effects of culture and religiosity on earnings opacity. Another extension would be to assess the differential effects of religiosity and political and social indicators, including measures of electoral rights, civil liberties, and economic freedom.

2. **Political Connectedness:** An investigation of the determinants of earnings opacity in 32 countries yielded unexpected results. First, elements of accounting order do not seem to affect earnings opacity. It is the political context rather than the technical that explicates better the level of accounting quality in general and the level of earnings opacity in particular in a given country. Second, earnings opacity is higher as a result of political connectedness of firms and lower as a result of a high degree of law enforcement and market capitalization of connected firms. What appears from the second results is that creating a culture based on law enforcement and market discipline is conducive to demand for more accountability and high quality of accounting. However, the

constraints created by political connectedness are more conducive to the supply of less accountability and lower quality of accounting. The answer to the problem of the quality of accounting internationally rests more with creating the "right" morals of a political society, than with toying with the limited technical discourse rituals offered by accounting.

3. Corruption: We have explored the causes that underlie the wide variations in earnings opacity internationally. Our explanation rests on the impact of corruption as it uses the lack of accounting quality to "camouflage" the ill-gained results. High corruption uses or creates a low quality accounting that is compatible with the unethical behavior of rent misappropriation or is a direct result of the unethical atmosphere. In effect, this study presents empirical results on the impact of corruption on different measures of earnings opacity. Based on a data set from 34 countries, the results of a regression model show a negative relationship between earnings opacity and the lack of corruption after controlling for economic development, human development, size of government and economic freedom. Where corruption is lower, the demand for earnings opacity is lower. Corruption creates a climate conducive to a low quality accounting.

4. Elements of Social, Economic, and Accounting Order: an investigation of the determinants of earnings opacity in 34 countries yielded unexpected results. First, elements of accounting order do not seem to affect earnings opacity as much as social and economic characteristics. It is the economic and the social context rather than the technical that explicates better the level of accounting quality in general and the level of earnings opacity in particular in a given country. Second, earnings opacity is higher as a result of higher rule of law, economic growth, and level of corruption, and lower as result of higher level of economic freedom and quality of life. What appears from the second results is that creating a culture based more on economic freedom and quality of life considerations are conducive to demands for more accountability and high quality of accounting. However, the constraints created by heavy rule of law, competitive economic growth and corrupt rent- seeking behavior are more conducive to the supply of less accountability and lower quality of accounting. The answer to the problem of the quality of accounting internationally rests more with creating the "right" morals of an economic and social society, then with "toying" with the limited "technical" discourse rituals offered by accounting.

5. **Quality of Government:** We assess the quality of government using proxies for voice and accountability, political stability, government effectiveness, regulatory quality, rule of law and control of corruption. We investigate the relationship between these measures and a composite measure of earnings opacity. The accounting relativism thesis implied is that the quality of government is negatively affected by the quality of accounting in general and the level of earnings opacity in

particular. The data on 34 countries show that, when using these measures of government performance, the differences in the quality of government internationally were indeed negatively related to the level of earnings opacity. Countries with low level of earnings opacity had better governments than countries with higher levels of earnings opacity. These results persist after controlling for market performance, economic freedom, newspaper circulation/population and emerging vs. developed countries.

These results present clear evidence of systematic influence of the quality of accounting on government performance. Government performance is surely in part determined by economic development, but it is also shaped by systematic variations in the earnings opacity in individual countries. The results call for a strengthening of the role and quality of accounting internationally as a way of promoting and achieving better quality from governments. In short, the accounting relativism of government performance adds to the economic, political and cultural relativisms.

6. Stock Market Wealth Effect and Economic Growth: This section examined how accounting quality, as measured by earnings opacity, may affect economic growth both directly and indirectly through the effect of stock market performance or economic growth. The results based on data from 34 countries indicate that the exogenous component of the stock market wealth effect- the component defined by earnings opacity-is positively associated with economic growth. However, the direct effect of earnings opacity on economic growth is negative as expected but statistically insignificant. Basically, cross- country differences in accounting quality affect the stock market performance. Countries with better accounting quality create a better condition for market performance, which in turn induce a rapid acceleration in long-run economic growth.

The results are subject to various limitations. The 1998-01 period used for the measurement of economic growth is short and reflects both high and low growth rates in various countries. In addition, other indicators can be used for all the variables used for the measurement of earnings opacity and stock market performance. Future research needs to investigate the impact of both longer periods for the measurement of economic growth and other indicators of earnings opacity and stock market performance on the relationship between economic growth, wealth effect and earnings opacity.

7. **Productivity of Nations:** A fundamental and proven thesis in economics is that a high level of output per worker is possible when countries achieve high rates of investment in physical capital and human capital, and because a high level of productivity is matched to these investments. Our empirical analysis suggests that success on each of these fronts is driven by the quality of accounting in general, and the level of earnings opacity in particular. This is in conformity with the thesis the quality of the accounting environment in which

individuals produce and transact enables individuals to capture as a private return the marginal social benefit of their actions. The significant impact of ethnic fractionalization and legal origin points to the necessary conditions of a good social infrastructure from our earnings opacity results. Three main conclusions can be made in terms of a country with high output per worker.

a) First, the country has adopted an accounting system based on low earnings opacity that protects outsiders from diversion and therefore favors production over diversion. It probably takes the form of mandated accounting techniques and a level of morality and ethics that support "good" accounting. By providing quality accounting, these countries channel talented people to produce rather than seek careers of rent seeking or corruption.

b) Second, the level of ethno linguistic fractionalization is low and/or reduced. The citizens of the country prefer to associate themselves with their state and country rather than their ethnicity and language.

c) Third, the legal system favors common law over civil law. This follows from findings that systematic differences among countries in the structure of laws and their enforcement, such as the historical origin of their laws, account for differences in financial development (La Porta et al., 1997 a, 1998 a). Countries with the common law legal origin have better protection of stakeholders than do countries with civil law legal origin (La Porta et al., 1998 a), and better corporate valuation (La Porta et al. 2002).

8. Investor Protection and Corporate Valuation: This paper examines how investor protection may affect corporate valuation both directly and indirectly through the effect of earnings opacity. The results based on data from 24 countries indicate that (a) earnings opacity is positively affected by the level of anti-director rights in line with a "penalty hypothesis" because insiders' incentives to hide their rent seeking activities are stronger when outsiders can effectively penalize them, and (b) the exogenous component of earnings opacity—the component defined by anti-director rights—is negatively associated with corporate valuation. The direct effect of civil law origin on corporate valuation is as expected, negative and significant. Basically, investor protection as measured by the anti- director rights affects positively the level of earnings opacity. Countries with a high level of anti-director rights are "plagued" by higher earnings opacity, which in turn lead to a lower corporate valuation. The role of investor protection appears more complex than presented in previous studies (e.g. La Porta et al. 2002). While the impact of civil law origin leads to lower corporate valuation as shown in previous studies, the impact of limiting director rights, as one form of investor protection, may lead investors to hide their rent seeking activities, resulting in higher levels of earnings opacity and lower corporate valuation. The control of the opportunistic use of accounting information that results in higher levels of earnings opacity internationally requires more than the imposition of investor protection laws. The evidence in this study expands our understanding of the dual role of investor protection and earnings opacity in shaping corporate finance, by clarifying the different roles of accounting and the law in delivering value to outside shareholders.

Notes

4. The core and traditional definition of rule of law in the U.S. still contains three basic values or concepts: (1) constitutionalism; (2) rule-based decision making; and (3) a commitment to neutral principles, such as federalism, separation of powers and textualism.

5. The law enforcement index used was found to be correlated with the "efficiency of the judicial system" score provided by La Porta et al. (1998), the law and order indicator provided by the International Country Risk Guide (ICRG), and the level of litigiousness in a country from Wingate (1997). The Pearson correlations of the law enforcement index used in the study with the three other legal enforcement indexes described earlier are high, ranging from 0.4632 to 0.6931.

6. The economic freedom index is made possible by the meticulous work of the Fraser Institute, the results of which were published in *Economic Freedom of the World 1975- 1995* by Gwartney et al. (1996). The index of economic freedom has 17 components that are allocated to four major areas: (1) money and inflation; (2) government operations and regulations; (3) takings and discrimination taxation; and (4) international exchange. In aggregating these components of economic freedom into a summary index, various alternatives are used to attach different weights to the components. This results in five possible summary indices: (a) an equal impact index: Ie; (b) a survey of knowledgeable people based index: Is1;

(c) a survey of a large number of people based index: Is2; (d) an average of the above three indices: AVG; and (e) a letter grade index: GRADE. AVG will be used in this study to measure the economic freedom of the countries investigated.

7. The core and traditional definition of the rule of law in the U.S. still contains three basic values or concepts: (1) constitutionalism; (2) rule-based decision making; and (3) a commitment to neutral principles, such as federalism, separation of powers, and textualism.

8. Two features—nonrivalry of consumption and non-excludability of benefits—are generally taken to be the defining characteristics of public goods. (Riahi-Belkaoui, 1984).

9. The Paul rule deduces from attribute-specific rank ordering performance that the degree of our performance of country i over country j increase monotonically, with the difference in their rank order.

10. It is appropriate to note that the judicial philosophy of common law countries allow judges to broadly interpret certain principles, such as fiduciary duty, and hence authorizes them to prohibit more forms of expropriation (La Porta, et al., 2002; Johnson et al., 2002).

11. Because of the use of fewer countries La Porta et al. (1998), this study does not distinguish between French, German and Scandinavian civil law origins.

12. This is part of a growing international accounting literature that examines the value relevance of accounting measures (Alford et al. (1993), Harris et al. (1994), Ali and Hwang (2000), Land and Lang (2002)), analyst forecasts (Ashbaugh and Pincus (2001), Chang et al. (2001)), earnings timeliness and conservatism (Ball et al. (2001)), the effects of institutional factors on earnings management (Leuz et al. (2001)), the impact of investor protection laws on accounting and audition (Francis, et al., 2001), and determinants of corporate transparency (Bushman, et al., 2001).

13. Similar evidence provided by Fan and Wong (2002) supports the inference that controlling insiders have both the opportunities and the incentive to induce less informative financial reports.

References

Acemoglu, Daron, (1995). "Reward structures and the allocation of talent." *European Economic Review.* January 39: 17-33.

Adsera, Alicia and Carles Boix. 2001. *Are you being served? Political accountability and quality of government.* Working Paper. University of Illinois at Chicago.

Agrawal, Anup, and Charles R. Knoeber, 2001, "Do some outside directors play a political role?" *Journal of Law and Economics,* 44: 179-198.

AINajjar, Fouad Kl, (2002). "Economic freedom and macroeconomic determinants of economic growth: Cross-country evidence." *Review of Accounting and Finance.* 1,3: pp. 1-14.

Alford, Al, J. Jones, R. Leftwich, and M. Zmijewski. (1993). "Relative informativeness of accounting disclosures in different countries." *Journal of Accounting Research.* 31 (Supplement): 183-233.

Ali, A.M. 1997. "Economic freedom, democracy and growth." *Journal of Private Enterprise.* 13:1-20.

Ali, A., and L-S Hwang. (2000). "Country-specific factors related to financial reporting and the value relevance of accounting data." *Journal of Accounting Research.* 38: 1-21.

Ang, James, and Carol Marie Boyer, 2000, *Finance and politics: special interest group influence during the nationalization and privatization of Conrail*, Working Paper, Florida State Univeristy.

Arestis, Philip, Demetriades, Panicos O, and Luintel, Kul B. (2001). "Financial development and economic growth: The role of stock markets." *Journal of Money, Credit, and Banking.* 33: pp16-41.

Arnold, P.J., 1991. "Accounting and the State: Consequences of merger and acquisition accounting in the U.S. hospital industry." *Accounting, Organizations and Society.* 16,2: 121-140.

Ashbaugh, Hl, and M. Pincus. (2001). "Domestic accounting standards, international accounting standards, and the predictability of earnings." *Journal of Accounting Research.*

Atje, R., and Jovanovic, B. (1993). "Stock markets and development." *European Economic Review.* 37: pp. 632-640.

Ball, R., S.P. Kothari, and A. Robin. (2000). "The effect of international institutional factors on properties of accounting earnings." *Journal of Accounting and Economics.* 29: 1-51.

Barro, R.J. and McCleary, R.M. (2003) *International determinants of religiosity,* National Bureau of Economic Research, Working Paper 10147.

Baumol, William J. (1990). "Entrepreneurship: Productive, unproductive, and destructive." *Journal of Political Economy.* 5: 893-921.

Bekaert, Geert; Harvey, Campbell R; Lundbland, Christian. (2001). "Does financial liberalization spur growth?" mimeo.

Belkaoui, A., and Maksy, M. (1985). "Welfare of the common man and accounting disclosure adequacy: An empirical investigation." *The International Journal of Accounting.* (Spring), 94.

Bencivenga, Valerie R. and Smith, Bruce D. (1991). "Financial intermediation and endogenous growth." *Review of Economic Studies.* 58: pp. 195-209.

Bencivenga, Valerie R. and Smith, Bruce D. and Ross M. Starr. (1995). "Transaction costs, technical choice, and endogenous growth." *Journal of economic theory.* 67: pp. 513-517.

Bhattacharya, S. (1979). "Imperfect information, dividend policy and the bird in the hand fallacy." *Bell Journal of Economics.* 10: pp. 259-270.

Bhattacharya, U., Daouk, Hl, & Welker, M. (2002). *The world price of earnings opacity*. Working Paper, Ohio University.

Bhattacharya, Utpal, Daouk, Hazem and Michael Welker. (2001). *The world price of earnings opacity.* Working paper. Queen's University. Kingston, Ontario, Canada. Bowen, R.M., D.

Burghstahler, and L.A. Daley. (1987). "The incremental information content of accrual versus cash flows." *The Accounting Review.* 62: pp. 723-747.

Burchell, S., Clubb, C., Hopwood, A., Hughes, J. and J. Nahapiet. 1980. "The roles of accounting in organizations and society." *Accounting Organizations and Society* 3:287-305.

Bushman, Robert; Piotroski, Joseph, and Abbie Smith. (2001). *What determines corporate transparency?* 2001. Working paper. University of Chicago.

Center for International Financial Analysis & Research (CIFAR). 1995. *International Accounting* th *and Auditing trends.* 4 Edition. Edited by V.B. Bavishi. Princeton, NJ:

CIFAR. Chang, J.J., T. Khanna, and K.G. Palpeu. (2000). *Analysts activity around the world.* Working Paper. The Wharton School of University of Pennsylvania, Philadelphia, PA.

Coleman, James. (1990). *Foundations of Social Theory.* Cambridge: Harvard University Press

Dasgupta, P. and M. Weale. 1992. "On measuring the quality of life." *World Development.* 20:119-131.

DeAngelo, H.L. DeAngelo, and D.J. Skinner. (1993). "Accounting choice in troubled companies." *Journal of Accounting Economics.* 17: pp. 113-144.

Dechow, P. (1994). "Accounting earnings and cash flows as measures of firm performance: The role of accounting accruals." *Journal of Accounting and Economics.* 17: pp. 3-42.

DeLong, Bradford, and Andrei Shleifer. 1993. "Princes and merchants: Government and city growth before the industrial revolution." *Journal of Law and Economics.* 671-702.

Demirguc-Kunt, Al, and V. Maksimovic. (1998). "Law, finance, and firm growth." *Journal of Finance.* 53: pp. 2107-2137.

Demsetz, Harold. (1967). "Toward a theory of property rights." *American Economic Review Papers and Proceedings.* 347-359.

De Soto, Hernando. 2000. *The mystery of capital: Why capitalism triumphs in the west and fails everywhere else.* Basic Books.

Dicey, A.V. (1915) *An introduction to the study of the law of the constitution.* Liberty Classicsth reprint of 8 ed., pp. 107-122.

Edlin, Aaron S. and Joseph E. Stiglitz. 1997. *Discouraging rivals: Managerial rent-seeking and economic inefficiencies.* NBER Working Paper No. W4145.

Easterly, W., & Levine, R. (1997). "Africa's growth tragedy: Politics and ethnic divisions." *Quarterly Journal of Economics,* 112, 1203-1250.

Ehrlich, Il, & Lui, F.T. (1999). "Bureaucratic corruption and endogenous economic growth." *The Journal of Political Economy,* 107(6), 270-293.

Faccio, Mara, and Larry H.P. Lang, 2002. "The ultimate ownership of Western European corporations." *Journal of Financial Economics*.

Fan, J., and T.J. Wong. (2002). "Corporate ownership structure and the in formativeness of accounting earnings in East Asia. *Journal of Accounting and Economics*.

Farr, W.K., Loid, R.A., and J.L. Wolfenbarger. 1998. "Economic freedom, political freedom and economic well-being: A causal analysis." *Cato Journal.* 18, 2: 247-262.

Fishman, Raymond, 2001. "Estimating the value of political connections," *American Economic Review,* 91: 1095-1102.

Francis, Jere, Khurana, Inder k. and Raynolde Pereira. (2001). *Investor protection laws, accounting and auditing around the world.* Working Paper. University of Missouri-Columbia.

Friedman, E., Johnson, S., Kaufmann, D., and P. Zoido-Lobatin. (2000). "Dodging the grabbing hand: The determinants of unofficial activity in 69 countries." *Journal of Public Economics.* 76: pp. 459-493.

Fukuyama, Francis. 1995. *Trust.* New York: Free Press.

Gaballero, Ricardo J. and Mohammad L. Hammom. 1998. "The macroeconomics of specificity." *Journal of Political Economy.* 106, 4.

Gernon, H. And Wallace, R.S.O. (1995) "International accounting research: a review of its ecology, contending theories and methodologies", *Journal of Accounting Literature,* Vol. 14, pp. 54-106.

Greif, R. (1994) "Cultural beliefs and the organization of society: a historical and theoretical reflection on collectivist and individual societies", *Journal of Political Economy,* Vol. 102, pp. 912-950.

Grief, Avner and Eugene Kandel. "Contract enforcement institutions: Historical perspecitive and current status in Russia." in Edward P. Lazear, ed. 1995. *Economic Transition in Eastern Europe and Russia: Realities of Reform.* Stanford, CA: Hoover Institution Press. Pp. 293- 321.

Grossman, Herschel I. and Minseong Kim. (1996). *Inequality, predation and welfare.* NBER Working paper. No. 5704. August.

Gwartney, J., Lawson, R., & Block, W. (1996). *Economic freedom of the world: 1975-1999.* Vancouver, BC: Fraser Institute.

Gwartney, Jim, Lawson, Robert and Dexter Samilda. (2000). *Economic freedom of the world: 2000 annual report.* Vancouver: The Fraser Institute.

Harris, Richard D.F. (1997). "Stock markets and development: A re-assessment. *European Economic Review.* 41: pp. 139-146.

Harris, T.S., M. Lang, and H.P. Moller. (1994). "The value relevance of German accounting measures: An empirical analysis." *Journal of Accounting Research.* 32(Autumn): 187-209.

Hausman, J.A. 1978. "Specification tests in econometrics." *Econometricsi* 4: 1251-1270.

Healey, P. (1985). "The effects of bonus schemes on accounting decisions." *Journal of Accounting and Economics.* 7: pp. 85-107.

Healy, P., & Whalen, J. (1999). "A review of the earnings management literature and its implications for standard setting." *Accounting Horizons,* 13, 365-383.

Hellman, Joel S., Geraint Jones, and Daniel Kaufmann. 2000. *Seize the State, seize the day. State capture, corruption, and influence in transition.* World Bank Policy Research Working Paper no. 24-44.

Henry, P. (2000). "Stock market liberalization, economic reform, and emerging market equity prices." *Journal of Finance.* 55: pp. 529-564.

Hermalin, B.E. 1992. "The effects of competition on executive behavior." *Rand Journal of Economics.* 23:350-365.

Holthausen, R. (1990). "Accounting method choice, opportunistic behavior, efficient contracting, and information perspectives." *Journal of Accounting and Economics.* 12: pp. 207-218.

Holthausen, R. and R. Leftwich. (1983). "The economic consequences of accounting choice: Implications of costly contracting and monitoring." *Journal of Accounting and Economics.* 5: pp. 77-117.

Iannaccone, L.R. (1998) "Introduction to the economics of religion", *Journal of Economic Literature,* Vol.36, pp. 1465-1496.

International Accounting Standards Committee. 1997. *Insight.* (October).

Johnson, Simon, and Todd Milton. 2002. "Cronyism and capital controls: Evidence from Malaysia." *Journal of Financial Economics,* forthcoming.

Jones, C.L. and R.E. Hall. (1997). *Fundamental determinants of output per worker across countries.* Working Paper. Stanford University.

Karras, Giorgios. (2002). "Openness and growth: Cross-sectional and time series evidence." *Review of Accounting and Finance.* 1,3: pp.1-14.

Kaufman, D., Kraay, A., & Zoido-Lobaton, P. (1999a). *Aggregating governance indicators.* World Bank Working Paper No. 2195. Washington: World Bank.

_____. (1999b). *Governance matters.* World Bank Working Paper No. 2196. Washington: World Bank

Knack, S., & Keefer, P. (1995). "Institutions and economic performance: Cross-country tests using alternative institutional measures." *Economics and Politics,* 7, 207-227.

Kroszner, Randall S., and Thomas Stratmann. 1998. "Interest group competition and the organization of congress: theory and evidence from financial services' Political Action Committees." *American Economic Review,* 88: 1163-1188.

Land, J., and M. Lang. (2002). *Empirical evidence on the evolution of international earnings.* Working Paper. Kenan-Flagler Business School. University of North Carolina, Chapel Hill, NC.

Landes, David. (1998). *The wealth and poverty of nations.* New York: W.W. Norton.

La Porta, R., Lopez-de-Silanes, F., Shleifer, A. and Vishny, R.W. (1997) "Legal determinants of external finance", *The Journal of Finance,* Vol.52, pp. 1131-1155.

_____. (1998). "Law and finance." *Journal of Political Economy.* 106: 1131-1155

_____. (1998). "Law and finance." *Journal of Institutional and Theoretical Economics* 154:1113-1155.

_____. (1999). "The quality of government." *Journal of economics, law and organization.* 15: 222-279.

_____. (1999b). *Investor Protection and Corporate Valuation*, NBER Working Paper 7403.

_____. (2000a). "Agency problems and dividend policies around the world." *Journal of Finance.* 55: 1-33.

_____. (2002). *Journal of Finance.* 3: 1147-1170.

Larson, R.K. (1992). "International accounting standards and economic growth: An empirical investigation of their relationship in Africa." *Research in Third World Accounting.* 2: pp. 27-43.

Lee, C.J. (1987). "Accounting infrastructure and economic development." *Journal of Accounting and Public Policy.* 6: pp. 75-85.

Leuz, Christin, Nanda, Dhananjay, and Peter D. Wysocki. 2001. "Investor protection and earnings management: An international comparison." Working Paper. Wharton School.

Levine, Ross, and Zervos, Saral (1998). "Stock markets, banks, and economic growth." *American Economic Review.* 88(3): pp. 537-558.

Levine, Ross. (1999). "Law, finance, and economic growth." *Journal of Finance Intermediation.* 8: pp. 8-35.

Levine, Ross. (2001). *Napoleon, bourses, and growth: With a focus on Latin America in market augmenting government.* Eds: Omar Azar and Charles Cadwell. Ann Arbor, MI: University of Michigan Press.

Ljungqvist, Lars and Thomas J. Sargent (1995). "The Swedish Unemployment Experience." *European Economic Review.* 5: 1043-1070.

Mauro, P. (1995). "Corruption and growth." *Quarterly Journal of Economics, 110,* 681-712.

Matolcsy, Zoltan. 1999. V. "Executive cash compensation and corporate performance during different economic cycles." *Working Paper.* University of Technology. Sydney, Australia.

Miller, P., 1990. *On the interrelations between accounting and the state.* 15, 4: 315-338.

Murphy, Kevin M., Andrei Shleifer, and Robert W. Vishny. (!991). "The allocation of talent: Implications for growth." *Quarterly Journal of Economics.* 2: 503-530.

Ndubizu, G.A. (1992). "Accounting disclosure methods and economic development: Criteria for globalizing capital markets." *International Journal of Accounting.* 27: pp. 1151-1163.

North, Douglass C. (1990). *Institutions, Institutional Change, and Economic Performance.* Cambridge, Cambridge University Press.

Olson, Mancur. (1965). *The Logic of Collective Action.* Cambridge: Cambridge University Press.

_____. (1982). *The Rise and Decline of Nations.* New Haven: Yale University Press.

Orts, Eric W. 1998. "Shirking and sharking: A legal theory of the firm." *Yale Law and Policy Review.*

Olson, Mancur. (1965). *The logic of collective action.* Cambridge: Harvard University Press.

_____. (1982). *The rise and decline of nations.* New Haven: Yale University Press.

_____. (1993). "Dictatorship, democracy, and development." *American Political Science Review.* 567-576. Paul, Satya. 1998. *A new social ranking rule.* Presented at the Fourth International Meeting of Society for Social Choice and Welfare. Vancouver, Canada.

_____. 2000, "Measuring the quality of life." *The Middle East Business and Economic Review.* 14, 1: 7-17.

Prakash, Prem and Alfred Rappaport. (1975). "Information interdependencies." *The Accounting Review.* 4: 723-734. Putman, Robert. (1993). *Making democracy work: Civic traditions in modern Italy.* Princeton: Princeton University Press.

Ramsey, F.I. 1969. "Test for specification errors in classical linear least squares regression analysis." *Journal of the Royal Statistical.* 31: (series B): 31.

Rapaczynski, Andrej. (1987). *Nature and Politics: Liberalism in the Philosophies of Hobbes, Locke, and Rousseau.* Ithaca: Cornell University Press.

Riali-Belkaoui, Ahmed. (1995). "Accounting information adequacy and macroeconomic determinants of economic growth: Cross-country evidence. *Advances in International Accounting.* 8: pp. 87-98.

_____. "Are you being fooled? Audit quality and quality of government." *The ICFAI Journal of Audit Practice.* 2004. pp 42-52.

_____. "Are you being fooled? Audit quality of earnings and quality of govermnent." *South Africa Journal of Accounting Research.*

_____. (2003). *Designed Accounting or Principled Accounting: What's Wrong With This Picture.* Westport, CT: Greenwood Publishing.

_____. (1999). "Disclosure adequacy and country risk." *American Business Review.* (Jume), 1-4.

_____. (2004)"Earnings opacity and the productivity of nations" *Review of Accounting and Finance.* pp. 130-144

_____. "Earnings Opacity, Stock Market Wealth Effect and Economic Growth." *Review of Accounting and Finance.* 2005. pp. 72-91.

_____. (2000). "Economic freedom, human development and accounting disclosure of global stock exchanges: An empirical investigation." *Accounting and Business Review.* 17,2: pp. 197-206.

_____. (1998). "Human development, economic development accounting disclosure requirements of global stock exchanges." *Journal of Global Business.* 9: 49-56.

_____. (2002). *International Accounting and Economic development: The Interactions of Economic and Social Indicators.* Westport, CT: Greenwood Publishing.

_____. "Investor Protection, Earnings Opacity, and Corporate Valuation." *Global Journal of Finance and Economics.* 3, 2004, pp. 130-144.

_____. "Is Earnings Management Affected by human development and economic freedom?" *Review of Accounting and Finance.* 3, 1, 2004.

_____. "Law, Religiosity and Earnings Opacity Internationally." *International Journal of Accounting Auditing, and Performance Evaluation.* Vol 1, 2004.

_____. (1996). "Political, financial and economic risks and accounting and disclosure requirements of global stock *exchanges. Research in Accounting Regulation.* 10: 179-194.

_____. "Publicly connected firms: Are they connected to earnings opacity?" *Research in Accounting Regulation.* Vol 17. 2004. pp 25-38.

_____. "Relationship between Tax Compliance Internationally and selected determinants of tax morale." *Journal of International Accounting, Auditing and Taxation.* 13, 2004, pp. 135-143.

_____. "The Effects of Economic and Social Variables in Earnings Opacity Internationally."

Roberts, Brian E., 1990. "A dead senator tells no lies: Seniority and the distribution of federal benefits." *American Journal of Political Science,* 34:31-58.

Rousseau, Peter L. and Wachtel, Paul (1998). "Financial intermediation and economic performance: Historical evidence from five industrial countries." *Journal of Money, Credit, and Banking.* Novemnber 30(4): pp. 657-678.

Saudagaran, Shahrokh and J. Diga. 1997. "Financial reporting in emerging capital markets: characteristics and policy issues." *Accounting Horizons.* 11:41-64.

Saudagaran, S. and Meek, G.K. (1997) "A review of research in the relationship between international capital markets and financial reporting by multinational firms", *Journal of Accounting Literature,* Vol. 16, pp. 127-159.

Scharfsein, D. 1988. "Product market competition and managerial slack."*Rand Journal of Economics.* 19:147-155.

Schleifer, A. (1997). "Government in transition." *European Economic Review, 41(3),* 385-410.

Schleifer, A., & Vishny, R.W. (1993). "Corruption." *Quarterly Journal of Economics, 108(3),* 599-617.

Schmidt, Klaus M. 1997. "Managerial incentives and product market competition." *Review of Economic Studies.* 64: 191-213.

Schrag, Joel and Suzanne Scotchmer. (1993). *The Self-Reinforcing Nature of Crime.* Working Paper. 93-11. Center for the Study of Law and Society, School of Law, University of California, Berkeley.

Sen, A.K. 1981. "Public auction and the quality of life in developing countries." *Oxford Bulletin of Economics and Statistics.* 43: 287-319.

Shauer, Frederick. 2000. *First amendment opportunism.* KSG Working Paper No. 00-011. John F. Kennedy School of Government. Harvard University.

Stiglitz, J.E. (1975). *Information and economic analysis in current economic problems.* In Parkin and Nobay (Eds). Cambridge University Press: pp. 27-52.

Stulz, Rene M., and Rohan Williamson. 2001. "Culture, openness and finance." Working Paper. Ohio State University.

Summers, Robert and Alan Heston. (1991). "The Penn World Table (Mark 5): An expanded set of international comparisons: 1950-1988." *Quarterly Journal of Economics.* 106: 327-368.

Talaga, J. and G. Ndubizu. (1986). "Accounting and economic development: Relationships among paradigms." *The International Journal of Accounting:* pp. 55-68.

Teoh, S.H., Welch, Il, & Wong, T.J. (1998). "Earnings management and the underperformance of seasoned equity offerings." *Journal of Financial Economics, 50,* 63-99.

Thursby, F.I. 1981. "A test for strategy for discriminating between auto-correlation and misspecification in regression analysis." *Review of Economics and Statistics.* 63:117-123.

_____. (1985). "The relationship among the specification test of Hausman, Ramsey and Chow. *Journal of the American Statistical Association.* 80: pp. 926-928.

Vishwanath, T. and D. Kaufmann. (1999). "Toward transparency in finance and governance." *The*th *World Bank,* Draft, September, 6 , 1999.

Wallace, O.R.S. and Gernon, H. (1991) "Frameworks for international comparative financial accounting", *Journal of Accounting Literature,* Vol. 10, pp. 209-264.

Watts, R. (1977). "Corporate financial statements, a product of the market and political processes." *Australian Journal of Management.* 2: pp53-78.

Watts, R. and J. Zimmerman. (1978). "Towards a positive theory of the determination of accounting standards." *The Accounting Review.* 53: pp.112-134.

Weber, M. (1930). *The Protestant Ethic and the Spirit of Capitalism.* Allen & Unwin, London.

Weingast, Barry R. (1995). "The economic role of political institutions: Market-perserving federalism and economic development." *Journal of Law, Economics, and Organization.* 11: 1-31.

White, H.A. 1980. "Heteroscedasticity-consistent covariance matrix estimator and a direct test for heteroscedasticity." *Econometrics*. 10:817-838.

Wu, P. 1973. "Alternative tests of independence between stochastic regressors and disturbances." *Econometrics*. 15: 737-750.

Figure 1. The Situation about Earnings Opacity

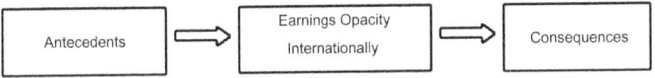

Figure 2. Determinants of Earnings Opacity Internationally

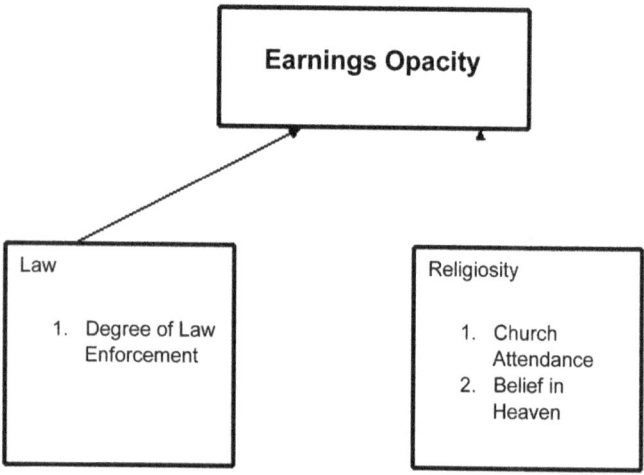

Figure 3. Determinants of Earnings Opacity Internationally

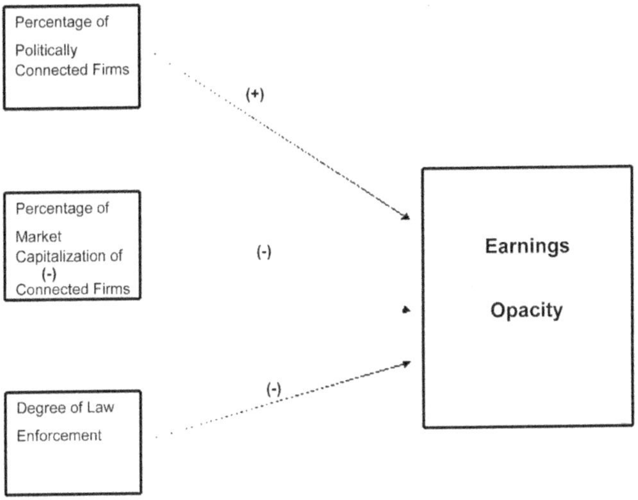

Figure. 4. Determinants of Earnings Opacity Internationally

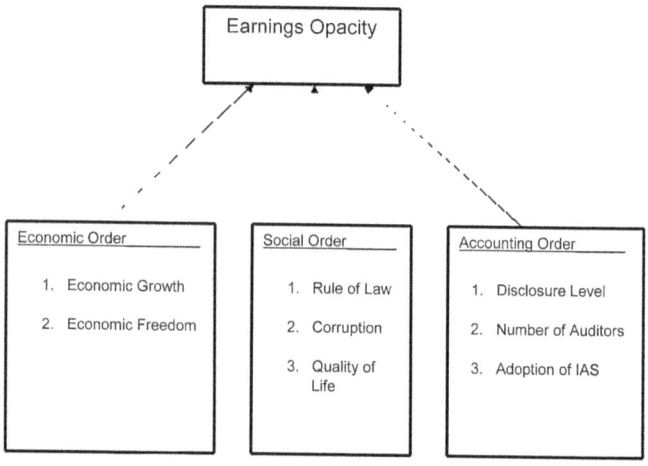

Figure 5. Economic Growth Model

Conventional Growth Determinants
1. Initial Income
2. Initial Human Development
3. Government Consumption

Market Wealth Effect
1. Market Wealth Effect

Earnings Opacity
1. Earnings Aggressiveness
2. Loss Avoidance
3. Earnings Smoothing
4. Overall Earnings Opacity

Economic Growth

Figure 6. Corporate Valuation Model

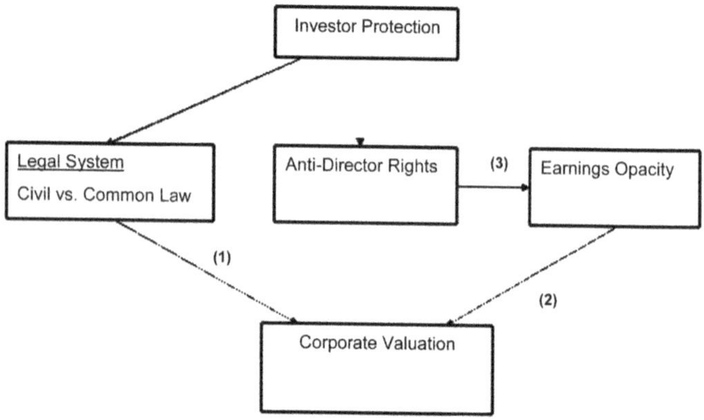

Figure 7. Antecedents and Consequences of Earnings Opacity Internationally

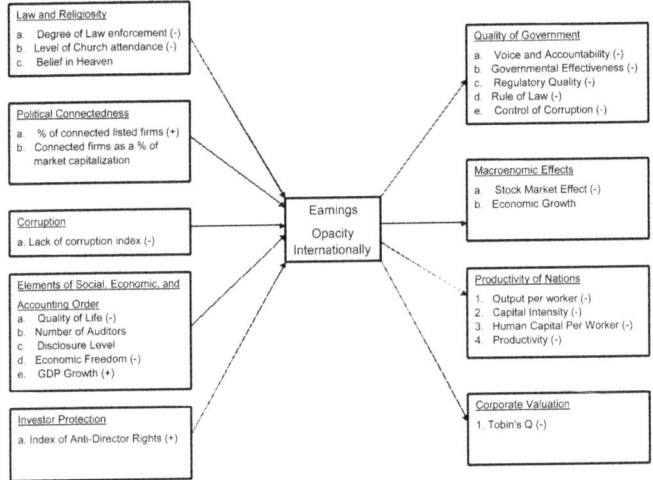

Table 1 Antecedents of Earnings Opacity Internationally

Independent Variables	Name	Description and Source
MCA	Monthly Church Attendance	Monthly fraction of the population that attended church or analogous houses of worship (Barro and McCleary, 2003)
BIH	Belief in Heaven	Fraction of people who hold a belief in heaven(Barro and McCleary, 2003)
DLE	Degree of Law Enforcement	It ranges from 2.98 to 10, with 10 indicating the best quality of the rule of law (Barro and McCleary, 2003)
PCLF	Percentage of Politically Connected Listed Firms	Ratio of connected firms over the total number of firms listed in a particular country (Faccio, 2002)
CFMC	Connected Firms as a Percentage of Market Capitalization	Ratio of market capitalization of connected firms over the overall capitalization of each country (Faccio, 2002)
CORR	Level of Corruption	Indication of subjective perception of public corruption (Kaufman et al., 1999 a,b). A higher index indicates lower corruption. The variable may be understood as the lack of corruption.
ROL	Rule of Law	Rule of law score obtained from Kaufman, Kray and Zoido-Lobaton, 1999

Independent Variables	Name	Description and Source
AD	Anti-director Rights Index	The index is formed by adding one when: (1) the country allows shareholders to mail their proxy vote, (2) shareholders are not required to deposit their shares prior to the General Shareholders Meeting, (3) cumulative voting or proportional representation of minorities or the board of directors is allowed, (4) an oppressed minorities mechanism is in place, (5) the minimum percentage of share capital that entitles a shareholder to call for an extraordinary shareholders' meeting is less than or equal to ten percent (the sample median), or (6) when shareholders have preemptive rights that can only be waived by a shareholder meeting. The range of the index is from zero to six (La Porta et al., 1998, 2002).

Table 2 Consequences of Earnings Opacity Internationally

Consequence Variable	Name	Description and Source
VA	Voice and Accountability	An indicator that measures the extent to which citizens of a country are able to participate in the selection of overnments. The indicator is oriented so that higher values correspond to better outcomes on a scale of -2.5 to 2.5 (Kaufman, Kraay and Zoido-Lobaton, 2002)
PS	Political Stability	An indicator that measures perception of the likelihood that the government in power will be destabilized or overthrown by possibly unconstitutional and/or violent means, including terrorism. The indicator is oriented so that higher values correspond to better outcomes on a scale of -2.5 to 2.5 (Kaufman, Kraay and Zoido-Lobaton, 2002)
ROL	Rule of Law	An indicator that measures the extent to which agents have confidence in and abide by the rules of society. The indicator is oriented so that higher values correspond to better outcomes on a scale of -2.5 to 2.5 (Kaufman, Kraay and Zoido-Lobaton, 2002)

Consequence Variable	Name	Description and Source
COC	Control of Corruption	An indicator that measures perception of corruption, conventially defined as the exercise of public power for private gain. The indicator is oriented so that higher values correspond to better outcomes on a scale of -2.5 to 2.5 (Kaufman, Kraay and Zoido-Lobaton, 2002)
LMMR	Market Return	Logarithm of one plus mean monthly returns scaled by the standard deviations of a country i for 1986-98 (Bhattacharya, Daouk, and Welker, 2001)
ECG	GNP Growth	GNP growth for the 1998-01 period for country i
GE	Government Effectiveness	An indicator that measures perceptions of the quality of public sector provision, the quality of the bureaucracy, the competence of civil servants, the independence of the civil service from political pressures, and the credibility of the government's commitment to policies in a single grouping. The indicator is oriented so that higher values correspond to better outcomes on a scale of -2.5 to 2.5 (Kaufman, Kraay and Zoido-Lobaton, 2002)

(Table 2 Continued on Next page)

Consequence Variable	Name	Description and Source
RQ	Regulatory Quality	An indicator that measures the incidence of market-unfriendly policies such as price controls or inadequate bank supervision, as well as perceptions of the burdens imposed by excessive regulation in areas such as foreign trade and business development. The indicator is oriented so that higher values correspond to better outcomes on a scale of -2.5 to 2.5 (Kaufman, Kraay and Zoido-Lobaton, 2002)
Y/L	Output per Worker	Level of output per worker computed on the basis of national income and product account and labor force data (Penn World Tables 5-6 of Summers and Heston 1991)
H/L	Human Capital per worker	Level of human capital per workier obtained after decomposing differences in output per worker into diffenences in capital intensity, human capital per worker and productivity (Jones and Hall, 1997)
(K/Y)	Capital Intensity	Level of capital intensity obtained after the decomposition of differences in output per worker (Jones and Hall, 1997)

Consequence Variable	Name	Description and Source
A	Productivity	Level of productivity obtained after the decomposition of differences in output per worker (Jones and Hall, 1997)
Tobin's Q	Tobin's Q as a measure of Corporate valuation.	The dependent variable of corporate valuation is Tobin's Q provided by La Porta et al. (2002) for their sample of 539 firms. It includes the largest 20 firms of market capitalization in each of the 27 countries that also have a shareholder who controls over 10 percent of the votes of the firm. The Tobin's Q is measured as the ratio of market value of assets to their replacement value. The market value of assets is proxied by the book value of equity minus deferred taxes plus the market value of common stock. The replacement value of assets is proxied by the book value of the assets (Worldscope, 1997)

Table 3 Control Variables Used

Control Variables	Name	Description and Source
LPCGNP	Log per capita GNP for country i	
RGDP	Ten year GDP growth	
AU	Number of auditors per 100,000 inhabitants	(Saudagaran and Diga, 1997, Table 6, p.51)
DISC	Financial disclosure level.	Disclosure level from the Center for International Financial Analysis and Research (CIFAR, 1995). The higher the number more is the disclosure
IAS	International accounting standards	Dummy variable used as a proxy for demand for international accounting harmonization 0. for completely independent standard setting and no use of IAS except for comparison with IAS 1. separate accounting standards that are based on an similar to IAS in most cases 2. IAS are used as national standards with some modifications for local conditions.Standards not covered by IAS are added (IASC, Insight, dated October 1997)
LOG GNP	Log of Gross National Product	The data taken from the World Bank correspond to the 1985-1998 average gross national product

Control Variables	Name	Description and Source
HDI	U.N. Human Development Index.	Generally considered as a more realistic measure of human development than mere GNP per head. The HDI is composed of three indicators: life expectancy, education, and income (United Nations, 1991
GE / GDP	Size of government	Government expenditures/GDP
EF	Economic Freedom	Economic freedom index from 1975-1995 (Gwartney, 1996)
Qualityoflife	Quality of life score	Quality of life for country i is measured as a. PR i using Paul rules b. BR i using Borda rules, and c. CR i using Copeland rules (Paul, 2002)
LDYDG	Dividend growth	Logarithn of one plus mean monthly yield over dividend growth for country i for 1986-1998. (Bhattacharya, Daouk, and Welker, 2001)
MMR	Market Return	Logarithm of one plus mean monthly returns scaled by standard deviation of returns for each country for 1986-88. (Bhattacharya, Daouk, and Welker, 2001)

(Table 3   Continued on Next page)

Control Variables	Name	Description and Source
EFI	Economic Freedom Index	An index based on principal component analysis of 23 components designed to identify the consistency of institutional arrangements and policies with economic freedom in seven areas: 1) size of government, 2) economic structure and use of markets, 3) monetary policy and price stability, 4) freedom to use alternative currencies, 5) legal structure and security of private ownership, 6) freedom to trade with foreigners, and 7) freedom of exchange in capital markets (Gwartney, Lawson and Serrida, 2000
NEWSC	Newspaper circulation/population	Circulation of daily newspaper/population (UNESCO statistical Yearbook, 1986)
MSOWC	Market share of World's Capital	The market share of world's capital was determined from the website of the International Federation of Stock Exchanges (www.FIBY.com)
NOA	Number of Auditors	The number of auditors per 100,000 population was obtained from Saudagaran and Diga (1997, Table 6, p. 51)
DL	Disclosure Level	The disclosure level was obtained from the Center of International Analysis and Research (CIFAR, 1995). The higher the number, more is the disclosure.

Control Variables	Name	Description and Source
EMERGE	Emerging Country	An indicator equal to one if the country was not treated as a "developed" country, zero otherwise (Bhattacharya, Daouk, and Welker, 2001)
EF	Ethnolinguistic fractionalization	Average value of different indices of ethnolinguistic fractionalization. Its values range from 0 to 1. The five components indices are 1) index of ethnolinguistic fractionalization, which measures the probability that two randomly selected people from a given country will not belong to the same ethnolinguistic group (the index is based on the number and size of population groups as distinguished by their ethnic and linguistic status); 2) probability of two randomly selected individuals speaking different languages; 3) probability of two randomly selected individuals
		do not speak the same language; 4) percent of the population not speaking the 'official' language; and 5) percent of the population not speaking the most widely used language (La Porta et al., 1999)
LO	Legal Origin	Company law or commercial code of each country with the value of 1 if it is based on the French commercial code

121

Table 4

Sample of Country
Name of Country
Australia
Austria
Belgium
Brazil
Canada
Chile
Denmark
Finland
France
Germany
Greece
Hong Kong
India
Indonesia
Ireland
Italy
Japan
Korea
Malaysia
Mexico
Netherlands
Norway
Pakistan
Portugal
Singapore

Sample of Country
Name of Country
South Africa
Spain
Sweden
Switzerland
Taiwan
Thailand
Turkey
U.K.
U.S.A.

Table 5 Determinants of earnings opacity

Dependent variable	Independent variables	
OEO(overall earnings opacity)	Intercept	10.499 (5.64)*
	LPCGNP	-0.057 (-0.29)
	MCA	-2.732 (-2.01)**
	BIH	0.165 (0.14)
	DLE	-0.472 (-2.77)**
	R (Adjusted)	41.62%
	F	5.10*
Wald test: 0.01.		
Reset F. value: 0.05		
Hausman F. value: 6.32*		
Variables depict		
LPCGNP: log of per capita GNP.		
MCA: monthly church attendance.		
BIH: belief in heaven.		
DLE: degree of law enforcement		
t values are between parentheses		

*Significant at $\alpha = 0.01$
**Significant at $\alpha = 0.05$

Table 6 Determinants of earnings opacity

Dependent Variable	OEO (Overall Earnings opacity)	
Independent Variables	1	2
Intercept	8.640 (13.05)*	6.017 (2.90)*
PCLF	0.072 (2.01)**	0.119 (2.32)**
CFMC	-0.037 (-2.15)**	-0.045 (-2.59)*
DLE	-0.373 (-4.96)*	-0.309 (-3.18)*
GL	_____	0.429 (0.84)
RGDP	_____	0.113 (0.98)
AU	_____	-0.002 (-1.28)
DISC	_____	0.025 (0.93)
ISA	_____	-0.501 (-1.52)
R	50.40%	52.51%
F	11.50*	4.18*
Waid Test	0.01	0.01
ResetF-Value	0.05	0.05
Hausman F-Value	9.35*	4.06*

(a) Variables such as PCLF, CFMC, and DLE one defined in Table 1. Other variables are defined as follows:

CL: Legal system with 1 for common law and 0 for civil law countries

RGDP: Ten year GDP growth

AU: Number of auditors per 100,000 inhabitants

DISC: Financial disclosure level

IAS: International accounting standards use.

(b) * Significant at α = 0.01; ** Significant at α = 0.05; *** Significant at α = 0.10

Table 7 Effects of Corruption on Earnings Opacity
(t- Values in Parentheses).

	Expected Sign	Earnings Opacity Index				
		EAG	LA	ES	AVR	Overall
	1	2	3	4	5
Intercept	?	6.815 (16.22)*	6.417 (22.63)*	6.141 (23.75)*	6.457 (25.07)*	11.044 (3.42)
Corruption	-	-1.165 (-3.66)*	-0.518 (-2.41)*	-0.484 (-2.47)*	-0.722 (-3.70)*	-0.299 (-3.47)*
Log GNP	-					-0.655 (-3.13)*
HDI	+					3.653 (-3.60)*
EFI	-					-0.739 (-3.26)*
GE/GDP	-					-0.009 (-3.59)*
Adjusted R		27.33%	12.76%	13.44%	27.83%	40.98%
F Statistic		13.41*	15.83*	6.12*	13.73*	14.89*

Note: Model 1: Earnings Opacity Index EAG = B 0 + B 1CORR; Model 2: Earnings Opacity IndexLA = B 0 + B 1CORR; Model 3: Earnings

Opacity Index ES = B 0 + B 1CORR; Model 4: Earnings Opacity IndexAVR = B 0 + B 1CORR; Model 5: Earnings Opacity Index = B0 + B 1CORR + B 2logGNP + B 3HDI + B 4EFI + B 5 GE/GDP

Table 8 Determinants of Earnings Opacity

Independent Variables	(1)	(2)	(3)
Intercept	7.485 (3.58)*	6.611 (3.12)*	6.575 (2.40)*
ROL	2.186 (4.50)*	2.004 (4.35)*	1.943 (3.71)*
AU	0.001 (1.06)	0.0008 (0.94)	0.0009 (0.94)
DISC	0.002(0.11)	0.007 (0.37)	0.011 (0.51)
IAS	0.216 (0.87)	0.190 (0.82)	0.222 (0.79)
EF	-0.763 (-3.85)*	-0.693 (-3.51)*	-0.714 (-2.91)*
EG	0.2708 (1.99)***	0.896 (2.27)**	0.317 (2.06)**
PR	0.0126 (2.10)**		
BR		0.028 (2.50)*	
CR			0.023 (2.65)*
COR R (adjusted) 2	-0.966 (-2.19)** 78.74%	-0.849 (1.97)*** 80.97%	-0.907 (-1.81)*** 76.13%
F	9.80*	11.11*	8.58*
Wald Test	0.01	0.01	0.01
F-Value	0.05	0.05	0.05
Hausman F-Value	7.52*	8.53*	7.34*

a) Variables are defined in Table 2

(b) t values are between parentheses

*Significant at α = 0.01

**Significant at α = 0.05

***Signification at α = 0.10

Table 9 Voice and Accountability and Earnings Opacity

Independent Variables	Model 1		Model 2		Model 3		Model 4		Model 5	
	2001	1998	2001	1998	2001	1998	2001	1998	2001	1998
1. Intercept	2.869	3.348	2.013	2.036	2.828	2.703	3.569	3.778	1.916	2.102
	(4.90)*	(6.14)*	(2.55)*	(2.98)*	(2.70)*	(2.79)*	(6.24)*	-6.04	(2.49)*	(3.17)*
2. OEO	-0.342	-0.424	-0.246	-0.276	-0.346	-0.403	-0.473	-0.547	-0.236	-0.284
	(-3.43)*	(-4.56)*	(-2.14)**	(-2.78)*	(-3.21)*	(-4.05)*	(-4.96)*	(-5.25)*	(-2.04)**	(-2.85)*
3. MMR			2.14	3.28						
			(2.70)**	(2.79)*						
4. EFI					0.007	0.078				
					-0.07	-0.83				
5. NEWSC							0.019	0.082		
							-0.37	-6.42		
6. EMERGE									0.545	0.709
									(2.01)**	(3.03)*

Adjusted R2	24.61%	37.49%	27.95%	48.44%	22.85%	37.28%	46.42%	55.71%	32.82%	52.46%
F	11.77*	20.79*	7.40*	16.50*	5.75*	10.51*	12.69*	15.73*	8.82*	18.66*

(1) * Significant at $\alpha = 0.01$
**Significant at $\alpha = 0.05$

Table 10 Regulatory Quality and Earnings Opacity

Independent Variables	Model 1		Model 2		Model 3		Model 4		Model 5	
	2001	1998	2001	1998	2001	1998	2001	1998	2001	1998
1. Intercept	1.982	1.689	0.875	0.794	0.157	0.316	2.496	1.217	0.646	0.756
	(4.49)*	(5.69)*	-1.6	(2.31)**	-0.666	-0.24	(4.00)*	(4.23)*	-1.26	(2.23)**
2. OEO	-0.209	-0.168	-0.085	-0.068	-0.133	-0.112	-0.338	-0.118	-0.047	-0.05
	(-2.79)*	(-3.33)*	(-1.78)***	(-1.76)***	(-1.95)***	(-2.55)*	(-3.25)*	(-2.47)**	(-1.75)***	(-1.76)***
3. MMR			2.768	2.24						
			(2.94)**	(3.79)*						
4. EFI					0.215	0.162				
					(3.30)*	(3.87)*				
5. NEWSC							0.197	0.09		
							(3.41)*	(3.38)*		
6. EMERGE									0.684	0.467
									(3.77)*	(3.90)*

Adjusted R2	17.01%	23.44%	33.04%	45.95%	36.57%	46.87%	40.15%	39.31%	40.70%	45.76%
F	7.77*	11.10*	9.14*	15.03*	10.23*	15.12*	10.06*	9.74*	11.98*	14.50*

(1) * Significant at α = 0.01
**Significant at α = 0.05
***Significant at α = 0.10

Table 11 Government Effectiveness and Earnings Opacity

Independent Variables	Model 1		Model 2		Model 3		Model 4		Model 5	
	2001	1998	2001	1998	2001	1998	2001	1998	2001	1998
1. Intercept	2.862 (4.90)*	3.135 (5.24)*	1.727 (2.27)**	1.423 (2.01)**	1.005 -1.05	0.044 -0.06	2.772 (5.07)*	2.498 (4.00)*	1.026 -1.54	0.994 -1.6
2. OEO	-0.323 (-3.25)*	-0.376 (-3.69)*	-0.196 (-1.76)***	-0.183 (-1.78)***	-0.246 (-2.50)*	-0.25 (-3.01)*	-0.354 (-3.88)*	-0.338 (-3.25)*	-0.102 (-1.73)***	-0.119 (-1.74)***
3. MMR			2.838 (2.16)**	4.281 (3.51)*						
4. EFI					0.219 (2.34)**	0.366 (4.63)*				
5. NEWSC							0.414 (2.28)*	0.197 (3.41)*		
6. EMERGE									0.953 (4.06)*	1.118 (5.11)*

Adjusted R2	22.43%	27.61%	30.42%	46.52%	31.66%	56.89%	46.40%	56.79%	47.41%	61.92%
F	10.54*	13.58*	8.22*	15.35*	8.41*	21.43*	12.69*	12.40*	15.42*	24.39*

(1) * Significant at $\alpha = 0.01$

**Significant at $\alpha = 0.05$

***Significant at $\alpha = 0.10$

Table 12 Political Stability and Earnings Opacity

Independent Variables	Model 1		Model 2		Model 3		Model 4		Model 5	
	2001	1998	2001	1998	2001	1998	2001	1998	2001	1998
1. Intercept	2.886	2.857	1.776	1.672	1.34	0.247	2.843	2.335	1.42	0.864
	(5.63)*	(4.94)*	(2.70)*	(2.23)**	-1.58	-0.3	(5.54)*	(3.66)*	(2.36)**	-1.4
2. OEO	-0.362	-0.376	-0.237	-0.243	-0.297	-0.266	-0.426	-0.368	-0.189	-0.137
	(-4.14)*	(-3.82)*	(-2.47)*	(-2.23)**	(-3.41)*	(-2.55)*	(-4.98)*	(-3.47)*	(-2.09)**	(-1.73)***
3. MMR			2.726	2.965						
			(2.45)**	(2.30)**						
4. EFI					0.182	0.307				
					(2.20)**	(3.81)*				
5. NEWSC							0.168	0.198		
							(3.55)*	-3.35		
6. EMERGE									0.785	1.043
									(3.70)*	(4.80)*

AHMED RIAHI-BELKAOUI

| Adjusted R2 | 32.80% | 29.13% | 41.90% | 37.52% | 39.76% | 50.64% | 62.40% | 47.02% | 52.18% | 57.93% |
| F | 17.11* | 14.56* | 12.90* | 10.91* | 11.56* | 17.42* | 20.75* | 12.98* | 18.46* | 23.04* |

(1) * Significant at α = 0.01
**Significant at α = 0.05
***Significant at α = 0.10

135

Table 13 Rule of Law and Earnings Opacity

Independent Variables	Model 1		Model 2		Model 3		Model 4		Model 5	
	2001	1998	2001	1998	2001	1998	2001	1998	2001	1998
1. Intercept	2.792	2.69	1.734	1.872	0.854	0.418	2.599	2	0.681	0.308
	(4.30)*	(4.2)*	(2.00)*	-1.55	-0.8	(-0.48)	(4.29)*	(3.06)*	-0.88	-0.5
2. OEO	-0.312	-0.301	-0.193	-0.14	-0.229	-0.229	-0.352	-0.274	-0.052	-0.02
	(-2.82)*	(-2.75)*	(-1.73)***	(-1.74)***	(-2.10)**	(-2.10)**	(-3.48)*	(-2.52)*	(-1.78)***	(-1.79)***
3. MMR			2.646	3.566						
			(1.77)***	(2.53)*						
4. EFI					0.227	0.367				
					(2.18)*	(4.27)*				
5. NEWSC							0.201	0.238		
							(3.59)*	(3.93)*		

6. EMERGE									1.137	1.285
									(4.55)*	(5.91)*
Adjusted R2	17.42%	16.55%	22.60%	28.59%	25.81%	46.11%	48.96%	45.03%	49.00%	60.50%
F	7.96*	7.55*	5.82*	7.61*	6.57*	14.69*	13.95*	12.06*	16.37*	25.51*

1) * Significant at $\alpha = 0.01$
**Significant at $\alpha = 0.05$
***Significant at $\alpha = 0.10$

137

Table 14 Control of Corruption and Earnings Opacity

Independent Variables	Model 1		Model 2		Model 3		Model 4		Model 5	
	2001	1998	2001	1998	2001	1998	2001	1998	2001	1998
1. Intercept	3.397	3.374	1.618	1.862	1.214	0.612	3.216	2.99	1.03	0.91
	-4.72	(5.14)*	(2.03)**	(2.01)**	-1.14	-0.61	(4.29)*	(4.20)*	-1.3	-1.39
2. OEO	-0.419	-0.419	-0.217	-0.246	-0.338	-0.305	-0.457	-0.413	-0.139	-0.116
	(-3.41)*	(-3.70)*	(-1.87)***	(-1.83)***	(-2.71)*	(-2.95)*	(-3.66)*	(-3.53)*	(-1.73)***	(-1.82)***
3. MMR			4.304	3.841						
			(3.23)*	(2.41)**						
4. EFI					0.239	0.328				
					(2.01)**	(3.33)*				
5. NEWSC							0.198	0.192		
							(2.85)*	(2.96)*		

138

6. EMERGE									1.237	1.27
									(4.41)*	(5.48)*
Adjusted R2	24.39%	27.83%	44.09%	34.27%	30.63%	45.11%	44.85%	44.59%	51.94%	61.79%
F	11.65*	13.73*	13.97*	9.60*	8.06*	14.15*	11.98*	11.86*	18.29*	26.88*

1) * Significant at $\alpha = 0.01$
**Significant at $\alpha = 0.05$
***Significant at $\alpha = 0$.

Table 15 Effect of Overall Earnings Opacity and
Stock Market Performance

Model: LMMR i = 0 + 1LGNP + 2 LDYDG i + 3 LOEO		
Dependant Variable (1)		
Independent Variable	(1)	(2)
Intercept (2)	-0.1274	0.04083
	(3.39)*	-0.45
LGNP (a)	0.0425	0.0278
	(4.73)*	(2.21)*
LDYDG (b)	3.2495	4.3802
	(1.98)**	(2.09)**
LOEO (a)		-0.1474
		(-2.14)**
F	12.24**	10.16**
Wald Test (3)		
R2 (adjusted)	39.10%	47.80%
Reset F-value	0.05	0.05
Hausman F-value	7.23	7.85

(1) Variable definitions: Variables are defined in Table 3. (a) indicates
that this variable is included as log (variable) and (b) indicates that this
variable is included as log (1 + variable)
(2) White's adjusted t-statistics are between parentheses.
*Significant at 0.01 level
**Significant at 0.05 level.

(3) Wald test for joint significance

Table 16 Effect of Stock Market Performance and
Earnings Opacity on Economic Growth

Model: ECG i = a 0 + a 1LGNP i + a 2 LDHI i + a 3 LGC/GDP i + a 4ELMMR i + a 5LOEO i + m i (2)		
Dependant Variable (1)	ECG(Per Capita GNP Growth for the period (1998-01)	
Independent Variable	(1)	(2)
Intercept (2)	3.0515	3.9841
	(4.34)*	(4.28)*
LGNP (a)	-0.7085	-0.683
	(3.02)*	(2.77)*
LDHI (a)	3.9433	3.7931
	(2.50)**	(2.30)**
LGC/GDP (a)	-0.7998	-0.7314
	(-3.82)*	(-3.69)*
ELMMR (3)	6.4353	5.8066
	(2.70)*	(2.03)**
LOEO (a)		-0.1633
		(-0.42)
F	10.08*	10.16**
R	58.29%	56.66%
Wald Test (3)	0.001	0.001
Reset F-value	0.50%	0.50%
Hausman F-value	8.42	8.47

(1) Variable definitions: Variables defined as in Table 3.

(a) indicates that this variable is included as log (variables)

(2) T Statistics are between parentheses.

 * Significant at a 0.01 level

 **Significant at a 0.05 level

(3) ELMMR = Estimated stock market performance from the results of equation (1) in Table 5.

Table 17 Level of output per worker and Earnings Opacity

	Model 1	Model 2
Independent Variables		
Intercept (1)	0.592	0.535
	(3.02)*	(3.22)*
OEO	-0.159	-0.119
	(-4.77)*	(-4.02)*
EF	_____	-0.598
		(-3.93)*
LO	_____	-0.109
		(1.61)
Adjusted R 2	39.69%	58.37%
F	22.72*	16.43*

(1) * Significant at = 0.01

Table 18 Capital Intensity and Earnings Opacity

	Model 1	Model 2
Independent Variables		
Intercept (1)	0.072	0.077
	-0.87	-1.1
OEO	-0.041	-0.029
	(-2.91)*	(-2.32)**
EF	_____	-0.193
		(2.99)*
LO	_____	-0.095
		(3.30)*
Adjusted R 2	18.48%	44.54%
F	8.48*	9.84*

(1) * Significant at = 0.01
**Significant at = 0.05
***Significant at = 0.10

Table 19 Human Capital per worker and Earnings Opacity

	Model 1	Model 2
Independent Variables		
Intercept (1)	0.11	0.092
	(1.92)***	-1.64
OEO	-0.021	-0.014
		(-1.83)***
EF		-0.114
		(-2.21)**
LO		-0.001
		(-0.06)
Adjusted R 2	10.70%	18.33%
F	4.96**	3.47**

(1) * Significant at = 0.01
 **Significant at = 0.05

Table 20 Productivity and Earnings Opacity

	Model 1	Model 2
Independent Variables		
Intercept (1)	0.346	0.304
	(1.92)***	-1.63
OEO	-0.085	-0.079
	(-2.91)*	(-2.37)**
EF	————	-0.152
		-0.381
LO	————	0.039
		-0.605
Adjusted R 2	18.49%	16.53%
F	8.49*	3.18**

(1) * Significant at = 0.01
**Significant at = 0.05

Table 21 Effects of Investor Protection on Earnings Opacity

The Table presents results of the determinants of earnings opacity. The dependent variable is the overall earnings score for each country. The independent variables are 1) the anti-director rights of the country, 2) the country stock market share of world's capital, 3) the number of auditors per 100,000 population and 4) the accounting disclosure level for the country. T-values are shown between parentheses

Intercept	11.273	(4.65)*
Anti-Director (AD)	0.456	2.60*
Market Share of World's Capital (MSOWC)	0.056	2.47**
Number of Auditors per 100,000 population (NOA)	0.002	2.39**
Disclosure Level (DL)	0.089	2.52**
F	3.31*	
R2 (Adjusted)	31.64%	
Wald Test	0.01	
Reset F. Value	0.05	
Hausman F. Value	3.22*	

* Significant at the 1 Percent Level
** Significant at the 5 Percent Level

Table 22 Corporate Valuation Model

The Table presents results of the corporate valuation model. The dependent variable is Tobin's Q. The independent variables are 1) civil law, a dummy variable that equals one if the legal origin of the company law or commercial code of the country is civil law and zero otherwise, 2) estimated overall earnings opacity from the regression results of equation (1) in Table 2, 3) the interaction between civil law and estimated overall earnings opacity and 4) the anti-director rights of the country. T values are between parentheses.

Intercept	5.113 (6.36)*	5.239 (5.84)**
Civil Law	-3.988 (-4.54)*	-4.072 (-4.38)*
Estimated Overall Earnings Opacity	-0.649 (-4.28)*	-0.654(-4.20)*
Civil Law * Estimated Overall Earnings Opacity	0.678 (4.12)*	0.685 (4.04)*
Anti-Director Rights (AD)	————	-0.021 (-0.35)
F	9.60*	6.91*
R (Adjusted)	52.86%	50.69%
Wald Test	1.00%	0.01
Reset F. Value	0.05	0.05
Hausman F. Value	6.82*	5.32*

* Significant at the 1 Percent Level
** Significant at the 5 Percent Level

Chapter 2:
Fraud

Fraud in the accounting environment is on the increase, causing enormous losses to firms, individuals, and society and creating a morale problem in the workplace. It takes place as corporate fraud, fraudulent financial reporting, white-collar crime, or audit failures. This chapter explicates the nature of fraud in the accounting environment, provides some theoretical explanations of the phenomenon from the field of criminology, and explores some outcome situations arising from corporate fraud.

NATURE OF FRAUD IN THE ACCOUNTING ENVIRONMENT

Fraud has many definitions. It is a crime. The Michigan criminal law states:

Fraud is a generic term, and embraces all the multifarious means which human ingenuity can devise, which are resorted to by one individual to get advantage over another by false representations. No definite and invariable rule can be laid down as a general proposition in defining fraud, as it includes surprise, trick, cunning and unfair ways by which another is cheated. The only boundaries defining it are those that limit human knavery.[1]

Fraud is the intentional deception of another person by lying and cheating for the purpose of deriving an unjust, personal, social, political, or economic advantage over that person.[2] It is definitively immoral.

Within a business organization fraud can be perpetrated for or against the firm. It is then *corporate fraud.* Management or a person in a position of trust can perpetrate it. It is then *management fraud* or *white-collar crime.* It may involve the use of an accounting system to portray a false image of the firm. It is then a form of *fraudulent financial reporting.* It may also involve a failure of the auditor to detect errors or misstatements. It is then an *audit failure.* In all these cases—corporate fraud, management fraud, white-collar crime, fraudulent financial reporting, audit failure—the accountant as preparer, auditor, or user stands to suffer heavy losses.

Corporate Fraud

Corporate fraud or economic crimes are perpetrated generally by officers, executives, and/or profit center managers of public companies to satisfy their short-term economic needs. In fact, the short term-oriented management style may create the need for corporate fraud, given the pressure to increase current profitability in the face of few opportunities and the need to take unwise risks with firm's resources. As confirmed by Jack Bologna:

Rarely is compensation based on the longer term growth and development of the firm. As a consequence of this myopic view of performance criteria, the executives and officers of many public companies have a built-in incentive or motivation to play fast and loose with their firm's assets and financial data.[3]

In fact, more than the pressure for short-term profitability, economic greed and avarice blot social values and lead to corporate fraud. Evidence from the Federal Bureau of Investigation shows that arrests from two categories of corporate fraud have climbed: fraud jumped 75 percent between 1976 and 1986, and embezzlement rose 26 percent.[4] In fact, corporate fraud goes beyond mere fraud and embezzlement. The situation points to a myriad of activities that may result in corporate fraud. The increase in corporate fraud in the United States and elsewhere is the result of the erosion in business ethics.

Fraudulent Financial Reporting

Fraudulent financial reporting is so rampant that a special commission was created to investigate it: the National Commission on Fraudulent Financial Reporting. The commission defined fraudulent financial reporting as "intentional or reckless conduct, whether act or omission, that results in materially misleading financial statements." Such reporting undermines the integrity of financial information and can affect a rage of victims: shareholders, creditors, employees, auditors, and even competitors. It is used by firms that are facing economic crises as well as by those motivated by misguided opportunism.

Common types of fraudulent financial reporting include

1. the manipulation, falsification, or altering of records or documents

2. the suppression or omission of the effects of completed transactions from records or documents

3. the recording of transactions without substance

4. the misapplication of accounting policies, and

5. the failure to disclose significant information

There is a deliberate strategy to deceive by distorting the information and the information records. This results from a number of documented dysfunctional behaviors: smoothing, biasing, focusing, gaming, filtering, and illegal acts. Such behaviors generally occur when managers have a low belief both in the analyzability of information and in the measurability and verifiability of data.[5] Of all these documented dysfunctional behaviors, the one most likely to result in fraudulent financial reporting is the occurrence of illegal acts by violation of a private or public law through various types of fraud. One type of fraud is within the accounting system. Examples include the following:

False input scams (creating fake debits)

a.   False or inflated claims from vendors, suppliers, benefits claimants, and employees or false refund or allowance claims by customers

b.   Lagging on receivable payments or customer bank deposits

c.   Check kiting

d.   Inventory manipulation and reclassification
     Arbitrary write-ups and write-downs
     Reclassification to lower value-obsolete, damaged, or "sample" status

e.   Intentional misclassification of expenditures
     Operational expense versus capital expenditures
     Personal expense versus business expense

f.   Fabrication of sales and cost of sales data

g.   Misapplication and misappropriation of funds and other corporate assets (theft and embezzlement)

h.   Computerized input and fraudulent access scams
     Data diddling and manipulation
     Impersonation and imposter terminal
     Scavenging
     Piggybacking
     Wiretapping
     Interception and destruction of input and source documents

Fabrication of batch or hash totals
Simulation and modeling fraud (fraudulent parallel systems)

i. Forgery, counterfeiting, or altering of source documents, authorizations, computer program documentation, or loan collateral

j. Overstating revenues and assets

k. Understating expenses and liabilities

l. Creating off-line reserves

m. Related party transactions

n. Spurious assets and hidden liabilities

o. "Smoothing" profits

p. Destruction, obliteration, and alteration of supporting documents

q. Exceeding limits of authority
False throughput scams

r. Salami slicing, trapdoors, Trojan horse, logic

s. Designed random error during processing cycle
Output scams

t. Scavenging through output

u. Output destruction, obliteration

v. Theft of output reports and logs

w. Theft of programs, data files, and systems programming and operations documentation[6]

Fraud does not always start with an illegal act. Managers are known to choose accounting methods in terms of their economic consequences. Various studies have argued that managerial preferences for accounting methods and procedures may vary, depending on the expected economic consequences of those methods and procedures. It has been well established that the manager's choice of accounting methods may depends on the effect on reported income,[7] the degree of owner versus manager control of the company,[8] and methods of determining managerial bonuses.[9] This effort to use accounting methods to show a good picture of the company becomes more pressing on managers who are facing some form of financial distress and are in need of showing the economic events in the most optimistic way. This may lead to suppressing or delaying the dissemination of negative information.[10] The next natural step for these managers is to use fraudulent financial reporting. To hide difficulties and to deceive investors, declining and failing companies have resorted to the following fraudulent reporting practices: (1) prematurely recognizing income, (2) improperly treated operating leases as sales, (3) inflating inventory by improper application of the last in, first out (**LIFO**) inventory method, (4) fictitious amounts in inventories, (5) failure to recognize losses through write-offs and allowances, (6) improperly capitalized or deferred costs and expenses, (7) unusual gains in operating income, (8) overvalued marketable securities, (9) "sham) year-end transactions to boost reported earnings and (10) changing their accounting practices to increase earnings without disclosing the changes.[11]

One factor in the increase of fraudulent financial reporting that has escaped scrutiny is the failure of accounting educational institutions to teach ways of detecting fraud and the importance of its detection to the entire financial reporting system. The emphasis in the university and the CPA examinations is with financial auditing rather than with forensic, fraud, or investigative reporting. J.C. Threadway Jr., chairman of the National Commission on Fraudulent Financial Reporting, sees it this way:

If you go back to the accounting literature of the 1920s or earlier, you'll find the detection of fraud mentioned as the objective of an audit much more prominently. Our work to date in looking at the way accounting and auditing are taught today in colleges and business schools indicates that fraud detection is largely ignored. In fact, there are texts currently in use that do not even talk about the detection of fraud.[12]

Because the Securities and Exchange Commission is dedicated to the protection of the interests of investors and the integrity of capital markets, it is concerned that adequate disclosures are provided for the public to allow a better judgment of the situation. One financial disclosure fraud enforcement program called for disclosures in four areas:

Liquidity problems, such as (1)decreased inflow of collections from sales to customers, (2) the lack of availability of credit from suppliers, bankers, and others, and (3) the inability to meet maturing obligations when they fall due.

Operating trends and factors affecting profits and losses, such as (1) curtailment of operations, (2) decline of orders, (3) increased competition, or (4) cost overruns on major contracts.

Material increases in problem loans must be reported by financial institutions.

Corporations cannot avoid their disclosure obligations when they approach business decline or failure.

Corporations need to adopt measures to reduce exposure on causes of fraudulent and questionable financial reporting practices. Examples of suggestions for the reduction of exposure include:

The formulation of desired behavior

The maintenance of effective system of internal control

The maintenance of effective financial organization with acknowledged responsibility for maintaining good financial reporting practices

The maintenance of effective internal audit function

Having the board of directors play an active role in reviewing financial reporting policies and practices

The monitoring of capabilities and circumstances of individuals in positions affecting the financial reporting

The promise and use of strong penalties for the violation of guidelines

Making sure that the performance targets are realistic

Being aware of high emphasis on short-term financial performance[13]

White-Collar Crime

White-collar crime was a concern for Durkheim, who was convinced that the "anomie state" of "occupational ethics" was the cause "of the incessant recurrent conflicts, and the multifarious disorders of which the economic world exhibits so sad a spectacle."[14] At the same time, Ross noticed the rise in vulnerability created by the increasingly complex forms of interdependence in society and the exploitations of these vulnerabilities by a new class that he called "criminaloid."[15] He argued that a new criminal was at large, one who picks pockets with a railway rebate, murders with an adulterant instead of a bludgeon, burglarizes with a "rake-off" instead of a jimmy, cheats with a company prospectus instead of a deck of cards, or scuttles his town instead of his ship.[16]

The phrase "white-collar crime" was originated in Edwin Sutherland's presidential address to the American Sociological Society in December 1939.[17] He defined it as "a crime committed by a person of respectability and high social status in the course of his occupation."[18] A debate followed, with Clinard and Reier's defining white-collar crime as restricted only to "illegal activities among business and professional men,"[19] and Harting's defining it as "a violation of law regulating business, which is committed for a firm by the firm or its agents in the conduct of its business."[20] Basically, one view of white-collar crime focused on occupation, and the other focused on the organization, but in fact the world of both occupation and organization is the world of white-collar crime and constitutes what the knife and gun are to street crime.[21] White-collar crimes have not been condemned as vehemently as other common crimes. One reason is that their crime is not to cause physical injury but to further organizational goals. In fact, individuals were found to consider organizational crimes far less serious than those with physical impact.[22] Another reason for the indifference to white-collar crime may be the possibility that members of the general public are themselves committing white-collar crimes on a smaller scale.[23] In addition, the white-collar criminal generally finds support for his or her behavior in group norms, which place him or her in a different position from the common criminal. As Aubert explains:

But what distinguishes the white-collar criminal in this aspect is that his group often has an elaborate and widely accepted ideological rationalization for the offenses, and is a group of great social significance outside the sphere of criminal activity—usually a group with considerable economic and political power.[24]

The white-collar criminal is motivated by social norms, accepted and enforced by groups that indirectly give support to the illegal activity. In many cases the organization itself is committing the white-collar crime, sometimes because it may be the only response to economic demands.

White-collar crime may be characterized by five principal components: (1) intent to commit the crime, (2) disguise of purpose, (3) reliance on the naivete of the victim(s), (4) voluntary victim action to assist the offender, and (5) concealment of the violation.[25] Unlike traditional crime, its objective is to steal kingly sums rather than small sums of money, and its modus operandi is to use technology and mass communications rather than brute force and crude tools. In addition, white-collar crime relies on the ignorance and greed of its victim.[26] it inflicts economic harm and physical harm and damages the social fabric.

Audit Failure

Auditors are expected to detect and correct or reveal any material omissions or misstatements of financial information. When auditors fail to meet these expectations, an audit failure is the inevitable result. The level of audit quality can avoid the incurrence of audit failures. Audit quality has been defined as the probability that financial statements contain no material omission or misstatements.[27] It has also been defined in terms of audit risk, with high-quality services reflecting lower audit risk.[28] Audit risk was defined as the risk that "the auditor may unknowingly fail to appropriately modify his opinion on financial statements that are materially misstated."[29]

Audit failures do, however, occur and, as a consequence, bring audit firms face-to-face with costly litigation and loss of reputation, not to mention court-imposed judgments and out-of-court settlements. The client's or user's losses lead to the litigation situation and the potential of payments to the plaintiff. Litigation can be used as an indirect measure of audit quality using an inverse relation—auditors with relatively low (high) litigation offer higher- (lower-) quality audits. This relation was verified in a study that indicated, as expected, that non-Big Eight firms as a group had higher litigation occurrence rates than the Big Eight and that supported the Big Eight as quality-differentiated auditors.[30]

But not all litigations follow directly from audit failures. In a study that described the role of business failures and management fraud in both legal actions brought against auditors and the settlement of such actions, Palmrose found that (1) nearly half of the cases that alleged audit failures involved business failures or clients with severe financial difficulties, and (2) most lawsuits that involved bankrupt clients also involved management fraud.[31] These findings point to the fact that business failures and management fraud play a great role in the occurrence of audit failures, which calls for the auditor to take a responsible attitude in the detection of fraud, as it may affect the audit quality, the audit risk, and the potential for costly litigations. As stated by Connor:

Establishing the requirement to identify the conditions underlying fraudulent reporting as an independent objective of the audit process would help to clarify auditor responsibility and increase auditor awareness of this responsibility.

161

Performance of the recommended procedures of management control review and evaluation and fraud risk evaluation would improve the probability of detecting conditions leading to misstated financial statements. The required focus on financial condition would help identify more effectively those entities that would qualify as business failure candidates in the near tem.[32]

Although management fraud and business failure may play a great role in audit failures, there are other reasons for such failures. For example, St. Pierre and Anderson's extended analysis of documented audit failures identified three other reasons: (1) error centering on the auditor's interpretation of generally accepted accounting principles; (2) error centering on the auditor's interpretation of generally accepted auditing standards or implementation of generally accepted auditing standards; and (3) error centering on fraud of the auditor.[33]

FRAMEWORK FOR FRAUD IN THE ACCOUNTING ENVIRONMENT

We have established that fraud is rampant in the accounting environment, taking the shape of corporate fraud, fraudulent financial reporting, white-collar crime, and audit failures. The main issue is to determine the causes and, above all, provide an explanation for the situation. Descriptive characteristics of the person or the situation that may lead to fraud in the accounting environment abound. For example, there is a need to watch for "red flags," which do not necessarily prove management fraud, but when enough of them exist, there is the potential for corporate fraud. Red flag characteristics to be wary of in the course of an audit include the following:

A person who is a wheeler-dealer
A person without a well-defined code of ethics
A person who is neurotic, manic-depressive, or emotionally unstable
A person who is arrogant or egocentric
A person with a psychopathic personality

Financial pressures lead to the following possible red flags within the industry

Unfavorable economic conditions within that industry
Heavy investments or losses
Lack of sufficient working capital
Success of the company dependent on one or two products, customers, or transactions
Excess capacity
Severe obsolescence
Extremely high debt
Extremely rapid expansion through new business or product lines
Tight credit, high interest rates, and reduced ability to acquire credit
Pressure to finance expansion through current earnings rather than through debt or equity
Profit squeeze (costs and expenses rising higher and faster than sales and revenues)
Difficulty in collecting receivables

Unusually heavy competition (including low-priced imports)

Existing loan agreements with little flexibility and tough restrictions

Progressive deterioration in quality earnings

Significant tax adjustments by the IRS

Long-term financial losses

Unusually high profits with a cash shortage

Urgent need for favorable earnings to support high price of stock, meet earnings forecast, and so on

Need to gloss over a temporary bad situation and maintain management position and prestige

Significant litigation, especially between stockholders and management

Unmarketable collateral

Significant reduction in sales backlog indicating future sales decline

Long business cycle

Existence of revocable and possibly imperiled licenses necessary for continuation of business

Suspension or delisting from a stock exchange[34]

Fear of a merger

Merchant cities as causes of fraudulent financial reporting organizational factors and personal circumstances:

By providing incentives for deception, by failing to persuade managers and employees that chances of detection are higher and penalties severe, and by failing to provide adequate moral guidance and leadership, corporations increase the use of illegal and unethical practices.[35]

Although these descriptive characteristics may be useful for detecting the potential for fraud in the corporate environment, they do not provide an adequate normative explanation of why fraud happens. The field of criminology offers various models and theories that are very much applicable to fraud in the accounting environment and may offer alternative explanations for the phenomenon.

The Conflict Approach

The consensus approach and the conflict approach are two major views that hypothesize about law and society.[36] Influenced by anthropological and sociological studies of primitive law, the consensus approach sees laws developing out of public opinion as a reflection of popular will. The conflict approach sees laws as originating in a political context in which influential interest groups pass laws that are beneficial to them. A third view argues for an integrated approach that focuses on the different functions of the consensus and conflict approaches, with the conflict approach ideal to explain the creation of criminal law and the consensus perspective, the operation of the law.

In the case of the accountant and fraud it can be argued, using the conflict approach, that accounting interest groups presented a favorable picture of their problematic situation by insisting that they can control for fraud and worked to get their view of the situation more widely recognized. The process led to less stringent regulation enacted for fraudulent reporting cases and white-collar crime. Basically, it fits with the notion that the criminal law that emerges after the creation of the state is designed to protect the interests of those who control the machinery of the state, including the accounting profession.

The consensus approach refers instead to the widespread consensus about the community's reaction to accounting fraud and to the legislation enacted. The consensus approach to accounting fraud may have resulted from either the ignorance or the indifference of the general public to the situation. Another explanation is the idea of differential consensus related to the support of criminal laws.[37] While serous crimes receive strong support for vigorous actions, crimes relating to the conduct of business and professional activities generate an apathetic response.

If one adopts a conflict model of crime, then the origin of the fraudulent practices in accounting may be linked to a society's political and economic development. As society's political and economic development reaches higher stages, institutions are created to accommodate new needs and to check aggressive impulses. In the process these restraining institutions created a system of inequality and spur the aggressive and acquisitive impulses that the consensus model of crime mistakes for part of human nature. The powerful elites rather than the general will arise to label the fraudulent practices in accounting as criminal because these crimes affect these elites as they are related to property and its possession and control. At the same time, members of that same elite constitute a major component of those participating in the fraudulent practices in accounting. Their motivation to engage in the practices remains the question.

The conflict model of crime would attribute the practices to a system of inequality that values certain kinds of aggressive behavior. Basically, those engaging in fraudulent practices in accounting are reacting to the life conditions of their own social class: acquisitive behavior of the powerful, on the hand, and the high-risk property crimes of the powerless, on the other. One would conclude that the focus of the attack on the fraudulent practices should be toward the societal institutions that led to the isolation of the individuals. It implies a reorganization of these institutions to eliminate the illegal possession of rights, privileges, and position.[38]

The Ecological Theory

An examination of some of the notorious accounting frauds, white-collar crimes, and audit failures may suggest that some criminal types are attracted to business in general and to accounting in particular. Therefore, the criminal cases are not indicative of a general phenomenon in the field but the result of the criminal actions of the minority of criminal types that have been attracted to the discipline of accounting. This approach is known as the "Lombrosian" view of criminology. But with the Lombrosian theory of a physical "criminal type" losing its appeal, the ecological theory appears as a more viable and better alternative to an explanation of the fraud phenomenon in accounting. It adopts as a basis of explanation of corporate fraud the concept of social disorganization, which is generally defined as the decrease in influence of existing rules of behavior on individual members of the group. Criminal behavior in the accounting field is to be taken as an indicator of a basic social disorganization. First, weak social organization of the discipline of accounting leads to criminal behavior. Second, with the social control of the discipline waning because of the general public indifference, some accountants are freed from moral sensitivities and are predisposed to corporate fraud, white-collar crime, and audit failure. Then the general public's failure to function effectively as an agency of social control is the immediate cause of corporate fraud, white-collar crime, fraudulent financial reporting, and audit failure. Basically, some accountants are freed from moral sensitivities when social control breaks down or fails to function properly.

The Cultural Transmission Theory

Unlike the ecological theory, which assumes that criminal behavior is a product of common values incapable of realization because of social disorganization, the cultural transmission theory attempts to identify the mechanisms that relate social structure to criminal behavior. One mechanism is the conception of differential association, which maintains that a person commits a crime because he or she perceives more favorable than unfavorable definitions of law violation. A person learns to become a criminal. As explained by Sutherland:

As part of the process of leaning practical business, a young man with idealism and thoughtfulness for others is inducted into white-collar crime. In many cases he is ordered by a manager to do things, which he regards as unethical or illegal, while in other cases he learns from those who have the same rank as his own how they make a success. He learns specific techniques for violating the law, together with definitions of situations in which those techniques may be used. Also he develops a general ideology.[39]

This mechanism assumes, then, that delinquents have different values from those of nondelinquents. Criminal behavior is the result of values that condone crime. Criminals have been socialized into the values that condone crime. They were transmitted into a culture of crime. Their behavior is an expression of specific values.[40]

Basically, what is implied is that fraudulent behavior in accounting is learned; it is learned indirectly or by indirect association with those who practice the illegal behavior. An accountant engages in fraud because of the intimacy of his or her contact with fraudulent behavior. This is called the process of "differential association." Sutherland explains:

It is a genetic explanation of both white-collar criminals and lower-class criminality. Those who become white-collar criminals generally start their careers in good neighborhoods and good homes, graduate from colleges with some idealism, and with little selection on their part, get into particular business situations in which criminality is practically a folk way. The lower-class criminals generally start their careers in deteriorated neighborhoods and families, find delinquents at hand from whom they acquire the attitudes towards, and the techniques of, crime through association with delinquents and through partial segregation from law-abiding people. The essentials of the process are the same for the two classes of criminals.[41]

Anomie Theories

Anomie, as introduced by Durkheim, is a state of normlessness or lack of regulation, a disordered relation between the individual and the social order, which can explain various forms of deviant behavior.[42] Merton's formulation of anomie focuses not no the discontinuity in the life experiences of an individual but on the lack of fit between values and norms that confuses the individual.[43] As an example in achieving the American Dream, a person may find himself or herself in a dilemma between cultural goals and the means specified to achieve them. The ways adopted include conformity, innovation, ritualism, retreatism, and rebellion.[44]

Conformity to the norms and use of legitimate means to attain success do not lead to deviance. Innovation refers to the use of illicit means to attain success and may explain white-collar crime in general and fraudulent accounting and auditing practices in particular. Merton states: "On the top economic levels, the pressures toward innovation not infrequently erase the distinction between business-like stirrings this side of the mores and sharp practices beyond themores."[45]

Ritualism refers to an abandoning of the success goal. "Though one draws in one's horizons, one continues to abide almost compulsively by institutional norms."[46] Retreatism is basically a tacit withdrawal from the race, a way of escaping from it all.

Finally, rebellion is a revolutionary rejection of the goals of success and the means of reaching it. Those adaptations are a result of the emphasis in our society on economic success and on the difficulty of achieving it.

Only when a system of cultural values extols, virtually above all else, certain common success-goals for the population at large while the social structure rigorously restricts or completely closes access to approved modes of reaching these goals *for a considerable part of the same population* does deviant behavior ensue on a large scale.[47] Interestingly enough, Merton goes as far as suggesting that deviance develops among scientists because of the emphasis on originality. Given limited opportunity and short supply, scientists would resort to devices such as reporting only data that support one's hypothesis, secrecy, stealing ideas, and fabricating data.[48]

Unlike Durkheim, Merton believes that anomie is a permanent feature of all modern industrial societies. Their emphasis on achievement and the pressures that result lead to deviance. The anomie thesis is further explored in the work of Cohen[49] and Cloward and Ohlin.[50] Cohen attributes the origins of criminal behavior to the impact of ambition across those social positions for which the possibilities of achievement are limited. What results is a nonutilitarian delinquent subculture.[51] Individuals placed in low social positions accept societal values of ambition but are unable to realize them because of lack of legitimate opportunities to do so. Cloward and Ohlin suggest that the resulting delinquent behavior is, however, conditioned by the presence or absence of appropriate illegitimate means.[52]

Corporate fraud, fraudulent reporting practices, white-collar crime, and audit failures are a result of anomie in modern societies. Basically, delinquent accountants emerge among those whose status, power, and security of income are relatively low

171

but whose level of aspiration is high, so that they strive to emerge from the bottom using even illegal ways. Fraudulent behavior among accountants is then the solution to status anxiety. It results from the discrepancy between the generally accepted values of ambition and achievement and the inability to realize them and the availability of appropriate illegitimate means.

A Framework for Fraud in Accounting

The various theories from the field of criminology offer alternative explanations for corporate fraud, white-collar crime, fraudulent financial reporting, and audit failures. They can be integrated in a framework to be used for identifying the situations most conductive to those phenomena (see Figure 2.1). Basically, the framework postulates that corporate fraud, white-collar crime, fraudulent financial reporting and audit failures occur most often in the following situations:

In which accounting and business groups have presented a favorable picture of their problematic situation by insisting that they can control for fraud and worked to get their view of the situation more widely recognized. What may exist is a situation in which the accountants and/or businessmen have stated that they are taking private actions to avoid public regulation of the phenomena, whereas in fact their actions were mere cosmetic changes or camouflage of serous problems in the profession. There have been many examples of situations in which the accounting profession has argued for private regulation of various problems that affect the profession, the discipline, and standard setting and has thwarted the actions of legislators who were trying to put a stop to the abuses. One has only to recall the failure of various congressional committees investigating the profession to enact any fundamental regulations to change the nature, character, structure, and behaviors of the profession to illustrate the point. From a conflict approach, this is clearly a situation in which the interests of those who control the machinery of the state, including the power of the accounting profession, are protected from stringent regulation.

Figure 2.1 A Framework for Fraud in Accounting

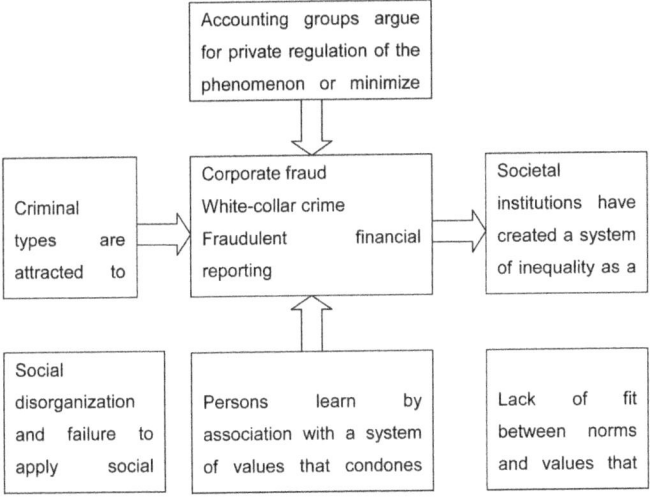

In which societal institutions have accumulated power, privileges, and position, creating a perception of inequality in those who are not members of these institutions. Basically, the situation may lead to an isolation of individuals in a situation in which the acquisitive behavior of the powerful is evident in their daily

173

lives. The lower-level accountant may react to this situation of powerlessness, inferiority, and exclusion by resorting to the various types of illegal activities covered in this chapter. It would be a mere reaction to a system of inequality that values aggressive behavior as explained by the conflict model.

In which firms in general have attracted some criminal types. This Lombrosian view of the phenomenon applies to various accounting frauds.

In which social disorganization in general and failure to apply social control exist. Basically, weak social organization of the discipline and failure of the general public to be concerned creates a climate conducive to fraud.

In which people are placed in a system of values that condones corporate fraud, white-collar crime, fraudulent financial reporting, and audit failures.

In which there is a lack of fit between values and norms that compose the person.

OUTCOME SITUATIONS THAT ARISE FROM CORPORATE FRAUD

Away from RICO to ADR

There is definitely a dramatic increase in the number of claims against certified public accountants (CPAs) and in the amounts sought by claimants as a result of the expanding scope of accountants' liability and the Racketeer-Influenced and Corrupt Organization (RICO) Act liability. RICO, originally used by people victimized by a "pattern of rack-eteering activity" to sue for treble damages and attorney fees, ahs been used more and more in commercial litigation growing out of fraudulent securities offerings, corporate failures, and investment disappointments. A situation in which code-fendent auditors (sometimes in alleged conspiracy with their client and its management) had violated the federal mail and securities fraud statutes by improperly auditing and issuing audit opinions on their client's financial statements on two or more specified occasions and by employing in the operations of their firms (in or affecting interstate commerce) the fees received for those audits, by reason of which plaintiffs were injured in their business or property, is claimed to allege a violation of statutory provisions of RICO.[53] Efforts were made in 1987 to reform the civil provisions of RICO. In fact, a Senate bill introduced by Senator Howard Metzenbaum continues to permit plaintiffs to seek multiple damages in cases otherwise punishable under the securities in the United States. This spells bad news for the accounting profession. Witness the following statement made by B.Z. Lee, the AICPA's choice for testifying to the need to reform RICO:

Of greatest concern to the accounting profession…is the fact that RICO continues to be used to evade the standards of the securities laws and to raise the stakes in ordinary litigation arising from securities transactinos.[54]

For now, fraudulent cases that involve auditors will continue to be prosecuted with RICO liability in mind. In these fraudulent cases accountants have found themselves named as codefendants. The rationale behind the courts' proneness to hold auditors liable for losses associated with business failures results from the belief that auditors "(1) can best prevent the losses associated with business failures and (2) are able to spread their liability through insurance."[55] What auditors face is a dangerous gamble that is trial by jury, especially with the risk of RICO-treble damage judgments. Not only may the average juror not understand the complexities of the cases, but the CPA may face the situation of claims without merit because his or her factual and legal positions may be misunderstood or rejected by the same jurors. The trial by jury may also be an expensive alternative even if the CPA's position prevailed. Witness the following assessment of the situation:

Even if the accountant ultimately prevails at trial, the costs of protracted litigation, including attorneys' fees and deposition costs, can be prohibitively high. Thus, even a win before a jury often translates into great pecuniary loss. Litigation costs and exposure aside, an additional substantial burden is placed on an accountant defendant who is called away from practice—losing both time and fees—and required to produce and review records, study claimants' documents and testimony, appear as a witness on deposition, attend depositions of others and be in attendance at trials.[56]

The trial by jury can also be detrimental to accountants because of the several often repeated arguments that are increasingly persuasive in courts. These arguments include the perceptions (a) that auditors are equipped to prevent the losses associated with business failures, (b) that accountants have deep pockets that can use their insurance to spread the losses, and (c) that equity calls for placing the blame for losses resulting from business failures on auditors.[57] What appear to be more beneficial options for resolving claims against CPAs are the alternative dispute resolution (ADR) methods: arbitration, court-assessed arbitration, mediation, and mistrial.

The AICPA's special committee on accountants' legal liability prepared in 1987 a paper on ADR as a flexible approach to resolving litigation with a client by transforming the typical confrontational position into one of cooperation to reach a mutually advantageous solution.[58] One suggestion made is for the accountant and his or her client to agree on some element of an engagement letter or on a separate agreement that any disputes between them will be determined by ADR procedures. The following two model paragraphs are offered for an engagement letter, one specifically for arbitration and the other for general procedure:

Model Arbitration Paragraph

Any controversy or claim arising out of or relating to our engagement to [describe service, e.g., audit the company's financial statements] shall be resolved by arbitration in accordance with the Commercial Arbitration Rules of the American Arbitration Association, and judgment on the award rendered by the Arbitrator(s) may be rendered in any Court having proper jurisdiction.

Model General ADR Paragraph

In the event of any dispute between us relating to our engagement to [describe engagement, e.g., audit the company's financial statements; prepare the company's tax returns], we mutually agree to try in good faith to resolve the dispute through negotiation or alternative dispute resolution techniques before pursuing full-scale litigation.[59]

Arbitration is now appearing as the more viable option. The pros for arbitration include (1) its informal nature, (2) the choice of knowledgeable professionals as arbitrators, (3) its low cost, (4) its avoidance of the wrong judgments by an unsophisticated jury, (5) the neutralizing of the hostility factor to professionals and sympathy factor to alleged victims prevalent in a jury trial, and (6) the elimination of the risk of a runaway jury's returning a verdict that far exceeds actual losses. These features are summed up as follows.

In arbitration, extensive and time-consuming discovery, which has become standard practice in litigation, is generally not permitted. During the preparatory stages of arbitration, lengthy depositions usually aren't allowed, and limited documentation is exchanged on an informal basis. At arbitration hearings, the rules of evidence are more relaxed. Because of the expertise of the members of the panel, the need for experts to make detailed explanations to unsophisticated jurors is substantially reduced. Fewer witnesses need to be called to testify, fewer technical requirements need to be met, and fewer technical evidentiary objections and arguments need to be made.[60]

Naturally, there are limitations to arbitration. The major limitations are the absence of judicial review and the loss of the court's requirement that evidence be legally admissible and weighed in accordance with legal principles. Other limitations are expressed as follows.

While the American Institute of CPAs' accountants' legal liability special committee has submitted proposed alternative dispute resolution and arbitration clauses, the inclusion of these clauses in the initial engagement letter may subject a member to a coverage defense in any subsequent litigation.... Arbitration includes numerous negative points such as limited discovery, limited appeal and a difficulty in confining the arbitrators' decision to case and statutory law. This is particularly true when a defense may involve a question of privity. These negative points severely affect the insurer's ability to defend an insured in a malpractice claim. It seems to me that a CPA may subject himself to an insurance coverage dispute by including an arbitration clause in the initial engagement letter, since the clause binds the CPA and his insurer to submit to future arbitration.[61]

The Liability Exposure Expands

With the number of lawsuits filed in 1987 reaching one private lawsuit for every fifteen Americans, accountants were not immune to the epidemic of lawsuits. The consequences include escalating judgments and legal costs and astronomical increases in the premiums for professional liability. Even the AICPA professional liability insurance plan increased the premium to 200 percent by the end of 1985, along with a coupling of deductibles and reduction in the maximum coverage available from $20 million in 1984 to $5 million in 1985. The situation is explained as follows: As a result of the premium increase, some medium-sized firms previously paying about $3,400 for $5 million in coverage saw their bills jump to $10,250. In addition, the deductible per claim doubled from $3,500 to $7,000.[62]

To make things worse, megasuits are now being filed against the eight largest accounting firms. Examples include (1) the $260 million damage suit filed in 1985 by the British government for alleged negligence against the auditors of the Delorean Motor Co. in Northern Oreland and (2) the $100 million judgment brought against an Australian accounting partnership in *Cambridge Credit Corporation Ltd. v. Hutcheson*.[63]

The nature of accounting liability has changed since the first English lawsuit against an auditor in 1887.[64] Two major suits had a profound effect: Judge (later Justice) Benjamin N. Cardozo's opinion in *Ultramares Corp. v. Touche* in 1931[65] and the McKesson & Robbins business fraud and settlement with accountants in 1938.[66] The *Ultramares Corp. v. Touche* decision was that accountants are liable for negligence to their clients and to those who they know will be using their work product. More precisely, Judge Cardozo held that accounts could not be held liable to third parties because it might expose accountants to a liability in an indeterminate amount for an indeterminate time to an indeterminate class. The hazards of business conducted on these terms are so extreme as to enkindle doubt whether a flaw may not exist in the implication of a duty that exposes to these consequences.[67]

The doctrine known as the "privity defense" has recently been eroded with a dramatic expansion in the scope of an auditor's availability for negligence. As Minow states: "The new theory seems to be that the accountant should be held responsible for a business that doesn't function properly."[68] The new *doctrine of indeterminate liability* extends the accountants' liability to any investor or creditor who can convince the court or a jury that the accountant, in hindsight, could have prevented a business failure or fraud by disclosing it. Another new doctrine known as the *fraud-on-the-market theory* allows investors to recover from defendants for alleged misrepresentations of which the investors were completely unaware as long as reliance on the statements by the market affected the price of the security bought or sold by the plaintiff. An example of the new doctrines came in 1983, when the New Jersey Supreme Court, in *Rosenblaum v. Adler,* held that the accountants can be held of negligence to any reasonable "third parties" relying on that information, especially that which the accountants are able to use and misuse:

Independent auditors have apparently been able to obtain liability insurance covering these risks or otherwise to satisfy their financial obligation. We have no reason to believe they may not purchase malpractice insurance policies that cover their negligence leading to misstatements relied upon by persons who received the audit from the company pursuant to a proper business purpose. Much of the additional costs incurred either because of more thorough auditing review or increased insurance premiums would be borne by the business entity and its stockholders or its customers.[69]

There is definitely a misperception of the accounting profession and its work product. Victor Earle, general counsel of Peat, Marwick, Main & Co., stated this misperception with prescience a decade ago:

The misconceptions in the public mind are at least fivefold: first, as to scope—that auditors make a 100% examination of the company's records, which can be depended upon to recover all errors or misconduct; second, as to evaluation—that auditors test the wisdom and legality of a company's multitudinous business decisions; third, as to precision—that the numbers set forth in a company's audited financial statements are immutable absolutes; fourth, as to reducibility—that the audited results of a company's operations for a year can be synthesized into a single number; and fifth, as to approval—that by expressing an option on a company's financial statement, the auditors "certify" its health and attractiveness for investment purpose.[70]

The liability exposure of U.S. accounting firms doing audits of overseas subsidiaries of American companies also increased tremendously in March 1988, when a federal judge ruled that United States-based accounting firms can be sued in U.S. courts for allegedly shoddy audits in other nations. The decision came after the Court denied a motion by Arthur Andersen & Co. to throw out a $260 million suit against it by the British government for allegedly negligent audits after the collapse of Delorean Motor Co.'s Irish unit. That the U.S. courts will have jurisdiction in such cases spells more trouble for American accounting firms, as U.S. courts are known to be far tougher on accountants than are English and European courts.[71]

In March 1988 the liability exposure took a different dimension when the Supreme Court made it easier for shareholders to file class-action lawsuits against companies that issue misleading information. In its ruling the Supreme Court endorsed the efficient market hypothesis, which maintains that all publicly available information is reflected in the market price. Therefore, shareholders who allege misleading information and security fraud don't have to prove that they have relied on the misleading information. Basically, nobody can hide anymore behind a white collar.[72]

Those developments put the accounting profession in a dangerous situation, as all business failures could be blamed on the accountant and as the normal risks of investment may be shifted from the investor to the accountant. Frivolous litigation may arise, leading the accounting profession to avoid serving riskier industries and to avoid innovations in its own practice. A case in point is the review of earnings forecasts. Minnow explains:

Accountants would be discouraged from innovations within their own practice, such as review of earnings forecasts, which, though potentially highly useful to the investing public, are necessarily speculative and, in the current climate, pose obvious litigation risks to accountants.[73]

Fraud Engagement: The Issues

Fraud as the intentional deception, misappropriation of resources, or distortion of data to the advantage of the perpetrator may involve either a manager or an employee.

183

Management fraud is the most difficult to detect and can cause irreparable damage. The conduct of an audit in accordance with generally accepted accounting principles does not anticipate deceit and may fail to detect fraud. The key to fraud prevention could be effective and functioning internal controls. However, some fraud schemes may be effectively designed to work within the framework of an effective internal control system. The level of assurance of these controls becomes the key, even though fraud is most associated with a problem of integrity and, therefore, not easily quantifiable. What may be needed besides the audit is a fraud engagement. This is different from an audit based on a generally accepted auditing standard in the following way:

In short, the fraud engagement requires a specialized program that is singularly designed for discovery. It is ideally concerned with what lies behind transactions, with regard to materiality, and is not concerned with the application of generally accepted accounting principles unless misapplication has led to fraudulent statements. In its purest form, therefore, it is a hybrid of auditing and management advisory services. And the individual searching for fraud must have a detection mentality that is tempered with a high level of innovation and skepticism.[74]

Fraud engagement should be looking for specially recurring fraud schemes and watch for specific indicators of fraud. Recurring fraudulent schemes include the following:

- Petty cash embezzlement, generally camouflaged by false or inadequate documentation

- Accounts payable fraud involving the formation of a dummy corporation to invoice the payer and receive the funds

- Cash inventory schemes in which inventory is purchased with cash or its equivalent, rather than by check, and is not placed on the books

- False payroll schemes involving the creation of a fictitious employee, with management cashing his or her spurious payroll checks

- Lapping schemes in which employees steal from one customer's account and attempt to cover the theft by applying to that account later collections from another customer

- Kickback schemes[75]

All of these schemes involve some diversion of assets or information followed by the prevention or deferral of the activities' disclosure. They can be detected if certain indicators or indicia are carefully watched, especially those indicators or indicia that are present time and again when fraud occurs. The following irregularities deserve closer scrutiny:

1. High rates of employee turnover, particularly in the accounting or bookkeeping departments

2. Refusal to use serially numbered documents or the undocumented destruction of missing numbers

3. Excessive and unjustified cash transactions

4. Excessive and unjustified use of exchange items, such as cashier's checks, traveler's checks, and money orders

5. Failure to reconcile checking accounts

6. Excessive number of checking accounts with a true business purpose

7. The existence of liens and other financial encumbrances before a bankruptcy, which may indicate that the bankruptcy was planned

8. Photocopies of invoices in files

9. A manager or employee who falls in debt

10. Excessive number of unexplained corporate checks bearing second endorsements

11. Excessive or material changes in bad-debt write-off

12. Inappropriate freight expenses in relation to historical sales or industry norms

13. Inappropriate ratio of inventory components

14. Business dealings with no apparent economic purpose

15. Assets apparently sold but possession maintained

16. Assets sold for much less than they are worth

17. Continuous rollover of loans to management or loans to employees not normally included in the loans accounts

18. Questionable changes in financial ratios, such as net income and inventory

19. Questionable leave practices, such as the failure or refusal of an employee to take leave[76]

It follows that auditors have to explain their role to that of police officers and engage in detecting and reporting fraud and financial weaknesses in the firms that they audit. The three-year examination of the auditing profession by the House Subcommittee on Oversight and Investigations that ended in 1988 had a nonnegotiable item for the profession, which is to be the voluntary protector of the investor or face legislation that will make this role mandatory.[77] For that, Congress will use the Treadway findings as a basis for the legislation and increase the SEC power to impose sanctions and push for criminal prosecution. One would not blame Congress, as the typical situation now shows a failure of auditing standards when they allow auditors to wait until a company has failed before notifying the SEC of possible fraud. A case in point is the ZZZZ Best One, in which Ernst and Whinney had good reason to believe long before ZZZZ Best collapsed that many of the statements made by the carpet cleaning company were fraudulent. It was over and of no use to anyone when Ernst and Whinney decided to make its knowledge of fraud public. Only after the bankruptcy did Ernst and whinney file documents with the SEC indicating that it had been tipped off that ZZZZ Best really was little more than a giant Ponzi schemes, costing investors more than $70 million.

Fraud auditing is then one solution to the problem of fraudulent financial reporting and fraud in general. It was referred to as the creation of an environment that encourages the detection and prevention of fraud in commercial transactions.[78] The advent of federal, criminal, and regulatory statutes involving business calls for some form of fraud auditing. When fraud auditing fails to connect the problems and frauds do happen, is there a role for forensic and investigative accounting? Forensic auditing deals with the relation and application of financial facts to legal problems.[79] What, then, is the difference between forensic accounting, fraud auditing, investigative auditing, and financial auditing? The answer to a survey among the staff members of Peat Marwick Lindquist Holmes, a Toronto-based firm of chartered accountants, is illustrative of the difference:

Forensic accounting is a general term used to describe any investigation of a financial nature that can result in some matter that has legal consequence.

Fraud auditing is a specialized discipline within forensic accounting, which involves the investigation of a particular criminal activity, namely fraud.

Investigative auditing involves the review of financial documentation for a specific purpose, which could relate to litigation support and insurance claims as well as criminal matters.[80]

Forensic accounting goes beyond routine auditing. It specializes in uncovering fraud in the ledger of business contracts and bank statements. Forensic auditors prepare a written profile of every key person involved with the company, including corporate officers, employees, and vendors. Keeping track of everything is the objective. The following comment by Douglas Carmichael illustrates the extent of the investigation under forensic auditing:

When the death of a company [occurs] under mysterious circumstances, forensic accountants are essential.... Other accountants may look at the charts. But forensic accountants actually dig into the body.[81]

THE POSITION OF THE ACCOUNTANTS IN THE COURTS

Do CPAs, because of their credentials as professionals, have special privileges in the legal system? The answer is that both as witnesses in the conduct of legal inquiry and as defendants in the law of torts, the accountants face a difficult and awkward situation.

Loss of Technical Privilege

The court requires of all witnesses that all relevant information be brought to court on pain of a charge of contempt. The best-known exception is the lawyer client privilege. The general rule of privilege of Federal Rule of Evidence 503 reads as follows:

A client has a privilege to refuse to disclose and to prevent any other person from disclosing confidential communications made for the purpose of facilitating the rendition of professional [sic] legal services to the client, (1) between himself or his representative and his lawyer or his lawyer's representative, or (2) between his lawyer and the lawyer's representative, or (3) by him or his lawyer to a lawyer representing another in a matter of common interest, or (4) between representatives of the client or between the client and a representative of the client, or (5) between lawyers representing the client.

The same privilege has also been given to the psychologist and the physician (Supreme Court Standard 504) and the clergyman (Supreme Court Standard 506). How about accountants? Do they function or rate sufficiently high to overweigh the value of requiring them to reveal their secrets to the court? The official decision of the courts is that accountants cannot join the privileged few.

As part of the audit process, accountants review contingencies that could affect a company's financial conditions as reflected in its financial statements. They are guided in their analysis by Statement of Financial Accounting Standards (SFAS) No. 5, "Accounting for Contingencies." One of the important contingencies examined is that the Internal Revenue Service (IRS) will audit the company's tax return and make material adjustments to it. The auditor is assumed to estimate the probabilities of such adjustments and their magnitude. In the process the auditor prepares a number of papers, including an audit program, reports to management, and tax accrual work papers. The tax accrual papers, which are the subject of a controversy, usually consist of (1) a summary analysis of the transactions recorded in the taxpayer's income tax accounts, (2) a computation of the tax provision for the current year, and (3) a memorandum that discusses items reflected in the financial statements as income or expense, when the ultimate tax treatment is unclear.

The controversy is that the IRS policy states that its agents may seek access to both audit and tax work papers of independent accountants. Section 7602 of the Internal Revenue Code gives the commissioner of internal revenue sweeping authority to summons relevant documents in an investigation of income tax liability. In fact, the section gives the IRS the power to (1) examine any books, papers, records, or other data that may be relevant or material to such inquiry; (2) summon people to produce such books, papers, records, or other data; and (3) give such testimony, under oath, as may be relevant or material to such inquiry.

Would the access of the IRS to the tax accrual papers threaten an accountant's ability to perform an effective audit of a company's financial statements? Most concerned accountants would view the IRS review of their work papers as a fishing expedition and a mind-scam. Most would expect the courts to give them the same treatment as attorneys and reject the mind-scam of accountants. In effect, in *Hickman v. Taylor* (1947) the Supreme Court rejected a mind-scam of attorneys because it destroys the mental privacy that a professional needs to work effectively. The accountants used the mind-scam argument to argue against the IRS' use of the auditor's work papers. The court's decisions, for some cases, were favorable to the accounting profession. This was true in *United States v. Humble Oil* (1974), *United States v. Powell* (1964), SEC *v. Arthur Young & Co.* (1979), *United States v. Matras* (1973), and *United States v. Coopers & Lybrand* (1977). Not all of the Court's decisions were favorable to accountants. This was true in United States v. Arthur Young & Co. (1981), United states v. Coopers & Lybrand (1975). In fact, the Supreme Court, in March 1984, overruled the Second Circuit of Appeals and said that the IRS was entitled to see the tax accrual work papers of Arthur Young & Co. in the IRS' probe of Amerada Hess Corp. for 1972 through 1974. The company was accused of setting up a slush fund for political contributions and payments to foreign officials. Arthur Young and Amerada Hess argued that the work papers were irrelevant to any IRS investigation because they were not used in preparing the tax returns. Moreover, they argued that accountants and clients are protected by the same privilege of confidentiality as lawyers. Both arguments were rejected. The Court maintained, first, that the papers were relevant and, second, that lawyers are "advocates" and "advisers" for their clients, but accountants play a "public watchdog" role as auditors. Chief Justice Burger wrote:

By certifying the public reports that collectively depict a corporation's financial status, the independent auditor assumes a public responsibility transcending any employment relationship with the client. The independent public accountant performing this special function owes ultimate allegiance to the corporations' creditors and stockholders, as well as to the investing public.

The decision is not a cause for joy in the accounting profession despite assurance from the IRS that it will seek work papers only in unusual cases and when it cannot get the information from the taxpayer. But will the IRS stick to the policy in the future? The decision raises many questions:

1. Will the decision lead companies to be less candid with their outside auditors about their tax pictures?

2. Should not the accountants be protected from disclosure by the privilege of confidentiality that applies to work done by accountants in much the same way that it applies to lawyers' work?

3. Are the outside auditors "watchdogs" or "advocates and advisers" to their clients?

4. Will the relationship between the auditors and their clients change toward less communication and more distortion?

5. Will the companies continue to self-disclose if they know that the CPA may have to give the contents of the disclosure to the IRS? Will it lead to less forthright disclosure?

6. Will the discovery of tax accrual work papers provide the IRS with a road map to the corporation's most aggressive interpretations of the Revenue Code?

7. Is the auditor's work-product privilege analogous to the attorney's work-product doctrine?

8. If candid communications between the taxpayer and the auditor are essential to ensure adequate reserves for tax contingencies, would it not be more appropriate that records of communications stating why a tax position was taken by the taxpayer and the settlement posture on that position should seldom, if ever, be discovered by the IRS?

9. Is the full disclosure of questionable positions required for effective revenue collection?

10. Why should corporations provide the IRS with the substance of the case against them?

11. Is the IRS at a disadvantage in its examination of tax returns because the taxpayer, or his or her agent, possesses the sources of information that the IRS needs to auditor the return?

12. Without client cooperation and self-disclosure, can the auditor review contingencies as required by SFAS No. 5 and be able to give an unqualified opinion, or is the auditor limited now to give only a qualified or adverse opinion or a disclaimer?

The Accountant as Defendant in the Law of Torts

The U.S. society is a litigious society. The price tag is enormous, with evidence showing that many civil cases that go to trial—with or without a jury—can easily cost the taxpayers more money than is at stake for any of the litigants. In a speech to the American Bar Association on February 12, 1984, Chief Justice Warren Burger observed: "Our system is too costly, too painful, too destructive, too inefficient for a truly civilized people." As a result, accountants find themselves affected in many ways by the litigation explosion.

What is affecting accountants started with prudent liability and the notion of strict liability, whereby "strict liability means that whenever a particular product emerges from an assembly line in a defective condition, the manufacturer will be liable for any injury that the defect causes."[82] The notion of strict product liability was later expanded to the area of professional liability affecting, in the process, architects, doctors, lawyers, accountants, and so on. In the case of the accountants, it meant that they should be held responsible for a business that does not function properly. This action has generated a flood of lawsuits against accountants. Each time a company fails, its independent auditors become one of the few potential defendants that are solvent and, therefore, likely targets for a suit. Given this situation, the first step is to identify the five potential sources of legal liability of accountants.

The first source of legal liability is the common liability to clients. This involves contractual liability, negligence liability, and problems of independence.

With respect to contractual liability, the auditor is bound by a contract with the client and an engagement letter specifying the scope of the auditor, that his or her audit examination is to be performed with due care and in accordance with professional standards, and that an opinion is to be issued regarding the quality of the client's financial statement.

195

Without this, the accountant would be subjected to legal liability.

With respect to negligence liability, it would arise not only from a breach of contract but also from a failure to observe professional standards and from lapses such as the following: (1) inadequate preparation by failing to prepare or revise the audit program for a client to take into account internal or external changes; (2) lapses in examination by omission or misapplication of a procedure required by the generally accepted standards; (3) inadequate supervision, review, and training of the audit staff; (4) shortcomings of evaluation and judgment; and (5) failure in reporting the right opinion. The accountant can avoid negligent liability if he or she can prove that (1) the client's own negligence contributed to the problem in the company; (2) the client failed to supervise the company's personnel, which contributed to the accountant's failure to fulfill his or her contract and to report the truth; (3) the client disregarded the auditor's recommendations; and (4) the client knew that reliance on the auditor's opinion is unjustified and that such reliance is a form of contributory negligence.

Problems of independence arise when the auditor issues an opinion on the financial statements while acting as an advocate for the client or as unjustifiably deferential to the client management's judgment. This usually happens when the accountant is also performing nonaudit accounting services for the client.

The second source of liability for accountants is the common liability to third parties. For a long time accountants were liable at common law for negligence in the performance of their professional engagements only to their clients. This is known as the *privity of contract doctrine.* The test of the privity of contract doctrine involving auditors came in *Ultramares Corp. v. Touche.*[83] In that case the defendant certified the accounts of a firm, knowing that banks and other lenders were guilty of negligence and fraudulent misrepresentation in not detecting fictitious amounts included in accounts receivable and accounts payable. In his opinion Justice Cardozo drew a sharp distinction between fraudulent conduct and merely negligent conduct, holding that the auditor would not be liable to third parties for the latter:

If liability for negligence exists, a thoughtless slip or blunder, the failure to detect a theft or forgery beneath the cover of deceptive entries, may expose accountants to a liability in an indeterminate amount for an indeterminate time to an indeterminate class. The hazards of a business conducted on these terms are so extreme as to rekindle doubt whether a flaw may not exist in an implication of a duty that espouses to these consequences. The court also stated, however, that if the degree of negligence is so gross as to amount to "constructive fraud," accountants' liability extends to third parties.

Then the defense of lack of privity eroded as the work of the auditors became more and more the subject of lawsuits by nonclient plaintiffs.

An accountant may be liable for ordinary negligence to third parties for whom the accountant knows the client has specifically engaged him or her to produce the accounting product.

This type of third party is known as the *primary beneficiary*. An accountant may also be liable for ordinary negligence to third parties, those known or reasonably foreseen by the accountant, as well as those who the accountant knows will rely on his or her work product in making a particular business decision. This type of third party is known as the *foreseen party*. This liability may extend to all third parties, including merely foreseeable third parties. In other words, users of financial statements beyond those actually foreseen could hold a CPA liable.

In addition, accountants may be found liable to third parties for actual or constructive fraud that is inferred from evidence of gross negligence. The plaintiff is required, in this case, to prove that the auditor knew the falsity (or its equivalent) of a representation. This knowledge is known as the *scienter,* and the requirement of its proof is the *scienter requirement.* In any case, fraud consists of the following elements: (1) false representation, (2) knowledge of a wrong and acting with the intent to deceive, (3) intent to induce action in reliance, (4) justifiable reliance, and (5) resulting damage.

The third source of liability for accountants arises under the federal securities laws. Everybody relies on accountants to play a role in producing accurate information. This main responsibility lies in making an independent verification of a company's financial statements. The Securities and Exchange Commission (SEC) perceives the purpose of an audit as a public accountant's examination intended to be an independent check on management's accounting of its stewardships. Thus, the accountant has a direct and unavoidable responsibility, particularly where his or her engagement relates to a company that makes filings with the commission or where there is a substantial public interest. That audit responsibility is exactly the reason for the potential legal liability of a CPA under the federal securities laws, specifically under Section 11 of the Securities Act of 1933; Section 10(b) of the Securities Exchange Act of 1934 and related Rule 10b-5; Section 12(2) of the 1933 act; Sections 9 and 18 of the 1934 act; Section 17(a) of the 1933 act; and Section 14 of the 1934 act.

Section 11 of the 1933 act defines the rights of third parties and auditors as follows:

In case any part of the registration statement...contained an untrue statement of a material fact or omitted to state a material fact required to be stated therein or necessary to make the statements therein not misleading, any person acquiring such security...may...sue...every accountant... who has with his consent been named as having...certified any part of the registration statement...with respect to the statement in such registration...which purports to have been...certified by him.

Section 11 lists among potential defendants every accountant who helps to prepare any part of the registration statement or any financial statement used in it. It imposes a civil inability on accountants for misrepresentations or omissions of material facts in a registration statement. The leading Section 11 case, *Escott v. Barchris Construction Corp.*,[84] was a class action against a bowling alley construction corporation that had issued debentures and subsequently declared bankruptcy. The court ruled that the accountants were liable for not meeting the minimum standard of "due diligence" in their review of subsequent events occurring to the effective date of the registration statement.

Section 10(b) of the 1934 act states:

It shall be unlawful for any person directly or indirectly, by the use of any means or instrumentality of interstate commerce, or of the mails or of any facility of any national securities exchange, a) to employ any device, scheme, or artifice to defraud, b) to make any untrue statement of a material fact or omit to state a material fact necessary in order to make the statements made, in the light of the circumstances under which they are made, not misleading, or c) to engage in any act, practice, or course of business which operates or would operate as a fraud or deceit upon any person in connection with the purchase or sale of any security.[85]

The elements of Section 10(b) violation are, therefore, (1) a manipulative or deceptive practice, (2) in connection with a purchase or sale, (3) which results in a loss to the plaintiff. Unlike the case in Section 11 of the 1933 act, here the plaintiff carries the burden of proof under Section 10(b). For a while the courts disagreed on the standard of performance to enforce against an accountant under Rule 10b-5. Then in 1976 the Supreme Court resolved the controversy in *Ernst & Ernst v. Hochfelder*[86] by ruling that some knowledge and intent to deceive are required before accountants can be held liable for violation of Rule 10b-5. In other words, the private suit must require the allegation of a scienter. Most lower courts have held that "recklessness" by a defendant is sufficient to satisfy the scienter requirement of Section 10(b), although mere negligence is not.

Section 12(2) of the 1933 act provides that any person who offers or sells a security by means of a prospectus or by oral statements that contain untrue statements or misleading opinions shall be liable to the purchaser for the damages sustained. Some courts have taken a broad view by implicating accountants as liable for aiding and abetting Section 12(2) violations.

Section 18(a) of the 1934 act imposes civil liability on accountants for filing a false or misleading statement. To escape liability, the defendant must prove that "he acted in good faith and had no knowledge that such statement was false or misleading."

Section 17(a) of the 1933 act states that it should be unlawful for any person in the offer or sale of securities (1) to defraud, (2) to obtain money or property by means of an untrue statement or misleading omission, or (3) to engage in any transaction, practice, or course of business that deceives a purchaser. This section does not state, however, whether a party violating the law is liable. The issue remains to be solved by the Supreme Court.

Section 14 of the 1934 act sets forth a comprehensive scheme governing solicitation of proxies. Rule 14a-9 outlaws proxy solicitation by use of false statements or misleading omissions.

The fourth source of liability for accountants arises under the Foreign Corrupt Practices Act (FCPA) of 1977. This act makes it illegal to offer a bribe to an official of a foreign country. It also require SEC registrants under the 1934 act to maintain reasonably complete and accurate records and an adequate system of internal control to prevent bribery. Until now the SEC has refused to take any action against perceived violations of the accounting provisions of the FCPA unless those violations are linked to breaches of other securities.

The fifth source of liability is the criminal liability under both federal and state laws. The criminal provisions are in the Uniform Mail Fraud Statute and the Federal False Statements Statute. All of these statutes make it a criminal offense to defraud another person through knowingly being involved with false financial statements. Four of the most widely publicized criminal prosecutions were the *Continental Vending, Four Seasons, National Student Marketing,* and *Equity Funding* cases, in which errors of judgment on the part of the auditors resulted in criminal liabilities. The SEC position on bringing criminal charges against auditors was once stated as follows:

While virtually all Commission cases are civil in character, on rare occasions it is concluded that a case is sufficiently serious that it should be referred to the Department of Justice for consideration of criminal prosecution. Referrals in regard to accountants have only been made when the Commission and the staff believed that the evidence indicated that a professional accountant certified financial statements that he knew to be false when he reported on them. The Commission does not make criminal references in cases that it believes are simply matters of professional judgment even if the judgments appear to be bad ones.[87]

CONCLUSIONS

The increase of fraud in the accounting environment is definitely an emerging problem for the accounting profession. The credibility of the profession and the field as a guarantor of the integrity of the financial recording system will suffer more unless drastic measures are taken to make the accountant and the auditor face the fraud problem as a major concern. The immorality of the phenomenon should be accentuated in special sources in the ethical problems of the profession. The education community should take the lead in sensitizing students to the existence, the gravity, the immorality, and the consequences of the problem. The short term-oriented management style that may account for a large proportion of corporate fraud needs to be de-emphasized because of its myopic view of the environment.

NOTES

1. *Michigan Law Review,* chap. 66, sect.1529.

2. J. Bologna, *Corporate Fraud: The Basics of Prevention and Detection* (Boston: Butterworth Publishers, 1984).

3. Ibid., 10.

4. "Ethics 101," *U.S. News and World Report,* March 14, 1988, p.76.

5. National Commission on Fraudulent Financial Reporting, *Report of the National Commission on Fraudulent Financial Reporting* (Washington, DC, April 1987), p.2.

6. Bologna, *Corporate Fraud*, p.63.

7. S. Lilien and V. Pastena, "Intermethod Comparability: The Case of the Oil and Gas Industry," *The accounting Review* (July 1981), pp.690-703.

8. D.S. Dhaliwal, G.L. Salamon, and E.D. Smith, "The Effect of Owner versus Management Control on the Choice of Accounting Methods," *Journal of Accounting and Economics* 1 (1982), pp.41-53.

9. P.M. Healey, "The Effect of Bonus Schemes on Accounting Decisions," *Journal of Accounting and Economics* 1-3 (1985), pp.85-107.

10. K.B. Schwartz, "Accounting Changes by Corporations Facing Possible Insolvency," *Journal of Accounting, Auditing and Finance* (Fall 1982), pp.32-43; K.A.

Merchant, *Fraudulent and Questionable Financial Reporting: A Corporate Perspective* (Morristown, NJ: Financial Executives Research Foundation, 1987), p.105.

11. J.M. Fedders and L.G. Perry, "Policing Financial Disclosure Fraud: The SEC's Top Priority," *Journal of Accountancy* (July 1984), p.59.

12. B. Lietbag, "Profile: James C. Treadway, Jr.," *Journal of Accountancy* (September 1986), p.80.

13. Merchant, *Fraudulent and Questionable Financial Reporting, p.38.*

14. E. Durkheim, *The Division of Labor in Society,* translated by George Simpson (New York: Free Press, 1964), p.2.

15. E.A. Ross, *Sins and Society* (Boston: Houghton Mifflin, 1907).

16. Ibid., p.7.

17. E. Sutherland, "White-Collar Criminality," *American Sociological Review* 5 (February 1940), pp.110-123.

18. E. Sutherland, *White Collar Crime* (New York: Dryden Press, 1949), p.9.

19. M.B. Clinard and R.F. Reier, *Sociology of Deviant Behavior* (New York: Holt, Rinehart, and Winston, 1979), p.viii.

20. F.E. Hartung, "White Collar Offenses in the Wholesale Meat Industry in Detroit," *American Journal of Sociology* 56 (1950), p.25.

21. S. Wheeler and M.L. Rothman, "The Organization as Weapon in White-Collar Crime," *Michigan Law Review* (June 1982), pp.1403-1476.

22. L.S. Shrager and O.F. Short Jr., "How Serious a Crime? Perceptions of Organizational and Common Crimes," in G. Geis and E. Stotland (eds.), *White-Collar Crime: Theory and Research* (London: Sage, 1980), p.26.

23. V. Aubert, " White Collar Crime and Social Structure," *American Journal of Sociology* (November 1952), p.265.

24. Ibid., p.266.

25. H. Edelhertz, E. Stotland, M. Walsh, and J. Weimberg, *The Investigation of White Collar Crime: A Manual for Law Enforcement Agencies* (Washington, DC: U.S. Government Printing Office, 1970).

26. A. Bequai, *White-Collar Crime: A 20th Century Crisis* (Lexington, Ma: Lexington Books, 1978), p.13.

27. Z.V. Palmrose, "An Analysis of Auditor Litigation and Audit Service Quality," *The Accounting Review* (January 1988), p.56.

28. L.E. DeAngelo, "Auditor Size and Audit Quality," *Journal of Accounting and Economics* (December 1981), pp.183-199.

29. American Institute of Certified Public Accountants, *Professional Standards,* Vol. 1 (New York: AICPA, 1985), SAS no.47.

30. Palmrose, "Analysis o fAuditor Litigation," p.72.

31. Z.-V. Palmrose, "Litigation and independent Auditors: The Role of Business Failures and Management Fraud," *Auditing: A Journal of Practice and Theory* (Spring 1987), pp.90-103.

32. J.E. Connor, "Enhancing Public Confidence in the Accounting Profession," *Journal of Accountancy* (July 1986), p.83.

33. K. St. Pierre and J. Anderson, "An Analysis of Audit Failures Based on Documented Legal Cases," *Journal of Accounting, Auditing and Finance* (Spring 1988), pp.229-247.

34. R.K. Elliott and J.J. Willingham, *Management Fraud: Detection and Deterrence* (New York: Petrocelli Books, 1980), p.10.

35. K.A. Merchant, *Fraudulent and Questionable Financial Reporting* (New York: Financial Executives Research Foundation, 1987), p.12.

36. J.T. Carey, *Introduction to Criminology* (Englewood Cliffs, NJ: Prentice-Hall, 1978), p.8.

37. D.L. Gibbons, "Crime and Punishment: A Study in Social Attitudes," *Social Forces* (June 1969), pp.391-397.

38. Carey, *Introduction to Criminology*, pp.36-41.

39. Sutherland, *White Collar Crime*, p.240.

40. W.B. Miller, "Lower Class Culture as a Generating Milieu of Gang Delinquency," *Journal of Social Issues* 14, 3 (1958), pp. 5-19.

41. Sutherland, "White Collar Criminality," p.12.

42. Durkheim, *The division of Labor in Society.*

43. R.K. Merton, "Social Structure and Anomie," *American Sociological Review* (October 1938), pp.672-682.

44. R.K. Merton, *Social Theory and Social Structure* (New York: Free Press, 1957), pp.31-60.

45. Ibid., p.144.

46. Ibid., p.150.

47. Ibid., p.146.

48. R.K. Merton, "Priorities in Scientific Discovery: A Chapter in the Sociology of Science," *American Sociological Review* (December 1957), pp.635-659.

49. A.K. Cohen, *Delinquent Boys: The Culture of the Gang* (New York: Free Press, 1955).

50. R.A. Cloward and L.E. Ohlin, *Delinquency and Opportunity* (New York: Free Press, 1960).

51. A.K. Cohen, "The Study of Social Disorganization and Deviant Behavior," in R.K. Merton, L. Boorm, and L.S. Cottrell Jr. (eds.), *Sociology Today: Problems and Prospects* (New York: Harper & Bros., 1959).

52. Cloward and Ohlin, *Delinquency and Opportunity*, p.72.

53. R.J. Gomley, "RICO and Professional Accountant," *Journal of Accounting, Auditing and Finance* (Fall 1982), pp.51-60.

54. "AICPA Testifies at RICO Hearings: Support Boucher Proposal," *Journal of Accountancy* (January 1988), p.82.

55. R.S. Banick and D.C. Broeker, "Arbitration: An Option for Resolving Claims Against CPAs," *Journal of Accountancy* (October 1987), p.124.

56. Ibid., p.126.

57. S.H. Collins, "Professional Liability: The Situation Worsens," *Journal of Accountancy* (November 1985), p.66.

58. American Institute of Certified Public Accountants, Special Committee on Accountants' Legal Liability, *Alternative Dispute Resolution* (New York: AICPA,1987).

59. Ibid., pp.2, 8.

60. Ibid., p.276.

61. J.D. Steward, "Arbitration," *Journal of Accountancy* (February 1988), p.1213.

62. Collins, "Professional Liability," p. 57.

63. Ibid., p.57.

64. *Leeds Estate, Building & Investment Co. v. Shepherd,* 36, Ch. D. 787 (18F7).

65. *Ultramares Corp. v. Torche,* 225 N.Y. 170, 174 N.E. 441 (1931).

66. See D.Y. Causey Jr., *Duties and Liabilities of Public Accountants* (Homewood, IL: Dow Jones-Irwin, 1982), pp. 16-17.

67. *Ultramares Corps. V. Torche,* 225 N.Y. 170, 174 N. E. 441, 444 (1931).

68. *N.N. Minow, "Accountants' Liability and the Litigation Explosion," Journal of Accountancy* (September 1984), p.72.

69. *Rosenblaum v. Adler,* Slip Op. A-39/85 (N.J., June 9, 1983), 21.

70. V. Earle, " Accountants on Trial in a Theater of the Absurd," *Fortune* (May 1972), p.227.

71. L. Berton, "Accounting Firms Can Be Sued in U.S. over Audits Done Abroad, Judge Rules," *Wall Street Journal* (March 10, 1988), p.2.

72. L.J. Tell, "Giliam's Legacy: Nobody Can Hide behind a White Collar," *Business Week* (February 8, 1988), p.69.

73. Minow, "Accountants' Liability and the Litigation Explosion," p. 80.

74. M.M. Levy, "Financial Fraud: Schemes and Indicia," *Journal of Accountancy* (August 1985), p.79.

75. Ibid., pp.79-86.

76. Ibid., pp.86-87.

77. S. Gaines, "From Balance Sheet to Fraud Beat," *Chicago Tribune* (February 28, 1988), sect. 7, p.5.

78. J.G. Bologna and R.J. Lindquist, *Fraud Auditing and Forensic Accounting* (New York: John Wiley & Sons, 1987), p.22.

79. Ibid., p.85.

80. Ibid., p.91.

81. D. Akst and L. Berton, "Accountants Who Specialize in Detecting Fraud Find Themselves in Great Demand," *Wall Street Journal* (February 26, 1988), sect. 2, p.17.

82. J. Weberman, *The Litigious Society* (New York: Basic Books, 1981), p.42.

83. *Ultramares Corp. v. Touche*, 255 N.Y. 170, 174, N.E. 441 (1931).

84. *Escott v. Barchis Construction Corp.* 283 F.Supp. 643 (S.D.N.Y. 1968).

85. Securities Act 1934, 17 C.F.R. Section 240. 10b-5 (1971).

86. *Ernst & Ernst v. Hochfelder*, 425 U.S. 185, 965 Ct. 1375, 47 L. Ed. 2d 668 (2nd ed.).

87. J.C. Burtow, "SEC Enforcement and Professional Accountants: Philosophy, Objectives and Approaches." *Vanderbilt Law Review* 78 (January 1975), p.88.

SELECTED REFERENCES

"AICPA Testifies at RICO Hearings: Support Boucher Proposal." *Journal of Accountancy* (January 1988), p.82.

Akst, D., and L. Berton. "Accountants Who Specialize in Detecting Fraud Find Themselves in Great Demand." *Wall Street Journal* (February 26, 1988), sect. 2, p.17.

American Institute of Certified Public Accountants. *Professional Standards,* Vol. 1. New York: AICPA, 1985, SAS no. 47.

American Institute of Certified Public Accountants, Special Committee on Accountants' Legal Liability. *Alternative Dispute Resolution.* New York: AICPA, 1987.

Aubert, V. "White Collar Crime and Social Structure." *American Journal of Sociology* (November 1952), p.265.

Banick, R.S., and D.C. Broeker. "Arbitration: An Option for Resolving Claims against CPAs." *Journal of Accountancy* (October 1987), p.124.

Bequai, A. *White-Collar Crime: A 20th Century Crisis.* Lexington, MA: Lexington Books, 1978, p.13.

Berton, L. "Accounting Firms Can Be Sued in U.S. over Audits Done Abroad, Judge Rules." *Wall Street Journal* (March 10, 1988), p.2.

Bologna, J. *Corporate Fraud: The Basics of Prevention and Detection.* Boston: Butterworth Publishers, 1984, p.39.

Bologna, J., and R.J. Lindquist. *Fraud Auditing and Forensic Accounting.* New York: John Wiley & Sons, 1987, pp.22, 91.

Carey, J.T. *Introduction to Criminology.* Englewood Cliffs, NJ: Prentice-Hall, 1978, pp.8, 36-41.

Causey, D.Y., Jr. *Duties and Liabilities of Public Accountants.* Homewood, IL: Dow Jones-Irwin, 1982, pp.16-17.

Clinard, M.B., and R.F. Reier. *Sociology of Deviant Behavior.* New York: Holt, Rinehart, and Winston, 1979.

Cloward, R.A., and L.E. Ohlin. *Delinquency and Opportunity.* New York: Free Press, 1960.

Cohen, A.K. *Delinquent Boys: The Culture of the Gang.* New York: Free Press, 1955, pp.77-82.

_____. "The Study of Social Disorganization and Deviant Behavior." In Robert K. Merton, Leonard Boorm, and Leonard S. Cottrell Jr. (eds.), *Sociology Today: Problems and Prospects.* New York: Harper & Bros., 1959.

Collins, S.H. "Professional Liability: The Situation Worsens." *Journal of Accountancy* (November 1985), pp.57, 66.

Connor, J.E. "Enhancing Public Confidence in the Accounting Profession." *Journal of Accountancy* (July 1986), p.83.

Durkheim, E. *The Division of Labor in Society,* translated by George Simpson. New York: Free Press, 1964, p.2.

Earle, V. "Accountants on Trial in a Theater of the Absurd." *Fortune* (May 1972), p.227.

Edelhertz, H., E. Stotland, M. Walsh, and J. Weimberg. *The Investigation of White Collar Crime: A Manual for Law Enforcement Agencies.* U.S. Department of Justice, LEAH. Washington, DC: Government Printing Office, 1970.

"Ethics 101." *U.S. News and World Report* (March 14, 1988), p.76.

Fedders, J.M., and L.G. Perry. "Policing Financial Disclosure Fraud: The SEC's Top Priority." *Journal of Accountancy* (July 1984), p.59.

Gaines, S. "From Balance Sheet to Fraud Beat." *Chicago Tribune* (February 28, 1988), sect. 7, p.5.

Gibbons, D.L. "Crime and Punishment: A Study in Social Attitudes." *Social Forces* (June 1969), pp. 391-397.

Gomley, R.J. "RICO and the Professional Accountant." *Journal of Accounting, Auditing and Finance* (Fall 1982), pp.51-60.

Hartung, F.E. "White Collar Offenses in the Wholesale Meat Industry in Detroit." *American Journal of Sociology* 56 (1950), p.25.

Leeds Estate, Building & Investment Co. v. Shepherd, 36, Ch. D. 787 (1887).

Levy, M.M. "Financial Fraud: Schemes and Indicia." *Journal of Accountancy* (August 1985), p.79.

Lietbag, B. "Profile: James C. Treadway, Jr." *Journal of Accountancy* (September 1986), p.80.

Merchant, K.A. *Fraudulent and Questionable Financial Reporting.* New York: Financial Executives Research Foundation, 1987, p.12.

Merton, R.K. "Social Structure and Anomie." *American Sociological Review* (October 1938), pp.672-682.

_____. "Priorities in Scientific Discovery: A Chapter in the Sociology of Science." *American Sociological Review* (December 1957), pp.635-659.

_____. *Social Theory and Social Structure.* New York: Free Press, 1957, pp. 131-60.

Michigan Law Review, ch. 66, sect. 1529.

Miller, W.B. "Lower Class Culture as a Generating Milieu of Gang Delinquency." *Journal of Social Issues* 14, 3 (1958), pp.5-19.

Minow, N.N. " Accountants' Liability and the Litigation Explosion." *Journal of Accountancy* (September 1984), pp.72, 80.

National Commission on Fraudulent Financial Reporting. *Report of the National Commission on Fraudulent Financial Reporting.* Washington, DC: Author, April 1987, p.2.

Palmrose, Z.-V. "Litigation and Independent Auditors: The Role of Business Failures and Management Fraud."

Auditing: A Journal of Practice and Theory (Spring 1987), pp.90-103.

_____. "An Analysis of Auditor Litigation and Audit Service Quality." *The Accounting Review* (January 1988), pp.56, 72.

Rosenblaum v. Adler, Slip Op. A-39/85. N.J. June 9, 1983, 21.

Ross, E.A. *Sins and Society.* Boston: Houghton Mifflin, 1907.

Russell, H.F. *Foozles and Fraud.* Altamonte Springs, FL: Institute of Internal Auditors, 1977.

Schwartz, K.B., and K. Merton, "Auditor Switches by Failure Firms." *The Accounting Review* (April 1985), pp.248-261.

Shrager, L.S., and O.F. Short Jr. " How Serious a Crime? Perceptions of Organizational and Common Crimes." In G. Geis and E. Stotland (eds.), *White-Collar Crime: Theory and Research.* London: Sage, 1980, p.26.

Steward, J.D. "Arbitration." *Journal of Accountancy* (February 1988), pp. 12-13.

St. Pierre, K., and J. Anderson. "An Analysis of Audit Failures Based on Documented Legal Cases." *Journal of Accounting, Auditing and Finance* (Spring 1982), pp.229-247.

Sutherland, E. "White-Collar Criminality." *American Sociological Review* (February 1940), pp. 210-231.

_____. *White Collar Crime.* New York: Dryden Press, 1949, p.9.

Tell, L. "Giliam's Legacy: Nobody Can Hide behind a White Collar." *Business Week* (February 8, 1988), p.69.

Uecker, W.C., A.P. Brief, and W.R. Kinney Jr. "Perception of the Internal and External Auditor as a Deterrent to Corporate Irregularities." *The Accounting Review* (July 1981), pp.465-478.

Ultramares Corp. v. Torche, 225 N.Y. 170, 179-180, 174 N.E. 441, 444 (1931).

Wheeler, S., and M.L. Rothman. "The Organization as Weapon in White-Collar Crime." *Michigan Law Review* (June 1982), pp. 1403-1476.

Chapter 3:
Slack

INTRODUCTION

Rational principles of management and accounting would dictate the planning and use of company resources in a manner emphasizing truth and accuracy in planning and optional efficiency in use. In reality, the prevailing principles of "designed" management and accounting favor the creation of organizational slack in the use of resources[1] and information distortion through slack budgeting in the planning and budgeting for the same resources.[2] Accordingly, this chapter reviews the research of this opportunistic behavior in management and accounting known as slack by differentiating between organizational slack and budgetary slack.

SLACK BEHAVIOR

Slack behavior refers to the tendency to deviate from principled management and accounting to designed management and accounting. It is a clear manifestation of opportunistic behavior by organizations and individuals.

Slack arises from the tendency of organizations and individuals to refrain from using all the resources available to them. It describes a tendency not to operate at peak efficiency. In general, two types of slack have been identified in the literature, organizational slack and budgetary slack. Organizational slack basically refers to an unused capacity, in the sense that the demands put on the resources of the organization are less than the supply of these resources. Budgetary slack is found in the budgetary process and refers to the intentional distortion of information that results from an understatement of budgeted sales and an overstatement of budgeted costs.

The concepts of organizational slack and budgetary slack appear in other literature under different labels. Economists refer to an X-inefficiency in instances where resources are either not used to their full capacity or effectiveness or are used in an extremely wasteful manner, as well as in instances where managers fail to make costless improvements. X-inefficiency is to be differentiated from allocative inefficiency, which refers to whether or not prices in a market are of the right kind, that is, whether they allocate input and output to whose users who are willing to pay for them.[3] Categories of inefficiency of a nonallocative nature, or X-inefficiency, include inefficiency in (1) labor utilization, (2) capital utilization, (3) time sequence, (4) extent of employee cooperation, (5) information flow, (6) bargaining effectiveness, (7) credit availability utilization, and (8) heuristic procedures.[4]

Agency theory also refers to slack behavior. The problem addressed by the agency theory literature is how to design an incentive contract such that the total gains can be maximized, given (1) information asymmetry between principal and agent, (2) pursuit of self-interest by the agent, and (3) environmental uncertainty affecting the outcome of the agent's decisions.[5] Slack can occur when managers dwell in an "excess consumption of perquisites" or in a "tendency to shrink." Basically, slack is the possible "shrinking" behavior of an agent.[6]

The literature in organizational behavior refers to slack in terms of defensive, tactical responses and deceptive behavior. By viewing organizations as political environments, the deceptive aspects of individual power-acquisition behavior become evident.[7] A variety of unobtrusive tactics in the operation of power,[8] covert intents and means of those exhibiting power-acquisition behaviors,[9] and a "wolf in sheep's clothing"[10] phenomenon, whereby individuals profess a mission or goal strategy while practicing an individual-maximization strategy, characterize these deceptive behaviors, which are desired to present an illusionary or false impression. V.E. Schein has provided the following examples of deceptive behaviors in communication, decision making, and presentation of self.

Communication. With regard to written or oral communications, there may be an illusion that these communications include all the information or that these communications are true, which masks the reality either of their consisting of only partial information or of their actually distorting the information.

Decision making. A manager may present the illusion that he or she is actually compromising or giving in with regard to a decision, whereas in reality he or she is planning to lose this particular battle with the long-range objective of winning the war. Or a manager or a subunit may initiate a particular action and then work on plans and activities for implementing a program. This intensive planning and studying, however, may in reality be nothing more than a delaying tactic, during which the actual program will die or be forgotten. Underlying this illusion that one is selecting subordinates, members of boards of directors, or successors on the basis of their competence may be the reality that these individuals are selected for loyalty, compliance, or conformity to the superior's image.

Presentation of self. Many managers exude an apparent confidence, when in reality they are quite uncertain. Still other managers are skilled in organizing participatory group decision-making sessions, which in reality have been set up to produce a controlled outcome.[11]

Schein then hypothesized that the degree to which these behaviors are deceptive seems to be a function of both the nature of the organization and of the kinds of power exhibited (work-related or personal)[12]. She relied on Cyert and March's dichotomization of organizations as either low- or high-slack systems.[13]

Low-slack systems are characterized by a highly competitive environment that requires rapid and nonroutine decision making on the part of its members and a high level of productive energy and work outcomes to secure an effective performance. High-slack systems are characterized by a reasonably stable environment that requires routine decision making to secure an effective performance.

Given these dichotomizations, Schein suggested that:

1. The predominant form of power acquisition behavior is personal in a high-slack organization and work-related in a low-slack organization.

2. The underlying basis of deception is the inherently overt nature of personal power acquisition behaviors in a high-slack organization and an organization's illusion as to how work gets done in a low-slack organization.

3. The benefits of deception to members are the provisions of excitement and personal rewards in a high-slack organization and the facilitation of work accomplishment and organizational rewards in a low-slack organization.

4. The benefits of deception to organization are to foster [the] illusion of a fast-paced, competitive environment in a high-slack organization and to maintain an illusion of workability of the formal structure in a low-slack organization.[14]

ORGANIZATIONAL SLACK

Nature of Organizational Slack

There is no lack of definitions for organizational slack, as can be seen from the definitions provided by Cyert and March,[15] Child,[16] Cohen, March, and Olsen,[17] March and Olsen,[18] Dimmick and Murray,[19] Litschert and Bonham,[20] and March.[21]

What appears from these definitions is that organizational slack is a buffer created by management in its use of available resources to deal with internal as well as external events that may arise and threaten an established coalition. Slack, therefore, is used by management as an agent of change in response to changes in both the internal and external environments.

Cyert and March's model explains slack in terms of cognitive and structural factors.[22] It provides the rationale for the unintended creation of slack. Individuals are assumed to "satisfice," in the sense that they set aspiration levels for performance rather than a maximization goal. These aspirations adjust upward or downward, depending on actual performance, and in a slower fashion than actual changes in performance. This lag in adjustment allows excess resources from superior performance to accumulate in the form of an organizational stabilizing force to absorb excess resources in good times without requiring a revision of aspirations and intentions regarding the use of these excess resources. "By absorbing excess resources it retards upward adjustment of aspirations during relatively good times...by providing a pool of emergency resources, it permits aspirations to be maintained during relatively bad times."[23]

Oliver E. Williamson has proposed a model of slack based on managerial incentives.[24] This model provides the rationale for managers' motivation and desire for slack resources. Under conditions where managers are able to pursue their own objectives, the model predicts that the excess resources available after target levels of profit have been reached are not allocated according to profit-maximization rules. Organizational slack becomes the means by which a manager achieves his or her personal goals, as characterized by four motives: income, job security, status, and discretionary control over resources.

Williamson makes the assumption that the manager is motivated to maximize his or her personal goals subject to satisfying organizational objectives and that the manager achieves this by maximizing slack resources under his or her control.

Williamson has suggested that there are four levels of profits: (1) a maximizing profit equal to the profit that the firm would achieve when marginal revenue equals marginal cost, (2) actual profit equal to the true profit achieved by the firm, (3) reported profit equal to the accounting profit reported in the annual report, and (4) minimum profit equal to the profit needed to maintain the organizational coalition. If the market is noncompetitive, various forms of slack emerge: (1) *slack absorbed as staff* equal to the difference between maximum and actual profit, (2) *slack in the form of cost* equal to the difference between reported and minimum profits, and

(3) *discretionary spending for investment* equal to the difference between reported and minimum profits.

Income smoothing can be used to substantiate the efforts of management to neutralize environmental uncertainty and to create organizational slack by means of an accounting manipulation of the level of earnings. J.Y. Kamin and J. Ronen have related organizational slack to income smoothing by reasoning that what often results in slack accumulation is aimed at smoothing earnings.[25]

They hypothesized that management-controlled firms were more likely to be engaged in smoothing as a manifestation of managerial discretion and slack. "Accounting" and "real" smoothing were tested by observing the behavior of discretionary expenses vis-à-vis the behavior of income numbers. Their results showed (1) that a majority of the firms behaved as if they were income smoothers and (2) that a particularly strong majority was found among management-controlled firms with high barriers to entry. This line of reasoning was pursued by Ahmed Belkaoui and R.D. Picur.[26] Their study tested the effects of the dual economy on income-smoothing behavior. It was hypothesized that a higher degree of smoothing of income numbers would be exhibited by firms in the periphery sector than by firms in the core sector in reaction to different opportunity structures and experiences. Their results indicated that a majority of the firms may have been resorting to income smoothing. A higher number were found among firms in the periphery sector.

Lewin and Wolf proposed the following statements as a theoretical framework for understanding the concept of slack:

1. Organizational slack depends on the availability of excess resources.

2. Excess resources occur when an organization generates or has the potential to generate resources in excess of what is necessary to maintain the organizational coalition.

3. Slack occurs unintentionally as a result of the imperfection of the resource allocation decision-making process.

4. Slack is created intentionally because managers are motivated to maximize slack resources under their control to ensure achievement of personal goals subject to the achievement of organizational goals.

5. The disposition of slack resources is a function of a manager's expense preference function.

6. The distribution of slack resources is an outcome of the bargaining process-setting organization and reflects the discretionary power of organization members in allocating resources.

7. Slack can be present in a distributed or concentrated form.

8. The aspiration of organizational participants for slack adjusts upward as resources become available. The downward adjustment of aspirations for slack resources, when resources become scarce, is resisted by organizational participants.

9. Slack can stabilize short-term fluctuations in the firm's performance.

10. Beyond the short term, the reallocation of slack requires a change in organizational goals.

11. Slack is directly related to organizational size, maturity, and stability of the external environment.[27]

Functions of Organizational Slack

Because the definition of slack is often intertwined with a description of the functions that slack serves, L.J. Bourgeois discussed these functions as a means of making palpable the ways of measuring slack.[28] From a review of the administrative theory literature, he identified organizational slack as an independent variable that either "causes" or serves four primary functions: "(1) as an inducement for organizational actors to remain in the system, (2) as a resource for conflict resolution, (3) as a buffering mechanism in the work flow process, or (4) as a facilitator of certain types of strategic or creative behavior within the organization."[29]

The concept of slack as an inducement to maintain the coalition was first introduced by C.I. Barnard in his treatment of the inducement/contribution ratio (VC) as a way of attracting organizational participants and sustaining their membership.[30] March and H.A. Simon later described slack resources as the source of inducements through which the inducement/contribution ratio might exceed a value of 1, which is equivalent to paying an employee more than would be required to retain his or her services.[31] This concept of slack was then explicitly introduced by Cyert and March as consisting of payments to members of the coalition in excess of what is required to maintain the organization.[32]

Slack as a resources for conflict resolution was introduced in L.R. Pondy's goal model.[33] In this model subunit goal conflicts are resolved partly by sequential attention to goals and partly by adopting a decentralized organizational structure. A decentralized structure is made possible by the presence of organizational slack.

A notion of slack as a technical buffer from the variances and discontinuities caused by environmental uncertainty was proposed by J.D. Thompson.[34] It was also acknowledged in Pondy's system model, which described conflict as a result of the lack of buffers between interdependent parts of an organization.[35] Jay Galbraith saw buffering as an information-processing problem:

Slack resources are an additional cost to the organization or the customer...The creation of slack resources, through reduced performance levels, reduces the amount of information that must be processed during task execution and prevents the overloading of hierarchical channels.[36]

According to Bourgeois, slack facilitates three types of strategic or creative behavior within the organization: (1) providing resources for innovative behavior, (2) providing opportunities for a satisficing behavior, and (3) affecting political behavior.[37]

First, as a facilitator of innovative behavior, slack tends to create conditions that allow the organization to experiment with new strategies[38] and introduce innovation.[39] Second, as a facilitator of suboptimal behavior, slack defines the threshold of acceptability of a choice, or "bounded search,"[40] by people whose bounded rationality leads them to satisfice.[41] Third, the notion that slack affects political activity was advanced by Cyert and March, who argued that slack reduces both political activity and the need for bargaining and coalition-forming activity.[42] Furthermore, W.G. Astley has argued that slack created by success results in self-aggrandizing behavior by managers who engage in political behavior to capture more than their fair share of the surplus.[43]

W. Richard Scott argued that lowered standards create slack—unused resources—that can be used to create ease in the system.[44] Notice the following comment:

Of course, some slack in the handling of resources is not only inevitable but essential to smooth operations. All operations require a margin of error to allow for mistakes, waste, spoil-age, and similar unavoidable accompaniments of work.[45]

But the inevitability of slack is not without consequences:

The question is not whether there is to be slack but how much slack is permitted. Excessive slack resources increase costs for the organization that are likely to be passed on to the consumer. Since creating slack resources is a rela-tively easy and painless solution available to organizations, whether or not it is employed is likely to be determined by the amount of competition confronting the organization in its task environment.[46]

Measurement of Organizational Slack

One problem in investing empirically in the presence of organizational slack relates to the difficulty of securing an adequate measurement of the phenomenon. Various methods have been suggested. In addition to these methods, eight variables that appear in public data, whether they are created by managerial actions or made available by environment, may explain a change in slack.[47] The model, suggested by Bourgeois, is as follows:

Slack = f(RE, DP, G&A, WC/S, D/E, CR, I/P, P/E)

where

RE = Retained earnings
DP = Dividend payout
G&A = General and administrative expense
WC/S = Working capital as a percentage of sales
D/E = Debt as a percentage of equity
CR = Credit rating
I/P = Short-term loan interest compared to prime rate
P/E = Price/earnings ratio

Here RE, G&A, WC/S, and CR are assumed to have a positive effect on changes and DP, D/E, P/E, and I/P are assumed to have a negative effect on changes in slack.

Some of these measures have also been suggested by other researchers. For example, Martin M. Rosner used profit and excess capacity as slack measures,[48] and Lewin and Wolf used selling, general, and administrative expenses as surrogates for slack.49 Bourgeois and Jitendra V. Singh refined these measures by suggesting that slack could be differentiated on an "ease-of-recovery" dimension.50 Basically, they considered excess liquidity to be a available slack, not yet earmarked for particular uses. Overhead costs were termed recoverable slack, in the sense that they are absorbed by various organizational functions but can be recovered when needed elsewhere. In addition, the ability of a firm to generate resources from the environment, such as the ability to raise additional debt or equity capital, was considered potential slack. All of these measures were divided by sales to control for company size.

Building on Bourgeois and Singh's suggestions, Theresa K. Lant opted for the four following measures:

1. Administrative Slack = (General and Administrative Expenses)/Cost of Goods Sold

2. Available Liquidity = (Cash + Marketable Securities – Current Liabilities)/Sales

3. Recoverable Liquidity = (Accounts Receivable + Inventory)/Sales

4. Retained Earnings = (Net Profit – Dividends)/Sales[51]

Lant used these measures to show empirically (1) that available liquidity and general and administrative expenses have significantly higher variance than profit across firms and across time and (2) that the mean change in slack is significantly greater than the mean change in profit. She concluded as follows:

These results are logically consistent with the theory that slack absorbs variance in actual profit. They also suggest that the measures used are reasonable measures for slack. Thus, it supports prior work which has used these measures and implies that further large sample models using slack as a variable are feasible since financial information is readily available for a large number of firms. Before these results can be generalized however, the tests conducted here should be replicated using different samples of firms from a variety of industries.[52]

Organizational Slack and Competition

The line of research studying the impact of market competition on internal efficiency of firms suggested results about competition reducing slack. Hart[53] and Scharfstein[54] use a hidden information model with a common shock transmitted via the market price to show that the (informational) effect of an increase in competition by entrepreneurial (profit-maximizing) firms on the internal efficiency of managerial firms depends on the specification of managers' preferences. This informational effect of competition was also confined in a hidden action model.[55] Similarly, when the strategic value of incentive contracts under much different market conditions is examined, it will appear that the increase in the intensity of completion leads to more X-inefficiency.[56] A similar negative relation between the intensity of completion and the degree of internal efficiency was observed in a Cournot principal-agent model, where the principal's managerial benefit of including the agent to minimize cost becomes smaller when competition increases.[57] In the case of multinational firms with multiple plants in different locations, the in-home competition may have an impact on slack under different economic conditions. For example, Kerschbamer and Tournas evaluated the impact of variations of product demand on the amount of internal slack in multiplant firms in a model in which facilities can produce output at a privately known cost up to a previously determined capacity level.[58] Their model shows the amount of slack to be pro-cyclical in the sense that as capacity constraints become tighter in booms, slack increases in booms, because the power of in-house competition is reduced, while the opposite is true in downturns.

BUDGETARY SLACK

Nature of Budgetary Slack

The literature on organizational slack shows that managers have the motives necessary to desire to operate in a slack environment. The literature on budgetary slack considers the budget as the embodiment of that environment and, therefore, assumes that managers will use the budgeting process to bargain for slack budgets. As stated by Michael Schiff and Lewin, "managers will create slack in budgets through a process of understating revenues and overstating costs."[59] The general definition of budgetary slack, then, is the understatement of revenues and the overstatement of costs in the budgeting process. A detailed description of the creation of budgetary slack by managers was reported by Schiff and Lewin in their study of the budget process of three divisions of multi-division companies.[60] They found evidence of budgetary slack through underestimation of gross revenue, inclusion of discretionary increases in personnel requirements, establishment of marketing and sales budgets with internal limits on funds to be spent, use of manufacturing costs based on standard costs that do not reflect process improvements operationally available at the plant, and inclusion of discretionary " special projects."

Evidence of budgetary slack has also been reported by others. A.E. Lowe and R.W. Shaw found a downward bias, introduced through sales forecasts by line managers, which assumed good performance where rewards were related to forecasts.[61] M. Dalton reported various examples of department managers' allocating resources to what they considered justifiable purposes, even though such purposes were not authorized in their budgets.[62] G. Shillinglaw noted the extreme vulnerability of budgets used to measure divisional performance given the great control exercised by divisional management in budget preparation and the reporting of results.[63]

Slack creation is a generalized organizational phenomenon. Many different organizational factors have been used to explain slack creation, in particular, organizational structure, goal congruence, control system, and managerial behavior. Slack creation is assumed to occur in cases where a Tayloristic organizational structure exists,[64] and it is also assumed to occur in a participative organizational structure.[65] It may be due to conflicts that arise between the individual and organizational goals, leading managers intentionally to create slack. It may also be due to the attitudes of management toward the budget and to worst views of the budgets as a device used by management to manipulate them.[66] Finally, the creation of slack may occur whether or not the organization is based on a centralized or decentralized structure.[67] With regard to this last issue, Schiff and Lewin have reported that the divisional controller appears to have undertaken the tasks of creating and managing divisional slack and is most influential in the internal allocation of slack.

Using agency theory, budgetary slack can be attributed to four conditions: "1) information asymmetry between the superior (the principal) and the subordinate's effort or output potential, 2) uncertainty in the relation between effort and output, 3) conflicting goals between the superior and the subordinate, and 4) opportunism or self-interest on the part of the subordinate."[68]

Budgeting and the Propensity to Create Budgetary Slack

The budgeting system has been assumed to affect a manager's propensity to create budgetary slack, in the sense that this propensity can be increased or decreased by the way in which the budgeting system is designed or complemented. Mohanmed Onsi was the first to investigate empirically the connections between the type of budgeting system and the propensity to create budgetary slack.[69] From a review of the literature, he stated the following four assumptions:

1. Managers influence the budget process through bargaining for slack by understating revenues and overstating costs.

2. Managers build up slack in "good years" and reconvert slack into profit in "bad years."

3. Top management is at a "disadvantage" in determining the magnitude of slack.

4. The divisional controller in decentralized organizations participates in the task of creating and managing divisional slack.[70]

Personal interviews of thirty-two managers of five large national and international companies and statistical analysis of a questionnaire were used to identify the important behavioral variables that influence slack buildup and utilization. The questionnaire's variables were grouped into the following eight dimensions;

1. Slack attitude, described by the variables indicating a manager's attitude to slack.

2. Slack manipulation, described by the variables indicating how a manager builds up and uses slack.

3. Slack institutionalization, described by the variables that make a manager less inclined to reduce his or her slack.

4. Slack detections, described by the variables indicating the superior's ability to detect slack based on the amount of information that he receives.

5. Attitude toward the top management control system, described by the variables indicating an authoritarian philosophy toward budgeting being attributed to top management by divisional managers.

6. Attitudes toward the divisional control system, described by variables on attitudes toward subordinates, sources of pressure, budget autonomy, budget participation, and supervisory uses of budgets.

7. Attitudes toward the budget, described by variables on attitude toward the level of standards, attitude toward the relevancy of budget attainment to valuation of performance, and the manager's attitude (positive or negative) toward the budgetary system in general, as a managerial tool.

8. Budget relevancy, described by variables indicating a manager's attitudes toward the relevancy of standards for his department's operation.[71]

Factor analysis reduced these dimensions to seven factors and showed a relationship between budgetary slack and what Onsi called "an authoritarian top management budgetary control system." Thus, he stated:

Budgetary slack is created as a result of pressure and the use of budgeted profit attainment as a basic criterion in evaluating performance. Positive participation could encourage less need for building up slack. However, the middle managers' perception of pressure was an overriding concern. The positive correlation between managers' attitudes and attainable level of standards is a reflection of this pressure.[72]

Cortland Cammann explored the moderating effects of subordinates' participation in decision making and the difficulty of subordinates' jobs based on their responses to different uses of control systems by their superiors.[73] His results showed that the use of control systems for contingent reward allocation produced defensive responses by subordinates under all conditions, which included the creation of budgetary slack. Basically, when superiors used budgeting information as a basis for allocating organizational rewards, their subordinates' responses were defensive. Allowing participation in the budget processes reduced this defensiveness.

Finally, Kenneth A. Merchant conducted a field study designed to investigate how managers' propensities to create budgetary slack are affected by the budgeting system and the technical context.[74] He hypothesized that the propensity to create budgetary slack is positively related to the importance placed on meeting budget targets and negatively related to the extent of participation allowed in budgeting processes, the degree of predictability in the production process, and the superiors' abilities to create slack. Unlike earlier studies drawn across functional areas, 170 manufacturing managers responded to a questionnaire measuring the propensity to create slack, the importance of meeting the budget, budget participation, the nature of technology in terms of work-flow integration and product standardization, and the ability of superiors to detect slack. The results suggested that managers' propensities to create slack (1) do vary with the setting and with how the budgeting system is implemented; (2) are lower where managers actively participate in budgeting, particularly when technologies are relatively predictable; and (3) are higher when a tight budget requires frequent tactical responses to avoid overruns.

The three studies by Onsi, Cammann, and Merchant provide evidence that participation may lead to positive communication between managers so that subordinates feel less pressure to create slack. This result is, in fact, contingent on the amount of information asymmetry existing between the principals (superiors) and the agents (the subordinates). Although participation in budgeting leads subordinates to communicate or reveal some of their private information, agents may still misrepresent or withhold some of their private information, leading to budgetary slack. Accordingly, Alan S. Dunk proposed a link between participation and budgetary slack through two variables: superiors' budget emphasis in their evaluation of subordinate performance and the degree of information asymmetry between superiors and subordinates:[75] "When participation, budget emphasis, and information asymmetry are high (low), slack will be high (low)."[76] The results, however, showed that low (high) slack is related to high (low) participation, budget emphasis, and information asymmetry. The results are stated as follows:

The results of this study show that the relation between participation and slack is contingent upon budget emphasis and information asymmetry, but in a direction contrary to expectations. The results provide evidence for the utility of participative budgeting, and little support for the view that high participation may result in increased slack when the other two predictors are high. Although participation may induce subordinates to incorporate slack in budgets, the results suggest that participation alone may not be sufficient. The findings suggest that slack reduction results from participation, except when budget emphasis is low.[77]

Budgetary Slack, Information Distortion, and Truth-Inducing Incentive Schemes

Budgetary slack involves a deliberate distortion of input information. Distortion of input information in a budget setting arises, in particular, from the need of managers to accommodate their expectations about the kinds of payoffs associated with different possible outcomes. Several experiments have provided evidence of such distortion of input information. Cyert, March, and W.H. Starbuck showed in a laboratory experiment that subjects adjusted the information that they transmitted in a complex decision-making system to control their payoffs.[78] Similarly, Lowe and Shaw have shown that in cases where rewards were linked to forecasts, sales managers tended to distort the input information and to induce biases in their sales forecast.[79] Dalton also provided some rich situational descriptions of information distortion in which lower-level managers distorted the budget information and allocated resources to what were perceived to be justifiable objectives.[80] Finally, a payoff structure can induce a forecaster to bias intentionally his or her forecast. R.M. Barefield provided a model of forecast behavior that showed a "rough" formulation of a possible link between a forecaster's biasing and the quality of the forecaster as a resource of data for an accounting system.[81]

Taken together, these studies suggest that budgetary slack, through systematic distortion of input information, can be used to accommodate the subjects' expectations about the payoffs associated with various possible outcomes. They fail, however, to provide a convincing rationalization of the link between distortion of input information and the subjects' accommodation of their expectations. Agency theory and issues related to risk aversion may provide such a lin. Hence, given the existence of divergent incentives and information asymmetry between the controller (or employer) and the controlee (or employee) and the high cost of observing employee skill or effort, a budget-based employment contract (i.e., where employee compensation is contingent on meeting the performance standard) can be Pareto-superior to fixed pay or linear sharing rules (where the employer and employee split the output).[82] However, these budget-based schemes impose a risk on the employee, as job performance can be affected by a host of uncontrollable factors. Consequently, risk-averse individuals may resort to slack budgeting through systematic distortion of input information. In practice, moreover, any enhanced (increased) risk aversion would lead the employee to resort to budgetary slack. One might hypothesize that, without proper incentives for truthful communication, the slack budgeting behavior could be reduced. One suggested avenue is the use of truth-inducing, budget-based schemes.[83] These schemes, assuming risk neutrality, motivate a worker to reveal truthfully private information about future performance and to maximize performance regardless of the budget.

Accordingly, Mark S. Young conducted an experiment to test the effects of risk aversion and asymmetric information on slack budgeting.[84] Five hypotheses related to budgetary slack were developed and tested using a laboratory experiment. The hypotheses were as follows:

Hypothesis 1: A subordinate who participates in the budgeting process will build slack into the budget.

Hypothesis 2: A risk-aversion subordinate will build in more budget slack than a non-risk-averse subordinate.

Hypothesis 3: Social pressure not to misrepresent productive capability will be greater for a subordinate whose information is known by management than for a subordinate having private information.

Hypothesis 4: As social pressure increases for the subordinate, there is a lower degree of budgetary slack.

Hypothesis 5: A subordinate who has private information builds more slack into the budget than a subordinate whose information is known by management.[85]

The results of the experiment confirmed the hypotheses that a subordinate who participates builds in budgetary slack and that slack is, in part, attributable to a subordinate's risk preferences. Given state uncertainty and a worker-manager information asymmetry about performance capability, the subjects in the experiment created slack even in the presence of a truth-inducing scheme. In addition, risk-averse workers created more slack than non-risk-averse workers did. Similarly, C. Chow, J. Cooper, and W. Waller provided evidence that, given a worker-manager information asymmetry about performance capability, slack is lower under a truth-inducing scheme than under a budget-based scheme with an incentive to create slack.[86]

Both Young's and Chow, Cooper, and Waller's studies were found to have limitations.[87] With regard to Young's study, William S. Waller found three limitations:

First, unlike the schemes examined in the analytical research, the one used in his study penalized outperforming the budget, which limits its general usefulness. Second, there was no manipulation of incentives, so variation in slack due to incentives was not examined. Third, risk preferences were measured using the conventional lottery technique of which the validity and reliability are suspect.[88]

With regard Chow, Cooper, and Waller's study, Waller found the limitations to be the assumption of state certainly and the failure to take risk preference into account. Accordingly, Waller conducted an experiment under which subjects participatively set budgets under either a scheme with an incentive for creating slack or a truth-incentive scheme like those examined in the analytical research. In addition, risk neutrality was induced for one-half of the subjects, and constant, absolute risk aversion for the rest, using a technique discussed by J. Berg, L. Daley, J. Dickhaut, and T. O'Brien that allows the experimenter to induce (derived) utility functions with any shape.[89] The results of the experiment show that when a conventional truth-inducing scheme is introduced, slack decreases for risk-neutral subjects but not for risk-averse subjects. Added to the evidence provided by the other studies, this study indicates that risk preference is an important determinant of slack, especially in the presence of a truth-inducing scheme.

Basically, there is preliminary evidence that risk-averse workers create more budgetary slack than risk-neutral ones. In addition, "truth-inducing incentive schemes" reduce budgetary slack for risk-neutral subjects but not for risk-averse subjects. It seems that resource allocations within organizations are mediated by perceptions of risk, where risk is a stable personal trait. Accordingly, D.C. Kim tested whether risk preferences are domain-specific, that is, whether latent risk preferences translate into differing manifest risk preferences according to the context.[90] He relied on an experiment simulating the public accountants' budgeting of billable bonus to test the hypothesis that subject preference for tight or safe budget behavior depends on the performance of coworkers and domain-specific risk preferences. The results supported the view that subordinates' risk preferences are influenced by a situation-dependent variable. As stated by Kim:

The reversal of risk preferences around a neutral reference point is statistically significant for both dispositionally risk-averse and dispositionally risk-seeking subjects. The dispositional variable also contributes to the explanation of variations in subjects' manifest risk preferences. Thus the propensity to induce budgetary slack seems to be a joint function of situations and dispositions.[91]

Budgetary Slack and Self-Esteem

The enhancement of risk aversion and the resulting distortion of input information can be more pronounced when self-esteem is threatened. It was found that persons who have low opinions of themselves are more likely to cheat than persons with higher self-esteem.[92] A situation of dissonance was created in an experimental group by giving out positive feedback about a personality test to some participants and negative feedback to others. All of the participants were then asked to take part in a competitive game of cards. The participants who received a blow to their self-esteem cheated more often than those who had received positive feedback about themselves. Could it also be concluded that budgetary slack through information distortion may be a form of dishonest behavior, arising from the enhancement of risk aversion caused by a negative feedback on self-esteem? A person's expectations can be an important determinant of his or her behavior. A negative impact on self-esteem would be more risk-averse than others and would be ready to resort to any behavior to cover the situation. Consequently, the person may attempt to distort the input information in order to have an attainable budget. Belkaoui accordingly tested the hypothesis that individuals given negative feedback about their self-esteem would introduce more bias into estimates than individuals given positive or neutral feedback about their self-esteem.[93] One week after taking a self-esteem test, subjects were provided with false feedback (either positive or negative) and neutral feedback about heir self-esteem score.

They were then asked to make two budgeting decisions, first one cost estimate and then one sales estimates for a fictional budgeting decision. The results showed that, in general, the individuals who were provided with information that temporarily caused them to lower their self-esteem were more apt to distort input information than those who ere made to raise their self-esteem. It was concluded that, whereas slack budgeting may be consistent with generally low self-esteem feedback, it is inconsistent with generally high or neutral self-esteem feedback.

Toward a Theoretical Framework for Budgeting

A theoretical framework aimed at structuring knowledge about biasing behavior was proposed by Kari Lukka.[94] It contains an explanatory model for budgetary biasing and a model for budgetary biasing at the organizational level.

The explanatory model of budgetary biasing at the individual level draws from the management accounting and organizational behavior literature and related behavioral research to suggest a set of intentions and determinants of budgetary biasing. Budgetary biasing is at the center of many interrelated and sometimes contradictory factors with the actor's intentions as the synthetic core of his or her behavior.

The model for budgetary biasing at organizational level shows that the "bias contained in the final budget is not the result of one actor's intentional behavior, but rather the result of the dialectics of the negotiations."[95] Whereas budgetary biases 1 and 2 are the original biases created in the budget by the controlling unit and the controlled unit, biases 3 and 4 are the final biases to end up in the budget after the budgetary negotiations, which are characterized by potential conflicts and power factors. The results of semistructured interviews at different levels of management of a large decentralized company verified the theoretical framework. The usefulness of this theoretical framework rests on further refinements and empirical testing.

Positive versus Negative Slack

Although the previous sections have focused on budgetary, or positive, slack, budgetary bias is, in fact, composed of both budgetary slack and an upward bias, or a negative slack. Whereas budgetary slack refers to bias in which the budget is designed intentionally so as to make it easier to achieve the forecast, upward bias refers to overstatement of expected performance in the budget. David T. Otley has described the difference as follows: "Managers are therefore likely to be conservative in making forecasts when future benefits are sought (positive slack) but optimistic when their need for obtaining current approval dominates (negative slack)."[96]

Evidence for negative slack was first provided by W.H. Read, who showed that managers distort information to prove to their superiors that all is well.[97] He cited several empirical studies of budgetary control that indicated that managers put a lot of effort and ingenuity into assuring that messages conveyed by budgetary information serve their own interests.[98] Following earlier research by Barefield, Otley argued that forecasts may be the mode, rather than the means, of people's intuitive probability distributions.[99] Given that the distribution of cost and revenue is negatively skewed, there will be a tendency for budget forecasts to become unintentionally biased in the form of negative slack. Data collected from two organizations verified the presence of negative slack.

REDUCING BUDGETARY SLACK: A BONUS-BASED TECHNIQUE

In general, firms use budgeting and bonus techniques to overcome slack budgeting. One such approach consists of paying higher rewards when budgets are set high and achieved and lower rewards when budgets are either set high but not met or set low and achieved. G.S. Mann presented a bonus system that gave incentives for managers to set budget estimates as close to achievable levels as possible.[100] The following two formulas were proposed:

Formula 1 applies for bonus if actual performance is equal to or greater than budget.

(multiplier no. 2 x budget goal) + [multiplier no.1 x (actual level achieved – budget goal)]

Formula 2 applies for bonus if actual performance is less than budget.

(multiplier no. 2 x budget goal) + [multiplier no.3 x (actual level achieved – budget goal)]

The three multipliers set by management served as factors in calculating different components of bonuses. They were defined as follows:

Multiplier no. 1 (which must be less than multiplier no. 2, and which in turn must be less than multiplier no.3) is used when actual performance is greater than budget. It provides a smaller bonus per unit for the part of actual performance that exceeds the budgeted amount.

Multiplier no. 2 is the rate per unit used to determine the basic bonus component. It is based on the budgeted level of activity which equals multiplier no. 2 times the budgeted level.

Multiplier no. 3 is the rate used to reduce the bonus when the chieved level is less than the budget (multiplier no. 3 times work of units by which actual performance fell short of budget).[101]

Figure 3.1 show an illustration of the application of the method and the effect of variations in multipliers or bonuses. As the figure shows, the manager will be rewarded for accurate estimation of the level of rates. In addition, the multipliers can be set with greater flexibility for controlling the manager's estimates.

Figure 3.1 Reducing Slack through a Bonus System

(1) Budget Slacks	(2) Actual Slacks	(3) State of Nature	(4) Bonus I	(5) Bonus II
			Multiplier No. 1 = $.05 Multiplier No. 2 = $.10 Multiplier No. 3 = $.15	Multiplier No. 1 = $.01 Multiplier No. 2 = $.10 Multiplier No. 3 = $.30
200,000	180,000	Overestimation	$17,000	$14,000
200,000	200,000	Actual = Budget	20,000	20,000
200,000	220,000	Underestimation	21,000	22,000

CONCLUSION

Organizational slack and budgetary slack are two hypotheti-
cal constructs to explain organizational phenomena that are
prevalent in all forms of organizations. Evidence linking
both constructs to organizational, individual, and contextual factors is growing and in the future may contribute to
an emerging theoretical framework for an understanding of
slack. Further investigation into the potential determinants
of organizational and budgetary slack remains to be done.
This effort is an important one because the behavior of slack
is highly relevant to the achievement of internal economic
efficiency in organizations. Witness the following comment:

The effective organization has more rewards at its disposal,
or more organizational slack to play with, and thus can
allow all members to exercise more discretion, obtain more
rewards, and feel that their influence is higher.[102]

NOTES

1. R.M. Cyert and J.G. March (eds.), *A Behavioral Theory of the Firm* (Englewood Cliffs, NJ: Prentice-Hall, 1963).

2. A.Y. Lewin and C. Wolf, "The Theory of Organizational Slack: A Critical Review," *Proceedings: Twentieth International Meeting of TIMS* (1976), pp.648-654.

3. H. Leibenstein, "Allocative Efficiency vs. X-Efficiency," *American Economic Review* (June 1966), pp.392-415.

4. H. Leibenstein, "X-Efficiency; From Concept to Theory," *Challenge* (September-October 1979), pp.13-22.

5. N. Choudhury, "Incentives for the Divisional Manager," *Accounting and Business Research* (Winter 1985), pp.11-21.

6. S. Baiman, "Agency Research in Managerial Accounting: A Survey." *Journal of Accounting Literature* (Spring 1982), pp.154-213.

7. D. Packard, *The Pyramid Climber* (New York: McGraw-Hill, 1962); E.A. Butler, "Corporate Politics-Monster or Friend?" *Generation* 3 (1971), pp.54-58, 74; A.N. Schoomaker, *Executive Career Strategies* (New York: American Management Association, 1971).

8. J. Pfeffer, "Power and Resource Allocation in Organizations," in B.M. Shaw and G.R. Salancik (eds.), *New Directions in Organizational Behavior* (Chicago: St. Clair Press, 1977).

9. V.E. Schein, "Individual Power and Political Behaviors in Organizations: An Inadequately Explored Reality," *Academy of Management Review* (January 1977), pp.64-72.

10. B. Bowman and W. Malpive, "Goals and Bureaucratic Decision-Making: An Experiment," *Human Relations* (June 1977), pp.417-429.

11. V.E. Schein, "Examining an Illusion: The Role of Deceptive Behaviors in Organizations," *Human Relations* (October 1979), pp.288-289.

12. Ibid., p.290.

13. Cyert and March, *A Behavioral Theory of the Firm.*

14. Schein, "Examining an Illusion," p.293.

15. Cyert and March, *A Behavioral Theory of the Firm.*

16. J. Child, "Organizational Structure, Environment, and Performance: The Role of Strategic Choice," *Sociology* 6, 1 (1972), pp.2-22.

17. M.D. Cohen, J.G. March, and J.P. Olsen, "A Garbage Can Model of Organizational Choice," *Administrative Science Quarterly* 17, 1 (1972), pp.1-25.

18. J.G. March and J.P. Olsen, *Ambiguity and Choice* (Bergen: Universitetsforlagt, 1976).

19. D.E. Dimmick and V.V. Murray, "Correlates of Substantive Policy Decisions in Organizations: The

Case of Human Resource Management." *Academy of Management Journal* 21, 4 (1978), pp. 611-623.

20. R.J. Litschert and T.W. Bonham, "A Conceptual Model of Strategy Formation," *Academy of Management Review* 3, 2 (1978), pp.211-219.

21. J.G. March, interview by Stanford Business School Alumni Association, *Stanford GSB* 47, 3 (1978-1979), pp.16-19.

22. Cyert and March, *A Behavioral Theory of the Firm.*

23. Ibid., p.38.

24. O.E. Williamson, "A Model of Rational Managerial Behavior," in Cyert and March, *A Behavioral Theory of the Firm*; O.E. Williamson, *The Economics of Discretionary Behavior: Managerial Objectives in a Theory of the Firm* (Englewood Cliffs, NJ: Prentice-Hall, 1964).

25. J.Y. Kamin and J. Ronen, "The Smoothing of Income Numbers: Some Empirical Evidence on Systematic Differences among Management-Controlled and Owner-Controlled Firms," *Accounting, Organizations and Society* (October 1978), pp.141-157.

26. A. Belkaoui and R.D. Picur, "The Smoothing of Income Numbers: Some Empirical Evidence on Systematic Differences between Core and Periphery Industrial Sector," *Journal of Business Finance and Accounting* (Winter 1984), pp. 527-545.

27. Lewin and Wolf, "The Theory of Organizational Slack," p.653.

28. L.J. Bourgeois, "On the Measurement of Organizational Slack," *Academy of Management Review* 6, 1 (1981), pp.29-39.

29. Ibid., p.31.

30. C.I. Barnard, *Functions of the Executive* (Cambridge, MA: Harvard University Press, 1938).

31. J.G. March and H.A. Simon, *Organizations* (New York: John Wiley and Sons, 1958).

32. Cyert and March, *A Behavioral Theory of the Firm*, p.36.

33. L.R. Pondy, "Organizational Conflict: Concepts and Models," *Administrative Science Quarterly* 12, 2 (1967), pp.296-320.

34. J.D. Thompson, *Organizations in Action* (New York: McGraw-Hill, 1967).

35. Pondy, "Organizational Conflict."

36. J. Galbraith, *Designing Complex Organizations* (Reading, MA: Addison-Wesley, 1973), p.15.

37. Bourgeois, "On the Measurement of Organizational Slack," p.34.

38. D.C. Hambrick and C.C. Snow, "A Contextual Model of Strategic Decision Making in Organizations," in R.L. Taylor, J.J. O'Connell, R.A. Zawaki, and D.D. Warrick

(eds.), *Academy of Management Proceedings* (1977), pp. 109-112.

39. Cyert and March, *A Behavioral Theory of the Firm*.

40. March and Simon, *Organizations*.

41. H.A. Simon, *Administrative Behavior* (New York: Free Press, 1957).

42. Cyert and March, *A Behavioral Theory of the Firm*.

43. W.G. Astley, "Sources of Power in Organizational Life" (Ph.D. diss., University of Washington, 1978).

44. W.R. Scott, *Organizations: Rational, Natural and Open Systems* (Englewood Cliffs, NJ: Prentice-Hall, 1981), p.216.

45. Ibid.

46. Ibid.

47. Bourgeois, "On the Measurement of Organizational Slack," p.38.

48. M.M. Rosner, "Economic Determinant of Organizational Innovation," *Administrative Science Quarterly* 12 (1968), pp.614-625.

49. A.Y. Lewin and C. Wolf, "Organizational Slack: A Test of the General Theory," *Journal of Management Studies* (forthcoming).

50. L.J. Bourgeois and J.V. Singh, "Organizational Slack and Political Behavior within Top Management Teams," Working paper, Graduate School of Business, Stanford University, 1983.

51. T.K. Lant, "Modeling Organizational Slack: An Empirical Investigation," Stanford University Research Paper no.856, July 1986.

52. Ibid., p.14.

53. O. Hart, "The Market Mechanism as an Incentive Scheme," *Bell Journal of Economics* 14 (1983), pp.366-382.

54. D. Scharfstein, "Product Market Competition and Managerial Slack," *Rand Journal of Economics* 14 (1988), pp.147-153.

55. B. Hermalin, "The Effects of Competition on Executive Behavior," *Rand Journal of Economics* 23 (1992), pp.350-365.

56. H. Horn, H. Lang, and S. Lundgren, "Competition, Long Run Contracts and Inefficiencies in Firms," *European Economic Review* 38 (1994), pp.213-233.

57. S. Martin, "Endogenous Firm Efficiency in a Cournot Principal-Agent Model," *Journal of Economic Theory* 59 (1993), pp.445-450.

58. R. Kerschbamer and Y. Tournas, "In-House Competition, Organizational Slack and the Business Cycle," Working paper, Department of Economics, University of Vienna, July 2000.

59. M. Schiff and A.Y. Lewin, "The Impact of People on Budget," *Accounting Review* (April 1970), pp.259-268.

60. M. Schiff and A.Y. Lewin, "Where Traditional Budgeting Fails," *Financial Executive* (May 1968), pp.51-62.

61. A.E. Lowe and R.W. Shaw. "An Analysis of Managerial Biasing Evidence from a Company's Budgeting Process," *Journal of Management Studies* (October 1968), pp.304-315.

62. M. Dalton, *Men Who Manage* (New York: John Wiley and Sons, 1961), pp.36-38.

63. G. Shillinglaw, "Divisional Performance Review: An Extension of Budgetary Control," in C.P. Bonini, R.K. Jaedicke, and H.M. Wagner (eds.), *Management Controls: New Directions in Basic Research* (New York: McGraw-Hill, 1964), pp.149-163.

64. C. Argyris, *The Impact of Budgets on People* (New York: Controllership Foundation, 1952), p.25.

65. E.H. Caplan, *Management Accounting and Behavioral Sciences* (Reading, MA: Addison-Wesley, 1971).

66. Argyris, *The Impact of Budgets on People.*

67. Schiff and Lewin, "Where Traditional Budgeting Fails," pp.51-62.

68. Stevens, D.E. "Determinants of Budgetary Slack in the Laboratory: An Investigation of Contracts for Self-Interested Behavior." Working paper, Syracuse University, March 2000, p.1.

69. M. Onsi, "Factor Analysis of Behavioral Variables Affecting Budgetary Slack," *Accounting Review* (July 1973), pp.535-548.

70. Ibid., p.536.

71. Ibid., p.539.

72. Ibid., p.546.

73. C.Cammann, "Effects of the Use of Control Systems," *Accounting Organizations and Society* (January 1976), pp.301-313.

74. K.A. Merchant, "Budgeting and the Propensity to Create Budgetary Slack," *Accounting, Organizations and Society* (May 1985), pp.201-210.

75. A.S. Dunk, "The Effect of Budget Emphasis and Information Asymmetry on the Relation between Budgetary Participation and Slack," *The Accounting Review* (April 1993), pp.400-410.

76. Ibid., p.400.

77. Ibid., pp.408-409.

78. R.M. Cyert, J.G. March, and W.H. Starbuck, "Two Experiments on Bias and Conflict in Organizational Estimation," *Management Science* (April 1961), pp.254-264.

79. Lowe and Shaw, "An Analysis of Managerial Biasing."

80. Delton, *Men Who Manage.*

81. R.M. Barefield, "A Model of Forecast Biasing Behavior," *Accounting Review* (July 1970), pp.490-501.

82. J.S. Demski and G.A. Feltham, "Economic Incentives in Budgetary Control Systems," *Accounting Review* (April 1978), pp.336-359.

83. Y. Ijiri, J. Kinard, and F. Purney, "An Integrated Evaluation System for Budget Forecasting and Operating Performance with a Classified Budgeting Bibliography," *Journal of Accounting Research* (Spring 1968), pp.1-28; M. Loeb and W. Magat, "Soviet Success Indicators and the Evaluation of Divisional Performance," *Journal of Accounting Research* (Spring 1978), pp.103=121; P. Jennergren, "On the Design of Incentives in Business Firms A Survey of Some Research," *Management Science* (February 1980), pp.180-201; M. Weitzman, "The New Soviet Incentive Model," *Bell Journal of Economics* (Spring 1976), pp.251-257.

84. M.S. Young, "Participative Budgeting: The Effects of Risk Aversion and Asymmetric Information on Budgetary Slack," *Journal of Accounting Research* (Autumn 1985), pp.829-842.

85. Ibid., pp.831-832.

86. C. Chow, J. Cooper, and W. Waller, "Participative Budgeting: Effects of a Truth-Inducing Pay Scheme and Information Asymmetry on Slack and Performance," Working paper, University of Arizona, Tucson, 1986.

87. W.S. Waller, "Slack in Participative Budgeting: The Joint Effect of a Truth-Inducing Pay Scheme and Risk Preferences," *Accounting, Organizations and Society* (December 1987), pp.87-98.

88. Ibid., p.88.

89. J. Berg, L. Daley, J. Dickhaut, and J. O'Brien, "Controlling Preferences for Lotteries on Units of Experimental Exchange," *Quarterly Journal of Economics* (May 1986), pp.281-306.

90. D.C. Kim, "Risk Preferences in Participative Budgeting," *The Accounting Review* (April 1992), pp.303-318.

91. Ibid., p.304.

92. E. Aronson and D.R. Mettee, "Dishonest Behavior as a Function of Differential Levels of Induced Self-Esteem," *Journal of Personality and Social Psychology* (January 1968), pp.121-127.

93. A. Belkaoui, "Slack Budgeting, Information Distortion and Self-Esteem," *Contemporary Accounting Research* (Fall 1985), pp.111-123.

94. K. Lukka, "Budgetary Biasing in Organizations: Theoretical Framework and Empirical Evidence," *Accounting, Organizations and Society* (February 1988), pp.281-301.

95. Ibid., p.292.

96. D.T. Otley, "The Accuracy of Budgetray Estimates: Some Statistical Evidence," *Journal of Business Finance and Accounting* (Fall 1985), p.416.

97. W.H. Read, "Upward Communication in Industrial Hierarchies," *Human Relations* (1962), pp.3-16.

98. G.H. Hofstede, *The Game of Budget Control* (London: Tavistock, 1968); A.G. Hopwood, "An empirical Study of the Role of Accounting Data in Performance Evaluation," *Journal of Accounting Research* (Supplement, 1972), pp.156-182; D.T. Otley, "Budget Use and Managerial Performance," *Journal of Accounting Research* (Spring 1978), pp.122-149.

99. R.M. Barefield, "Comments on a Measure of Forecasting Performance," *Journal of Accounting Research* (Autumn 1969), pp.324-327; Otley, "The Accuracy of Budgetary Estimates."

100. G.S. Mann, "Reducing Budget Slack," *Journal of Accountancy* (August 1988), pp.18-122.

101. Ibid., p.119.

102. C. Perrow, *Complex Organizations: A Critical Essay* (Glenview, IL: Scott, Foreman, and Company, 1972), p.140.

SELECTED REFERENCES

Antle, R., and G. Eppen. "Capital Rationing and Organizational Slack in Capital Budgeting." *Management Science* (February 1985), pp.163-174.

Argyris, C. *The Impact of Budgets on People.* New York: Controllership Foundation, 1952.

Aronson, E., and D.R. Mettee. "Dishonest Behavior as a Function of Differential Levels of Induced Self-Esteem." *Journal of Personality and Social Psychology* (January 1968), pp.121-127.

Barefield, R.M. "A Model of Forecast Biasing Behavior." *Accounting Review* (July 1970), pp.490-501.

Bernea, A., J. Ronen, and S. Sadan. "Classifactory Smoothing of Income with Extraordinary Items." *Accounting Review* (January 1976), pp.110-122.

Belkaoui, A. *Conceptual Foundations of Management Accounting.* Reading, MA: Addison-Wesley, 1980.

_____. "The Relationships between Self-Disclosure Style and Attitudes to Responsibility Accounting." *Accounting, Organizations and Society* (December 1981), pp.281-289.

_____. *Cost Accounting: A Multidimensional Emphasis.* Hinsdale, IL: Dryden Press, 1983.

_____. "Slack Budgeting, Information Distortion and Self-Esteem." *Contemporary Accounting Research* (Fall 1985), pp.111-123.

Belkaoui, A., and R.D. Picur. "The Smoothing of Income Numbers: Some Empirical Evidence of Systematic Differences between Core and Periphery Industrial Sectors." *Journal of Business Finance and Accounting* (Winter 1984), pp.527-545.

Bourgeois, L.J. "On the Measurement of Organizational Slack." *Academy of Management Review* 6, no. 1 (1981), pp.29-39.

Bourgeois, L.J., and J.V. Singh. "Organizational Slack and Political Behavior within Top Management Teams." *Academy of Management Proceedings* (1983), pp.43-47.

_____. "Organizational Slack and Political Behavior within Top Management Teams." Working paper, Graduate School of Business, Stanford University, 1983.

Bourgeois, L.J. and W.G. Astley, "A Strategic Model of Organizational Conduct and Performance." *International Studies of Management and Organization* 9, 3 (1979), pp.40-66.

Brownell, P. "Participation in the Budgeting Process When It Works and When It Doesn't." *Journal of Accounting Literature* (Spring 1982), pp.124-153.

Caplan, E.H. *Management Accounting and Behavioral Sciences.* Reading, MA: Addison-Wesley, 1971.

Carter, E. "The Behavioral Theory of the Firm and Top-Level Corporate Decisions." *Administrative Science Quarterly* 16, 4 (1971), pp.413-428.

Child, J. "Organizational Structure, Environment, and Performance: The Role of Strategic Choice." *Sociology* 6, 1 (1972), pp.2-22.

Chow, D. "The Effects of Job Standard Tightness and Compensation Scheme on Performance: An Exploration of Linkages." *Accounting Review* (October 1983), pp.667-685.

Christensen, J. "The Determination of Performance Standards and Participation." *Journal of Accounting Research* (Autumn 1982), pp.589-603.

Cohen, M.D., J.G. March, and J.P. Olsen, "A Garbage Can Model of Organizational Choice." *Administrative Science Quarterly* 17, 1 (1972), pp.1-25.

Collins, F. "Managerial Accounting Systems and Organizational Control: A Role Perspective." *Accounting, Organizations and Society* (May 1982), pp.107-122.

Conn, D. "A Comparison of Alternative Incentive Structures for Centrally Planned Economic Systems." *Journal of Comparative Economics* (September 1979), pp.261-278.

Cyert, R.M., and J.G. March. "Organizational Factors in the Theory of Oligopoly." *Quarterly Journal of Economics* (April 1956), pp.44-66.

_____. (eds.). *A Behavioral Theory of the Firm.* Englewood Cliffs, NJ: Prentice-Hall, 1963.

Cyert, R.M., J.G. March, and W.H. Starbuck. "Two Experiments on Bias and Conflict in Organizational Estimation." *Management Science* (April 1961), pp.254-264.

Dalton, M. *Men Who Manage.* New York: John Wiley and Sons, 1961.

Demski, J.S., and G.A. Feltham. "Economic Incentives in Budgetary Control Systems." *Accounting Review* (April 1978), pp.336-359.

Dunk, A.S. "The Effect of Budget Emphasis and Information Asymmetry on the Relation between Budgetary Participation and Slack." *The Accounting Review* (April 1993), pp.400-410.

Gonik, J. "Tie Salesmen's Bonuses to Their Forecasts." *Harvard Business Review* (May-June 1978), pp.116-123.

Hopwood, A.G. "An Empirical Study of the Role of Accounting Data in Performance Evaluation." *Journal of Accounting Research* (Supplement, 1972), pp.156-182.

Irjiri, Y., J. Kinard, and F. Putney. "An Integrated Evaluation System for Budget Forecasting and Operating

Performance with a Classified Budgeting Bibliography." *Journal of Accounting Research* (Spring 1968), pp.1-28.

Itami, H. "Evaluation Measures and Goal Congruence under Uncertainty." *Journal o f Accounting Research* (Spring 1975), pp.163-180.

Jennergren, p. "On the Design of Incentives in Business Firms   A Survey of Some Research." *Management Science* (February 1980), pp.180-201.

Karpik, P., and A. Riahi-Belkaoui. "A Comparison of the Financial Characteristics of Companies in the Core and Periphery Economies." *Advances in Quantitative Analysis in Finance and Accounting* 2 (1993), pp.105-139.

Kerr, S., and W. Slocum Jr. "Controlling the Performances of People in Organizations." In W. Starbuck and P. Nystrom (eds.), *Handbook of Organizational Design,* Vol. 2. New York: Oxford University Press, 1981, pp. 116-134.

Kim, D.C. "Risk Preferences in Participative Budgeting." *The Accounting Review* (April 1992), pp.303-319.

Lecky, P. *Self-Consistency.* New York: Island Press, 1945.

Leibenstein, H. "Allocative Efficiency vs. X-Efficiency." *American Economic Review* (June 1996), pp.392-415.

_____. "X-Efficiency: From Concept to Theory." *Challenge* (September-October 1979), pp.13-22.

Levinthal, D., and J.G. March. "A Model of Adaptive Organizational Search." *Journal of Economic Behavior and Organization* (May 1981), pp.307-333.

Lewin, A.Y., and C. Wolf. "The Theory of Organizational Slack: A Critical Review." *Proceedings: Twentieth International Meeting of TIMS* (1976), pp.648-654.

Litschert, R.J., and T.W. Bonham. "A Conceptual Model of Strategy Formation." *Academy of Management Review* 3, 2 (1978), pp.211-219.

Locke, E., and D. Schweiger. "Participation in Decision Making: One More Look." In B. Staw (ed.), *Research in Organizational Behavior.* Greenwich, CT: JAI Press, 1979, pp.265-339.

Loeb, M., and W. Magat. "Soviet Success Indicators and the Evaluation of Divisional Performance." *Journal of Accounting Research* (Spring 1978), pp.103-121.

Lowe, A.E., and R.W. Shaw. "An Analysis of Managerial Biasing: Evidence from a Company's Budgeting Process." *Journal of Management Studies* (October 1968), pp.304-315.

March, J.G., and H.A. Simon. *Organizations.* New York: John Wiley and Sons, 1958.

Mezias, S.J. "Some Analytics of Organizational Slack." Working paper, Graduate School of Business, Stanford University, November 1985.

Miller, J., and J. Thornton. "Effort, Uncertainty, and the New Soviet Incentive System." *Southern Economic Journal* (October 1978), pp.432-446.

Mitroff, I.I., and J.R. Emshoff. "On Strategic Assumption-Making: A Dialectical Approach to Policy and Planning." *Academy of Management Review* 4, 1 (1979), pp.1-12.

Moch, M.K., and L.R. Pondy. "The Structure of Chaos: Organized Anarchy as a Response to Ambiguity." *Administrative Science Quarterly* 22, 2 (1977), pp.351-362.

Parker, L.D. "Goal Congruence: A Misguided Accounting Concept." *Abacus* (June 1976), pp.3-13.

Riahi-Belkaoui, A. *The New Foundations of Management Accounting.* Westport, CT: Quorum Books, 1992.

Schein, V.E. "Examining an Illusion: The Role of Deceptive Behaviors in Organizations." *Human Relations* (October 1979), pp.287-295.

Schiff, M. "Accounting Tactics and the Theory of the Firm." *Journal of Accounting Research* (Spring 1966), pp.62-67.

Schiff, M., and A.Y. Levin. "Where Traditional Budgeting Fails." *Financial Executive* (May 1968), pp.51-62.

_____. "The Impact of People on Budgets." *Accounting Review* (April 1970), pp.259-268.

_____. *Behavioral Aspects of Accounting.* Englewood Cliffs, NJ: Prentice-Hall, 1974.

Simon, H.A. *Administrative Behavior.* New York: Free Press, 1957.

Singh, J.V. "Performance, Slack and Risk Taking in Strategic Decisions: Test of a Structural Equation Model." Ph.D. diss., Stanford Graduate School of Business, 1983.

_____. "Performance, Slack, and Risk Taking in Organizational Decision Making." *Academy of Management Journal* (September 1986), pp.562-585.

Stolzenberg, R.M. "Bringing the Boss Back In: Employer Size, Employee Schooling, and Socioeconomic Achievement." *American Sociological Review* 43 (1978), pp.42-53.

Swieringa, R.J., and R.H. Moncur. "The Relationship between Managers' Budget Oriented Behavior and Selected Attitudes, Position, Size and Performance Measures." *Journal of Accounting Research* (Supplement, 1972), p.19.

Thompson, J.D. *Organizations in Action.* New York: McGraw-Hill, 1967.

Waller, W.S., and C. Chow. "The Self-Selection and Effort of Standard-Based Employment Contracts: A Framework and Some Empirical Evidence." *Accounting Review* (July 1985), pp.458-476.

Watchel, H.M. "The Impact of Labor Market Conditions on Hard-Core Unemployment." *Poverty and Human Resources* (July-August 1970), pp.5-13.

Weitzman, M. "The New Soviet Incentive Model." *Bell Journal of Economics* (Spring 1976), pp.251-257.

Williamson, O.E. "A Model of Rational Managerial Behavior." In Richard M. Cyert and James G. March (eds.), *A Behavioral Theory of the Firm.* Englewood Cliffs, NJ: Prentice-Hall, 1963, pp.113-128.

_____. *The Economics of Discretionary Behavior: Managerial Objectives in a Theory of the Firm.* Englewood Cliffs, NJ: Prentice-Hall, 1964.

Winter, S.G. "Satisficing, Selection, and the Innovating Remnant." *Quarterly Journal of Economics* 85 (1971), pp.237-257.

Young, M.S. "Participative Budgeting: The Effects of Risk Aversion and Asymmetric Information on Budgetary Slack." *Journal of Accounting Research* (Autumn 1985), pp.829-842.

Appendix 3A. Slack Budgeting, Information Distortion and Self-Esteem

INTRODUCTION

Psychological variables are very helpful in explaining some of the accountant's behavioral patterns and can contribute to the development of better management accounting systems (Belkaoui, 1980; Collins, 1982). Personality traits and behavioral factors may be indicative of different accounting behavior and effectiveness. For example, self-disclosure was found to be positively related to attitudes to responsibility accounting (Belkaoui, 1981), and Gordon's Personality Profile and the Ohio State Leadership Behavior Description Questionnaire were found to be a predictor of budgeting behavior (Hopwood, 1972; Swieringa and Moncur, 1972). Slack creation is another important managerial behavior in need of explanation, correction, and/or control. An evaluation of the effectiveness of a firm's control system requires, among other things, the identification of the behavioral factors that lead to slack creation (Onsi, 1973, p.535). accordingly, this appendix reports on research designed to provide insights into the relationships between individual characteristics and slack creation. More specifically, it examines slack budgeting as a case of information distortion and investigates empirically the effects of self-esteem feedback on information distortion.

THEORY

Slack Budgeting and Information Distortion[1]

The literature on the behavioral implications of budgets as instruments of planning and control has found its way into most cost accounting textbooks (Belkaoui, 1983). It is suggested that the budget in its dual role of being a planning tool and a control device may give rise to slack. Cyert and March (1963) defined organizational slack as the difference between "the total resources available to the firm and the total necessary to maintain the organizational coalition" (p.36). Slack arises from imperfections in the organizational process of resource allocation. Slack may be distributed in the form of additional dividends and excessive wages beyond the minimum required to obtain a healthy coalition of all the participants in the organization or be undistributed as idle cash and securities. In examining the relationships between the controller and the controlled within the organization, Schiff and Lewin (1970) argued that these relationships revolved around the budget process and that the "controlled" exercise significant influence on the outcome of the budgets by the incorporation of slack into their budgets.[1] In brief,

---

1 *Source:* A. Riahi-Belkaoui, "Slack Budgeting, Information Distortion and Self-Esteem," *Contemporary Accounting Research* (Fall, 1985), pp. 11-123. Reprinted with permission.

since the budget is an expression of the performance criteria and because managers bargain and participate in its formation, the budget process may become the vehicle for slack. Thus, organizational slack is a general organizational phenomenon that may be reflected in slack budgeting behavior. In an accounting framework, slack budgeting is, in general, operationally defined as the process of understating revenues and overstating costs. Lowe and Shaw (1968) report also on downward and upward bias introduced in sales forecasts by line managers that may indicate the existence of negative slack in some cases.

Slack creation is a generalized organizational phenomenon. Various organizational factors have been used to explain slack creation, namely, organizational structure, goal congruence, control system, and managerial behavior. Basically (1) it is assumed to occur in cases where a Tayloristic organizational structure exists (Argyris, 1952, p.25), although it is also assumed to occur in a participative organization structure (Caplan, 1971, p.85); (2) it may be due to conflicts arising between the individual and organizational goals leading managers to intentionally create slack (March and Simon, 1958, p.84; Williamson, 1964; Parker, 1976, p.12); (3) it may be due to the attitudes of management toward the budget and to the workers' views of budgets as devices used by management to manipulate them (Argyris, 1952); and (4) it may occur whether or not the organization is based on a centralized or decentralized structure (Schiff and Lewin, 1970, p.264).

Whatever the sources or causes of slack creation, slack involves a deliberate distortion of input information. Distortion of

275

input information in a budget setting in particular arises from a need by managers to accommodate their expectations about the kinds of payoff associated with different possible outcomes. For example, Cyert, March, and Starbuck (1961) (hereafter referred to as CMS) showed in a laboratory experiment that subjects adjusted the information that they transmitted in a complex decision-making system to control their payoffs. Similarly, Lowe and Shaw (1968) have shown that in cases where rewards were related to forecast, sales managers tended to distort the input information and to induce biases in their sales forecasts. Dalton (1961) also provided some rich situational descriptions of information distortion in which lower-level managers distorted the budget information and allocated resources to what were perceived to be justifiable objectives. Finally, given the existence of a payoff structure that may induce a forecaster to intentionally bias his or her forecast, Barefield (1970) provides a model of forecast behavior that shows a "rough" formulation of a possible link between a forecaster's biasing and the quality of the forecaster as a source of data for an accounting system. All these studies seem to suggest that slack budgeting through systematic distortion of input information may be used to accommodate the subject's expectations about the payoffs associated with various possible outcomes. They fail, however, to provide a better rationalization of the link between distortion of input information and the subject's accommodation of expectations. Agency theory- and risk aversion-related issues may provide such a link. Hence, given the existence of divergent incentives and information asymmetry between controller (or employer) and controlee (or employee) and the high cost of observing employee skill or effort, a budget-based employment contract (i.e., employee compensation is contingent on meeting the performance standard) can be Pareto-superior to fixed pay or linear sharing rules (where the employer and employee split the output) (Demski and Feltham, 1978). However, these budget-based schemes impose a risk on the employee (since job performance may be affected by a host of uncontrollable factors). Consequently, risk-averse individuals may resort to slack budgeting through systematic distortion of input information. Moreover, any enhanced (increased) risk aversion would, in practice, lead the employee to resort to slack budgeting.

Self-Esteem

The enhancement of risk aversion and the resulting distortion of input information may be more pronounced when self-esteem is threatened. It was found that persons who have low opinions of themselves are more likely to cheat than persons with high self-esteem (Aronson and Mettee, 1968). A situation of dissonance was created in an experimental group by giving out positive feedback about a personality test to some participants and negative feedback to others. Then, all the participants were asked to take part in a competitive game of cards. The participants who received a blow to their self-esteem cheated more than those who had received positive feedback about themselves. Could it also be concluded that slack budgeting through information distortion may be a form of dishonest behavior arising from enhancement of risk aversion caused by negative feedback on self-esteem? A person's expectations may be an important determinant of his or her behavior. Negative feedback on self-esteem may lead an individual to develop an expectation of poor performance. At the same time the individual who is gen negative feedback about his or her self-esteem would be more risk-averse than others and would be ready to resort to any behavior to cover the situation. Consequently, he or she may attempt to distort the input information in order to have an attainable budget. Accordingly, one hypothesis may be stated as follows: *Individuals given negative feedback about their self-esteem will introduce more bias into estimates than individuals given positive or neutral feedback about their self-esteem.*

METHOD

A laboratory experiment was used to investigate the impact of self-esteem feedback on input information distortion in a budgeting task. The subjects were sixty male and female students drawn from the fourth-year undergraduate accounting theory class, the second-year graduate managerial accounting class, and the introductory undergraduate accounting class in the Faculty of Administration at the University of Ottawa who agreed to cooperate and participate in the experiment. Students rather than managers were used in order to better isolate the impact of self-esteem on input information distortion, given that managers may be influenced by a host of other organizational factors to create slack. The subjects were told that they were participating in a study concerned with the correlation between self-esteem scores and "estimation aptitudes." They were told that the Tennessee Self-Concept Scale (TSCS) would be used to measure their self-esteem, and the "estimation aptitudes" would be ascertained upon the completion of a budgeting test (Fitts, 1965).

All subjects were given the TSCS and were informed of its nature and intent. The test belongs to a wide variety of instruments that have been employed to measure the self-concept. The instrument is simple for the subject to understand, which explains its popularity as a means of studying and understanding human behavior. Sociologist, psychiatrists, theologians, philosophers, educators, and psychologists have increasingly come to view the self-concept as a central construct for the understanding of people and their behavior. Consequently, a whole theoretical school, known as self-theory, ahs evolved, as evidenced by works of people like Rogers (1951), Snygg and Combs (1949), Lecky (1945), Wylie (1961), and others. Self-theory is strongly phenomenological in nature and is based on the general principle that people react to their phenomenal world in terms of the way that they perceive this world. Self-theory holds that people's behavior is always meaningful and that we understand each person's behavior only if we can perceive his or her phenomenal world as he or she does. The TSCS was devised for the purpose of measuring the self-concept. Although subject to the limiitaions of any verbal or pencil-and-paper type of scale, the TSCS is nevertheless applicable to a broad range of people and situations (Fitts and Hammer, 1969; Fitts, 1970, 1972a, 1972b, 1972c; Fitts et al., 1971; Thompson,1972). It yields a number of measures and scores and is well standardized. Among these scores are:

The self-criticism score (SC): High scores indicate a normal, healthy openness and capacity for self-criticism.

The positive score (P): Scores on ninety items are summed to provide a total P score, which reflects general esteem. In general, people with high scores tend to like themselves, feel that they are persons of value and worth, have confidence in themselves, and act accordingly. People with low scores are doubtful about their own worth and unhappy and have little faith or confidence in themselves (Fitts, 1965, p.1).

Other scores are provided by the TSCS. To avoid any confusion, only the positive score is used in this study. The subjects were provided with sufficient information about the TSCS and the positive scores to consider it relevant and important.

A week after the administration of the TSCS and before participating in a budgeting paper-and-pencil test, subjects were assigned to one of three experimental conditions: positive, neutral, and negative feedback on self-esteem scores. This manipulation of self-esteem was done by disclosing the highest, lowest, and average scores in the class and by either (1) communicating the right score, (2) having the subject's score equal to the highest score in the class, or (3) having the subject's score equal to the lowest score in the class. In general, the first alternative was communicated to those whose right score was around the average score in the class, the second alternative to those with low scores, and the third alternative to those with high scores. The last two alternatives were aimed at temporarily inducing either an increase in self-esteem or a decrease in self-esteem. *The first alternative, where no change in self-esteem was sought, was intended for control purposes.*[2]

The highest scores were 405 for the positive score and 46 for the self-criticism score. The lowest scores were 261 for the positive score and 23 for the self-criticism score. The average scores were 310 for the positive score and 32 for the self-criticism score. The provision of such a range of scores for the false feedback groups was assumed to be high enough to generate a blow to the self-esteem of the subject.[3] To avoid any confusion, the subjects were provided with only the positive scores.

The experimental material included four pages: one page for instructions; one page for the positive, neutral, or negative feedback on their self-esteem scores; and the last two pages for a paper-and-pencil test requiring the subject to make cost and sales estimates.

The instructions stated:

The purpose of this experiment is to correlate the estimation ability with self-esteem characteristics. In order to get a true measure of a person's estimation ability, it is necessary to keep in mind the estimation's objective function which is first, to insure that the budget is attainable and, second, that the budget is accurate. In order to accomplish this, I am having you engage in the estimation of both cost and sales for a fictional situation. It is important that you keep the estimation's objective function in mind when making your decision. The second page gives your self-esteem score. The last two pages constitute the budgeting situation.

The second page for the feedback on the self-esteem scores stated:

In the middle of the semester, you were asked to complete the Tennessee Self-Concept Scale. The test belongs to a wide variety of instruments which have been employed to measure the self-concept. The test gives a measure of self-esteem. Persons with high scores tend to like themselves, feel that they are persons of value and worth, have confidence in themselves, and act accordingly. Your score was ___. The highest, the lowest, and the average scores in your class were respectively ___, ___, ___.

The last two pages of the experimental material included a paper-and pencil budgeting test requiring each subject to make ten estimates on the basis of the estimates of others. Two versions of the budgeting test were presented: a cost version and a sales version. The cost version reads as follows:

Assume that you are the controller of a manufacturing company considering the production of a new product. You are required to submit your estimate of the unit cost of the product if 500,000 units are produced. Your two assistants A and B, in whom you have equal confidence, presented you with preliminary estimates. For each of the cases below, indicate your estimate of costs you would submit.

The sales version reads as follows:

Assume that you are the marketing manager of a manufacturing concern considering the production of a new product. You are required to submit your estimate of the sales volume of the product if the price is set at$10.80. Your two assistants A and B, in whom you have equal confidence, presented you with preliminary estimates. For each of the cases below, indicate what estimate of sales you would submit.

Each question was followed by a list of ten pairs of numbers, representing the ten pairs of estimates by the two subordinates. The experiment involved in each case the choice between two estimates of cost and two estimates of sales. The cost estimates are indicated below:

Cost Estimates Presented to Participants

Cases	A's Estimate	B's Estimate	Your Estimate
(1)	$1.54	$6.75	$_____
(2)	$8.42	$4.56	$_____
(3)	$3.25	$7.52	$_____
(4)	$1.25	$4.35	$_____
(5)	$6.54	$4.70	$_____
(6)	$1.80	$7.30	$_____
(7)	$6.89	$1.65	$_____
(8)	$3.25	$7.52	$_____
(9)	$4.74	$1.54	$_____
(10)	$3.20	$5.35	$_____

The sales estimates were similar in value except that the cost estimates are expressed in dollars, and those for sales in units. However, the sales estimates were presented in various different orders to obscure the similarities in values. One such order of sales estimates is indicated below:

Sales Estimates Presented to Participants

Cases	A's Estimate	B's Estimate	Your Estimate
(1)	320,000 units	535,000 units	_____ units
(2)	474,000	154,000	_____
(3)	325,000	752,000	_____
(4)	689,000	165,000	_____
(5)	180,000	730,000	_____
(6)	654,000	470,000	_____
(7)	125,000	435,000	_____
(8)	325,000	752,000	_____
(9)	842,000	456,000	_____
(10)	154,000	675,000	_____

The three types of feedback on self-esteem scores (negative, neutral, and positive) and the two types of budgeting decisions (cost and sales estimates) resulted in the 2 x 3 x N factorial design in Table 3A.1. The group receiving the correct and hence neutral feedback was intended to be the control group in this experiment.

Table 3A.1 Diagram of the Two-Factor Sample
Experiment

Negative		Types of feedback sample experiment		
		Correct	Positive	
Types of budgeting	Cost	n = 20	n = 20	n = 20
decisions	Sales	n = 20	n = 20	n = 20

The nature of the task is assumed to lead the subjects to build in slack. First, it asks for an attainable budgets. Second, the courses being taken by the subjects and taught by the experimenter emphasize the notion of a biased payoff schedule within an organization. Therefore, following the argumentation provided by CMS (1961, p.254), if the payoffs are perceived to be biased or if they are perceived to depend on considerations other than the relations between the estimate and the true value, the tactical decision on biasing the estimate becomes important to the estimator.

RESULTS

Each subject's cost and sales estimates, E, were transformed into a summary statistic, x, which represented the weight assigned to the larger of the two given numbers in the pair presented to the subject such that

$$E = XU + (1 - X)L$$

where U is the upper number, and L the lower number.

Upper and lower limits of the ten pairs ranged from 125 to 842 and included two pairs in which the difference was approximately 200; two pairs in which the difference was approximately 300; two pairs in which the difference was approximately 400; two pairs in which the difference was approximately 550; one pair in which the difference was 521; and one pair in which the difference was 386.

The use of a linear combination of the two estimates was considered superior to a single reliance on the mean. In effect, the summary statistic, x, highlights the bias brought by the subject to his or her estimates better than a single use of the mean estimate. It is used in the study as the database for the analysis of variance. The mean estimate does not highlight the bias because it gives equal weight to the observations.

The analysis of variance is summarized in Table 3A.2. The main effects were significant. The nature of the feedback on self-esteem had an impact on the weight assigned to the largest estimate ($F_{obs} = 6.71 > F_{.95} (2, 54) = 3.20$), and the nature of the budgeting decision had an impact on the weight assigned by the subject to the highest estimate ($F_{obs} = 5.71 > F_{.95} (1, 54) = 4.00$). The interaction effects were also significant ($F_{obs} = 5.44 > F_{.95} (1, 54) = 3.20$). The nature of the interaction effects is indicated by an inspection of the cell means. These means are shown in Table 3A.3. A geometric representation of these means is also given in Figure 3A.1. This figure presents the profiles corresponding to the simple main effects of the type of feedback on self-esteem for each of the budgeting decisions. A response of 0.5 is unbiased, and responses of > 0.5 for cost estimates and < 0.5 for sales estimates represent slack creation. The profiles for the cost and sales decisions appear to have different slopes indicating that an analysis of the simple effects is warranted. Only one simple effect is significant. Given negative feedback on self-esteem, the impact of the budgeting decision on the weights assigned to the highest estimate is different (F_{obs} = 14.2 > $F_{.95}$ (1, 54) = 4.00). In fact, in the case of negative feedback, thirteen of the cost response points were superior to 0.5, and fourteen of the sales response points were inferior to 0.5.

However, the experimental data do not indicate a difference in the weights assigned given a neutral (F_{obs} = 0.9) or positive (F_{obs} = 1.01) feedback on self-esteem. Although the results are not significant, the positive feedback caused slack to be incorporated with cost estimation. If the positive feedback were significant, the evidence in this study would have been consistent with a curvilinear hypothesis that invalid feedback on self-esteem causes the incorporation of slack. Given the results of this study, however, the evidence seems more consistent with the linear hypothesis that negative feedback on self-esteem causes the incorporation of slack.

Table 3A.2 Summary ANOVA for Gain and Simple Effects

Source of variation	SS	Y	MS	F
A (Budgeting decision)	0.68	1	0.68	5.71*
A for b_1 (negative feedback)	(1.690)[1]	(1)	(1.690)	(14.2)*
A for b_2 (neutral feedback)	(0.115)	(1)	(0.115)	(0.9)
A for b_3 (positive feedback)	(0.221)	(1)	(.0221)	(1.01)
B (feedback on self-esteem)	1.6	2	0.8	6.71*
B for a_1 (cost decision)	(0.546)	(2)	(0.273)	(2.29)
B for a_2 (sales decision)	(0.955)	(2)	(0.473)	(3.9)
AB	1.336	2	0.668	5.44*
Within cell	6.474	54	0.119	
Total	10.090	59		

Notes:
*significant at .05 level.
[1]data for simple effects are in parentheses.
Legend: SS = Sum of squares; Y = Degrees of freedom; MS = Mean square; F = F statistic.

Table 3A.3 Mean of Cells Summary Table

	Negative Feedback	Neutral Feedback	Positive Feedback
Cost	0.81	0.50	0.75
Sales	0.23	0.65	0.54

Figure 3A.1 Profiles of Simple Effects of Feedback on Self-Esteem (Mean Weight Assigned to the Highest Estimate)

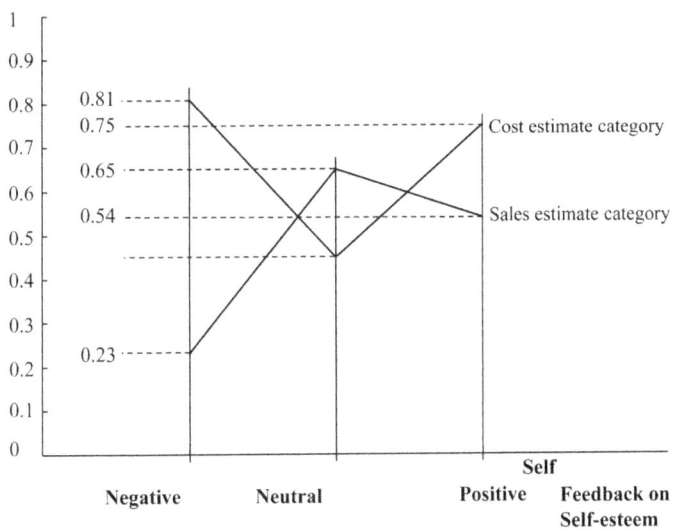

DISCUSSION

The above results suggest that inaccurate but neutral or positive feedback on self-esteem may not result in observed differences in the cost of sales budgeting decisions. An inaccurate but favorable feedback on self-esteem does not seem to lead to a slack budgeting behavior and distortion of input information. Similarly, negative but inaccurate feedback does lead to a difference in the type of budgeting decision, cost or sales. The inaccurate and negative feedback of self-esteem seems to result in the distortion of input information. An examination of Figure 3A.1 shows that given negative feedback on self-esteem, subjects tend to overestimate cost and underestimate sales.

These results seem to support the findings of CMS in part. They support the same idea that "cost and sales would tend to be estimated with a bias even though the bias might be in a different direction for each type of estimate." They also support their main proposition that "estimates within a complex decision making system involve attempts by the estimators to control their payoffs." Two differences arise, however, when comparing the scope of both results. First, the differences in the cost and sales estimation decisions result, in our study, in the creation of slack. Our subjects tend to overestimate cost and underestimate sales. Second, our results show that the bias introduced by the estimators is caused by the inaccurate and negative feedback on self-esteem.

One possible interpretation consistent with the observed effect may be related to the cognitive dissonance theory.

Inaccurate and negative feedback on self-esteem may lead to enhanced risk aversion and increased dissonance, and since dissonance and risk aversion lead to an effort to reduce them, and since the only means of reduction in this experiment is the budget, slack budgeting behavior is expected.[4]

Another possible interpretation is that slack budgeting behavior occurs as a result of being consistent with an enhanced risk aversion due to a negative self-concept. The inaccurate and negative feedback on self-esteem apparently accentuates the risk aversion, leading to a distortion of input information. In other words, a shock to one's self-esteem will cause one to be willing to be a party to cheating to achieve success. Given the nature of the task, the behavior is similar to that which would be exhibited by an increase in one's risk aversion. Two words of caution to qualify this conclusion are necessary. First, this study did not assess risk aversion directly, and, therefore, one cannot infer from the analysis that individuals with negative feedback on self-esteem are indeed risk averters. Second, future research should incorporate an incentive scheme; otherwise, the effects in the negative case may be overstated.

To be consistent with the work of Rogers (1951), the slack budgeting behavior may be altered by first changing the self-concept in a positive direction and thereby reducing the risk aversion. Clearly, any planning or control system within a firm must take into account the predisposition and biases created in the planner by the nature of the feedback on his or her performance and consequently on his or her self-esteem: an inaccurate and negative feedback on self-esteem may induce slack. So, the control of slack during the budget-setting period should be emphasized in the case of those employees who had previously received invalid feedback on their performance and self-esteem. In short, if an individual in an organization is tempted to use slack budgeting, it may be easier for him or her to yield to this temptation if his or her self-esteem has been lowered by inaccurate negative feedback. It is, however, appropriate to caution that the suggestions derived from the findings are tentative pending replication and further demonstrations of the external validity of this experiment.

One possible improvement would be to investigate whether the results of this study are due solely to the effects of negative and positive feedback on the subjects or are due to their perceived level of self-esteem. A second possible improvement would be to investigate the effects on estimation of accurate information concerning high and low self-esteem. To do so, the experiment should include individuals with high and low levels of self-esteem who either receive no feedback concerning their self-esteem levels (additional control group) or who receive accurate feedback concerning their self-esteem (additional experimental group). Another possible improvement would be to design an experiment dealing with more than the two budgetary items examined in this experiment, namely, cost and sales volume.

CONCLUSION

Certain hypotheses on slack budgeting were deduced from an examination of the nature of the feedback of self-esteem on the distortion of input information. Three main results appear. First, it can be said that the nature of the feedback on self-esteem has an impact on organizational estimation decisions. Second, the experiment also indicates that the nature of the budgeting decision leads to a different estimation figure. Finally, the negative and inaccurate feedback of self-esteem appears to accentuate the distortion of input information and the creation of slack. Until the impact of accurate feedback of self-esteem is investigated, this study's findings indicate that negative feedback should not be released before it has been categorically proven to be accurate.

NOTES

1. Various organizational processes grounded in the development and maintenance of coalitions as well as a variety of group and political behaviors may constitute other cases in which these relationships may be either successfully resolved or not.

2. Parametric and nonparametric tests ($\alpha = .10$) failed to reject the hypothesis of no differences in the TSCS scores of the three types of subjects (four-year undergraduate, first-year undergraduate, and second-year graduate).

3. At the end of the experiment the subjects were debriefed and given their correct TSDS scores.

4. In other words, to reduce the risk aversion and to reach more consonance, subjects reverted to a slack budgeting behavior.

REFERENCES

Argyris, C. *The Impact of Budgets on People.* New York: The controllership Foundation, 1952.

Aronson, E., and D.R. Mettee. "Dishonest Behavior as a Function of Differential Levels of Induced Self-Esteem." *Journal of Personality and Social Psychology* (January 1968), pp.121-127.

Barefield, R.M. "A Model of Forecast Biasing Behavior." *The Accounting Review* (July 1970), pp.490-501.

Belkaoui, A. *Conceptual Foundations of Management Accounting.* Reading, MA: Addison-Wesley, 1980.

_____. "The Relationships between Self-Disclosure Style and Attitudes to Responsibility Accounting." *Accounting, Organizations and Society* (December 1981), pp.281-289.

_____. *Cost Accounting: A Multidimensional Emphasis.* Hinsdale, IL: Dryden Press, 1983.

Caplan, E.H. *Management Accounting and Behavioral Sciences.* Reading, MA: Addison-Wesley, 1971.

Collins, F. "Managerial Accounting Systems and Organizational Control: A Role Perspective." *Accounting, Organizations and Society* (May 1982), pp.107-122.

Cyert, R.M., and J.G. March. *A Behavioral Theory of the Firm.* Englewood Cliffs, NJ: Prentice-Hall, 1963.

Cyert, R.M., J.G. March, and W.H. Starbuck. "Two Experiments on Bias and Conflict in Organizational Estimation." *Management Science* (April 1961), pp.254-264.

Dalton, M. *Men Who Manage*, New York: John Wiley, 1961.

Demski, J.S., and G.A. Feltham. "Economic Incentives in Budgetary Control Systems." *The Accounting Review* (April 1978), pp.336-359.

Fitts, W.F. *Manual for the Tennessee Self-Concept Scale.* Nashville, TN: Counselor Recording and Tests, 1965.

_____. *Interpersonal Competence: The Wheel Model.* Nashville, TN: Counselor Recording and Tests, 1970.

_____. *The Self-Concept and Behavior: Overview and Supplement.* Nashville, TN: Counselor Recording and Tests, 1972a.

_____. *The Self-Concept and Performance.* Nashville, TN: Counselor Recording and Tests, 1972b.

_____. *The Self-Concept and Psychopathology.* Nashville, TN: Counselor Recording and Tests, 1972c.

Fitts, W.F., J.L. Adams, G. Radford, W.C. Richard, B.K. Thomas, M.M. Thomas, and W. Thompson. *The Self-Concept and Self-Actualization.* Nashville, TN: Counselor Recording and Tests, 1971.

Fitts, W.F., and W.T. Hammer. *The Self-Concept and Delinquency.* Nashville, TN: Counselor Recording and Tests, 1969.

Hopwood, A.G. "An Empirical Study of the Role of Accounting Data in Performance Evaluation." *Empirical Research in Accounting: Selected Studies,* suppl. to *Journal of Accounting Research* 10 (1972), pp.194-209.

Lecky, P. *Self-Consistency.* New York: Island Press, 1945.

Lowe, A.E., and R.W. Shaw. "An Analysis of Managerial Biasing: Evidence from a Company's Budgeting Process." *The journal of Management Studies* (October 1968), pp.304-315.

March, J.G., and H.A. Simon. *Organizations.* New York: John Wiley, 1958.

Onsi, M. "Factor Analysis of Behavioral Variables Affecting Budgetary Slack." *The Accounting Review* (July 1973), pp.535-548.

Parker, L.D. "Goal Congruence: A Misguided Accounting Concept." *Abacus* (June 1976), pp.3-13.

Rogers, C.R. *Client Centered Therapy.* Boston: Houghton Miffin, 1951.

Schiff, M., and A.Y. Lewin. "The Impact of People on Budgets." *The Accounting Review* (April 1970), pp.259-268.

Snygg, D., and A.W. Combs. *Individual Behavior.* New York: Harper and Row, 1949.

Swieringa, R.J., and R.H. Moncur. "The Relationship between Managers' Budget Oriented Behavior and Selected Attitudes, Position, Size and Performance Measures." *Empirical Research in Accounting: Selected Studies,* suppl. to *Journal of Accounting Research* 10 (1972), p.19.

Thompson, W. *Correlates of the Self-Concept.* Nashville, TN: Counselor Recording and Tests, 1972.

Williamson, O.E. *The Economy of Discretionary Behavior: Managerial Objectives in the Theory of the Firm.* Englewood Cliffs, NJ: Prentice-Hall, 1964.

Wylie, R.C. *The Self-Concept: A Critical Survey of Pertinent Research Literature.* Lincoln: University of Nebraska Press, 1961.

CHAPTER 4:
SMOOTHING

INTRODUCTION

Income smoothing is a clear form of designed accounting. It is a deliberate attempt by management to show stable earnings by reaching the variations in earnings fluctuations and securing an acceptable earnings growth. The complexity of the phenomenon warrants examination of its nature, history, the motivations behind its construction, smoothing dimensions, and variables used, as well as the objects of smoothing. Because it may take different forms depending on different contextual confirmations, income smoothing may have different impacts that also warrant examination. All of these issues are discussed in this chapter.

ACCOUNTING POLICY AND CHANGES

Firms need to make choices among the different accounting methods in recording transactions and preparing their financial statements. These choices, as dictated by generally accepted accounting principles, represent the accounting policies of the firm. They are best defined by the Accounting

Principles Board (APB) in its Opinion 22, *Disclosure of Acceding Polices* (April 1972), paragraph 6:

The *accounting policies* of a reporting entity are the specific accounting principles and the methods of applying those principles that are judged by the management of the entity to be the most appropriate in the circumstances to present fairly financial position, changes in financial position, and results of operations in accordance with generally accepted accounting principles and that accordingly have been adopted for preparing the financial statements.

Firms also make accounting changes as part of their accounting policies. The general belief is that firms make accounting changes to make performance problems. The accounting literature explains the changes in accounting principles and estimates in terms of management's desire to reach definite objectives such as income smoothing[1] or the reduction of agency costs associated with a violation of debt covenants. A summary of existing research results suggests that as the tightness of debt covenant increases, firms are more likely to loosen the tightness of covenant restrictions through appropriate accounting changes.[2] In fact, two studies that examined the accounting changes of (1) successful and unsuccessful firms[3] and (2) firms facing or experiencing bond rating changes[4] provide some evidence consistent with the assertion that managers can modify income through judicious accounting changes.

Accounting regulators have tried to limit management's ability to use accounting changes to increase or decrease net income. Since 1970, APB No. 20 has stipulated that accounting changes should be accounted for as a cumulative effect change, requiring the reporting in the comparative income statements of the cumulative effect of change in the net income of the period of the change as well as the disclosure in the notes of the effect of adopting the new accounting principle on income before extraordinary income and net income (and on related per share amounts) of the period change. Similarly, the Securities and Exchange Commission's (SEC) accounting Release No. 177 required that accounting changes be made to more preferable accounting methods, using reasonable business judgment in the choice. While both pronouncements act as a control mechanism, they do not eliminate management's ability to increase and/or decrease income through accounting changes. SEC Chairman Arthur Levitt contended that public companies have used six accounting practices to manage corporate earnings:

1. overstatement of restructuring changes to clean up the balance sheet;

2. classification of a significant portion of the price of an acquired entity as in-process research and development so that the amount can be written off as a onetime charge;

3. creation of large liabilities for future expenses (recorded as part of the accounting for an acquisition) to protect future earnings;

4. use of unrealistic assumptions to estimate liabilities for items such as sales returns, loan losses, and

warranty costs so that the overaccrual can be reversed to improve earnings during a subsequent period;

5. intentional inclusion of errors in the company's books and justifying the failure to correct the errors by arguing materiality; and

6. recognition of revenue before the earnings process is complete.[5]

INCOME SMOOTHING HYPOTHESIS

Nature of Income Smoothing

Income smoothing may be viewed as the deliberate normalization of income in order to reach a desired trend or level. As far back as 1953, Heyworth observed "more of the accounting techniques which may be applied to affect the assignment of net income successive accounting periods...for smoothing or leveling the amplitude of periodic net income fluctuations."[6] What followed were arguments made by Monsen and Downs[7] and Gordon[8] that corporate managers may be motivated to smooth their own income security, with the assumption that stability in income and rate of growth will be preferred over higher average income streams with greater variability. More specifically, Gordon theorized on income smoothing as follows:

Proposition 1: The criterion that a corporate management uses in selecting among accounting principles is the maximization of its utility or welfare.

Proposition 2: The utility of management increases with (1) its job security, (2) the level and rate of growth in the management's income, and (3) the level and rate of growth in the corporation's size.

Proposition 3: The achievement of the management goals stated in Proposition 2 is dependent in part on the satisfaction of stockholders with the corporation's performance; that is, other things being equal, the happier the stockholders, the greater the job security, income, and so on of the management.

Proposition 4: Stockholders' satisfaction with a corporation increases with the average rate of growth in the corporation's income (or the average rate of return on its capital) and the stability of its income. This proposition is as readily verified as Proposition 2.

Theorem: Given that the above four propositions are accepted or found to be true, it follows that management would, within the limits of its power, that is, the latitude allowed by accounting rules, (1) smooth reported income and (2) smooth the rate of growth in income. By "smooth the rate of growth in income" we mean the following: if the rate of growth is high, accounting practices that reduce it should be adopted, and vice versa.[9]

The best definition of income smoothing was provided by Beidleman as follows:

Smoothing of reported earnings may be deemed as the intentional dampening or fluctuations about some level of earnings that is currently considered to be normal for a firm.

In this sense smoothing represents an attempt on the part of the firm's management to reduce abnormal variations in earnings to the extent allowed under sound accounting and management principles.[10]

Given the above definition, what needs to be explicated are the motivation of smoothing, the dimensions of smoothing, and the instruments of smoothing.

History of Income Smoothing

Most of the literature on income smoothing attributes the origin of the concept to one of the three works by Gordon et al.,[11] Hepworth,[12] and White.[13] However, an article by Buckmaster[14] on income smoothing in accounting and business literature prior to 1954 identifies up to thirty-four works from 1893 to 1953 that contain some kind of reference to the smoothing properties of an accounting method or to an accounting practice used in such a way as to dampen the fluctuations of reported income. The article reports on pages that focus on the balance sheet and secret reserves that result in the reduction of the volatility of income time-series and those that examined the last in, first out (LIFO) base-stock inventory debate as it related to income smoothing.

Secret reserves were created by management in order to "avoid the distribution of firm assets as dividends, by creating a contra asset account or a liability or by failing to record assets and/or writing them off as expenses or directly to surplus (retained earnings)."[15] The secret reserves can also be created by the recording of unusually large amounts of depreciation in good years,[16] the write-down of assets,[17] the classification of extraordinary losses as extraordinary deprecitoin,[18] the use of flexibility in the capitalize/expense decisions for plant and equipment related costs,[19] the charging of large amounts of capital expenditures to expenses in periods of high profits,[20] the practice of overly excessive repairs in good years and inadequate repairs in bad years,[21] and the making of excessive provisions for bad debt and valuing inventories at below cost.[22]

Base-stock inventory was also used for smoothing purposes and dampening of business cycles. As Warshaw explains:

The leveling of inventory gains and losses, with the comparative stability of yearly profits which this method brings about…exerts a subconscious effect upon business policy which is very desirable. Prices of manufacturing articles are kept in more proper relation to prices of raw material. The management is not elated by apparent profits or depressed by apparent losses. Such elation and depression are responsible for most business follies. The normal stock inventory automatically creates a reserve that strengthens the basis for credit, gives stability, and makes expansion safe. Moreover, it has the great advantage of being a concrete suggestion for mitigating the security of business cycles.[23]

Warshaw's arguments were later supported by Davis[24] and Cotter.[25] Cotter mentioned the smoothing prosperities of LIFO and the advantages of (a) dampening the business cycles, (b) avoiding overexpansion of credit, (c) avoiding demands for excessive dividends, and (d) better information for pricing decisions.[26]

Motivation of Smoothing

As early as 1953 Heyworth claimed that motivations behind smoothing include the improvements of relations with creditors, investors, and workers, as well as dampening of business cycles through psychological processes.[27] Gordon proposed that:

1. The criterion that a corporate management uses in selecting among accounting principles is to maximize its utility or welfare.

2. The same utility is a function of job security, the level and rate of growth of salary, and the level and growth rate in the firm's size.

3. Satisfaction of shareholders with the corporation's performance enhances the status and rewards of managers.

4. The same satisfaction depends on the rate of growth and stability of the firm's income.[28]

These propositions culminate in the need to smooth as explained in the following theorem:

Given that the above four propositions are accepted or found to be true, it follows that a management should, within the limits of its power, i.e., the latitude allowed by accounting rules,

(1) smooth reported income and (2) smooth the rate of growth in income. By smoothing the rate of growth in income we mean the following: If the rate of growth is high, accounting practices which reduce it should be adopted and vice-versa.[29]

Beidleman considers two reasons for management to smooth reported earnings.[30] The first argument rests on the assumption that a stable earnings stream is capable of supporting a higher level of dividends than a more variable earnings stream, having a favorable effect on the value of the firm's shares as overall riskiness of the firm is reduced. He states:

To the extent that the observed variability about a trend of reported earnings influences investors' subjective expectations for possible outcomes of future earnings and dividends, management might be able favorably to influence the value of the firm's shares by smoothing earnings.[31]

The second argument attributes to smoothing the ability to counter the cyclical nature of reported earnings and likely reduce the correlation of a firm's expected returns with returns on the market portfolio. He states:

To the degree that auto-normalization of earnings is successful, and that the reduced covariance of returns with the market is recognized by investors and incorporated into their evaluation process, smoothing will have added beneficial effects in share values.[32]

It results from the need felt by management to neutralize environmental uncertainty and dampen the wide fluctuations in the operating performance of the firm subject to an intermittent cycle of good and bad times. To do so, management may resort to organizational slack behavior,[33] budgetary slack behavior,[34] or risk-avoiding behavior.[35] Each of these behaviors necessitates decisions affecting the incurrence and/or allocation of discretionary expenses (costs) that result in income smoothing.

In addition to these behaviors intended to neutralize environmental uncertainty, it is possible to identify organizational characterizations that differentiate firms in their extent of smoothing. For example, Kamin and Ronen[36] examined the effects of the separation of ownership and control on income smoothing, under the hypothesis that management-controlled firms are more likely to be engaged in smoothing as a manifestation of managerial discretion and budgetary slack. Their results confirmed that income smoothing is higher among management-controlled firms with high barriers to entry.

Management was also assigned to circumvent news of the constraints of generally accepted accounting principles by attempting to smooth income numbers so as to convey their expectations of future cash flows, enhancing in the process the apparent reliability of predictions based on the observed smoothed series of numbers.[37] Three constraints are presumed to lead managers to smooth:

1. the competitive market mechanisms, which reduce the options available to management;

2. the management compensation scheme, which is linked directly to firm's performance; and

3. the threat of management displacement.

This smoothing is not limited to high-level management and external accounting; it is also presumed to be used by lower-level management and internal accounting in the form of organizational slack and slack budgeting.[38]

Types of Smoothing

An early definition of income smoothing states that it "moderates year-to-year fluctuations in income by shifting earnings from peak years to less successful periods."[39] A more recent definition of income smoothing sees the phenomenon as "the process of manipulating the time profile of earnings or earnings reports to make the reported income less variable, while not increasing reported earnings over the long run."[40] Both definitions seem to imply that there is only one form of income smoothing used to dampen fluctuations of earnings toward an expected level of earnings. Of the studies that distinguished between potentially different types of smoothing, the article by Eckel[41] provides the more exhaustive classification of the different types of smooth income statements. The first distinction is made between an intentional or designed smoothing and a natural smoothing. The second distinction is to classify the intentional or designed smoothing with either an artificial smoothing or a real smoothing. These various types of smoothing are explicated next.

Intentional or designed smoothing refers specifically to the deliberate designing choices made to dampen earnings fluctuations around a desired level. Therefore, intentional or designed smoothing is essentially an accounting smoothing that uses the existing flexibility in generally accepted accounting principles and the choices and combinations available to smooth income. It is therefore essentially a form of the designed accounting that is the objective of this book.

Natural smoothing, unlike designed smoothing, is a natural product of the income-generating process, rather than the result of actions taken by management. Eckel gives the following example: "For example, one would expect the income generating process of public utilities to be such that income streams would be naturally smooth."[42]

Designed smoothing may be accomplished by either artificial or real smoothing. Artificial smoothing is the result of resorting to accounting manipulations to smooth income. As stated by Eckel:

These manipulations do not represent underlying economic events or affect cash flows, but shift costs and/or revenues from one period to another. For example, a firm would increase or decrease reported income smoothing by changing its actuarial assumptions concerning pension costs.[43]

Finally, real smoothing involves the deliberate choice and timing of transactions that can affect cash flows and control underlying choices of purchasing, hiring production, investment, sales, capital budgeting, research and development, advertising, and other decisions. It is basically a choice of business conduct to deliberately alter the cash flows of a corporation toward dampening earnings fluctuations. It can be either an attempt to control economic events or an attempt to construct economic events with the intention of affecting cash flows and smooth earrings. The actions taken by management in real smoothing are intended to alter the firm's production and/or investment decisions at year-end based on the knowledge of how the firm has performed up to that time of the year.[44]

The Smoothing Object

Basically, the smoothing object should be based on the most visible and used financial indication, which is the profit. Because income smoothing is not a visible phenomenon, the literature speculates on various expressions of profit as the most likely object of smoothing. These expressions include (1) net income-based indicators generally before extraordinary items and before or after tax, (2) earnings per share-based indicators generally before extraordinary gains and losses and adjusted for stock splits and dividends. The researchers choose net income- or earnings per share-based indicators as the object of smoothing because of the belief that management's long-term concern is with the net income, and users have a kind of functional fixation on the bottom figure, whether it is income or earnings per share. This is simplistic reasoning, as management may find it necessary and practical to smooth sales, and fixed sales commitments have only the flexibility of smoothing expenses. Similarly, a firm with good control on its expenses may find it more practical to smooth its sales revenues.

The Dimensions of Smoothing

The dimensions of smoothing are basically the means used to accomplish the smoothing of income numbers. Dascher and Malcolm distinguished between real smoothing and artificial smoothing as follows:

Real smoothing refers to the actual transaction that is undertaken or not undertaken on the basis of its smoothing effect on income, whereas artificial smoothing refers to accounting procedures which are implemented to shift costs and/or revenues from one period to another.[45]

These types of smoothing may be indistinguishable. For example, the amount of reported expenses may be lower or higher than in previous periods because of either deliberate actions on the level of the expenses (real smoothing) or the reporting methods (artificial smoothing). For both types, an operational test proposed is to fit a curve to a stream of income calculated two ways, excluding a possible manipulative variable and including it.[46]

Artificial smoothing was also considered by Copeland and defined as follows:

Income smoothing involves the repetitive selection of accounting measurement or reporting rules in a particular pattern, the effect of which is to report the stream of income with a smaller variation from trend than would otherwise have appeared.[47]

Besides real and artificial smoothing, other dimensions of smoothing were considered in the literature. A popular classification adds a third smoothing dimension, namely, classificatory smoothing. Barnes et al. distinguished between three smoothing dimensions as follows:

1. *Smoothing through events' occurrence and/or recognition.* Management can time actual transactions so that their effects on reported income would tend to dampen its variations over time. Mostly, the planned timing of events' occurrences (e.g., research and development) would be a function of the accounting rules governing the accounting recognition of the events.

2. *Smoothing through allocation over time.* Given the occurrence and the recognition of an event, management has more discretionary control over the determination over the periods to be affected by the events' quantification.

3. *Smoothing through classification (hence, classifactory smoothing).* When income statement statistics other than net income (net of all revenues and expenses) are the object of smoothing, management can classify intraincome statement items to reduce variations over time in that statistic.[48]

Basically, real smoothing corresponded to the smoothing through events' occurrence and/or recognition, while artificial smoothing corresponded to the smoothing through the allocation over time.

The Smoothing Variables

The smoothing devices or instruments are the variables used to smooth the chosen performance indicator. Copeland suggested the following five conditions as necessary for a smoothing instrument:

A. Once used, it must not commit the firm to any particular future action.

B. It must be based upon the exercise of professional judgment and be considered within the domain of "generally accepted accounting principles."

C. It must lead to material shifts relative to year-to-year differences in income.

D. It must not require a "real" transaction with second parties, but only a reclassification of internal account balances.

E. It must be used, singularly or in conjunction with other practices, over consecutive periods of time.[49]

Beidelman suggested two different and less restrictive criteria:

1. It must permit management to reduce the variability in reported earnings as it strives to achieve its long-run earnings (growth) objective.

2. Once used, it should not commit the firm to any particular action.[50]

Examples of smoothing instruments used include:

1. Switch from accelerated to straight-line depreciation[51]

2. Choice of cost or equity method[52]

3. Pension costs[53]

4. Dividend income[54]

5. Gains and losses on sale of securities[55]

6. Investment tax credit[56]

RESEARCH FINDINGS ON INCOME SMOOTHING

Sector and Country Analysis

It is possible to identify organizational characterizations, sector classifications, and country classifications that differentiate among different firms in their extent of smoothing.

1. With respect to the organizational characterizations, Kamin and Ronen[57] examined the effects of the separation of ownership and control on income smoothing under the hypothesis that management-controlled firms are more likely to be engaged in smoothing as a manifestation of managerial discretion and budgetary slack. Their results confirmed that a majority of the firms examined behave as if they were smoothers, and a particularly strong

majority is included among management-controlled firms with high barriers to entry.

2. With respect to sectorial classifications, Belkaoui and Picur[58] tested the effects of a dual economy on income-smoothing behavior. The main hypothesis was that a higher degree of smoothing of income numbers will be exhibited by firms in the periphery sector than firms in the core sector as a reaction to differences in the opportunity structures, experiences, and environmental uncertainty. Their results indicated that a majority of U.S. firms may be resorting to income smoothing, with a higher number included among firms in the periphery sector. However, using an income variability method of analysis, those results could not be replicated using a U.S. sample[59] or a Canadian samples.[60] in a Finnish context, Kinnunen et al.[61] found that one-sector firms may have more opportunities and more predisposition to income-smoothing behavior than firms operating in the more peripheral sector of the Finnish economy. The following explanation is provided for the Finnish results:

As an explanation for these findings, it can be argued that compared with the periphery sector, Finnish accounting rules provide the sector firms more opportunities to exploit certain earnings management instruments (such as accounting for depreciation of fixed assets, untaxed reserves, pension liabilities, exchange losses and R&D [research and development] costs). Furthermore, because these firms sell their products in highly competitive international markets, and are very much dependent on those markets, they presumably face a higher degree of environmental uncertainty than firms in the periphery sector. Therefore, the core sector firms are more apt to use income smoothing in the conventional sense.[62]

3. With regard to country classifications excluding the United States, the evidence shows a certain degree of income smoothing in Japan,[63] the United Kingdom,[64] Canada,[65] France,[66] and Singapore.[67]

Job Security and Anticipatory Smoothing

The general idea behind income smoothing is that the manager may take actions that increase reported income when income is low and take actions that decrease reported income when income is high. This is possible through either the flexibility allowed within generally accepted accounting principles or deliberate changes in operations. We may ask about the motivations of managers engaged in income smoothing. Fudenberg and Tirole[68] analytically show that income smoothing to increase job security arises in equilibrium if the following assumptions hold:

1. Managers enjoy nonmonetary private benefits (incumbency rents) from running the firm.

2. The firm is not committed to long-term incentive contract, which results in managers' dismissal in case of poor performance.

3. This is information decay in the sense that current earnings are more important than previous earnings in management's performance evaluation.

Because of these assumptions, managers in good times save for bad times. In other words:

First, when current earnings are relatively low, but expected future earnings are relatively high, managers will make accounting choices that increase current period discretionary accruals. In effect, managers in this setting are "borrowing" earnings from the future. Second, when current earnings are relatively high, but expected future earnings are relatively low, managers will make accounting choices that decrease current year discretionary accruals. Managers are effectively "saving" current earnings for possible use in the future.[69]

DeFond and Park[70] investigated the intuition derived from the Fudenberg-Tirole model by examining the effects of current relative premanaged earnings and expected future relative earnings on the behavior of discretionary accruals. Their evidence suggests that when current earnings are "poor," and expected future earnings are "good," mangers "borrow" earnings from the future for use in the current period. Conversely, when current earnings are "good" and expected future earnings are "poor," mangers "save" current earnings for possible use in the future. These findings that managers of firms experiencing poor (good) performance in the current period and expecting good (poor) performance in the next period choose income-increasing (income-decreasing) discretionary accruals in order to reduce the threat of being dismissed did not directly examine the link between job security and income smoothing. Accordingly, Ahmed et al.[71] hypothesized that the extent of income smoothing varies directly with managers' job security concern as proxied by the degree of competition in a firm's product markets, product durability, and capital-intensity. Basically, the argument is that managers of rims in more competitive industries, durable goods industries, and capital-intensive businesses are likely to have greater job security concerns than managers of other firms and therefore are more likely to engage in a greater extent of income smoothing. The results were consistent with the predictions. Using a different methodology, Elgers et al.[72] were able to provide results indicating that patterns in measured discretionary accruals and relative earnings performance are consistent with the theory that managers smooth earnings based on both current-year results and expected next-year results, a phenomenon better labeled as "anticipatory income smoothing."

Stockholders' Wealth and Income Smoothing

The only literature in income smoothing maintained and/or established a positive relationship between income smoothing and shareholders' wealth. The statements and/or findings are as follows:

1. Stockholder satisfaction is bound to increase with the rate of growth in a firm's income and the stability of its income.[73]

2. The possibility that analysts may become more enthusiastic about self-smoothers increases the interest in the firm's market shares and may have a favorable effect on share value and cost o fcapital.[74]

3. Income variability may be shown to be significantly correlated with both overall and systematic risk measures.[75]

4. Smoothing may imply a direct, cause-effect relationship between earnings fluctuations and market risk.[76]

5. By allowing management to select alternative accounting techniques, owners can capitalize upon managers' expertise.[77]

6. Smooth income reduces the probability of financial ratio covenants' leading to a reduction in the cost of default and renegotiation.[78]

7. Smooth income reduces the probability o financial ratio covenants' leading to a reduction in the cost of default and renegotiation.[79]

8. Firms that do not smooth have higher unexpected returns from earnings surprises than firms that smooth income.[80]

9. Institutional investors avoid firms that exhibit large variations in earnings. A smoother income stream is preferred.[81]

Other analyses of the impact of income smoothing on stockholders" wealth were more market-based. Nichelson et al.[82] found lower returns, lower risk, and larger firm sizes for smoothing firms. Wang and Williams[83] found that firms with a smooth income series were less risky and had a market response four times as large as that for the other firms. This favorable impact of smoothing is evaluated as follows:

Contrary to the widespread view that managers engage in income smoothing to increase their own welfare at the expense of stockholders, this study documents consistent evidence indicating that accounting income smoothing can be beneficial to the firm's stockholders and prospective investors. Specifically, the analysis demonstrated that income smoothing may enhance the informational value of earnings and reduce the riskiness of the firm.[84]

Chaney et al.[85] presents evidence that managers smooth income around their arrangements of the firm's permanent earnings. Income smoothing becomes a long-term strategy to communicate a firm's permanent earnings using discretionary accruals to remove (or offset) a portion of the transitory component of reported earnings. The evidence shows that (1) if the current year's income before discretionary accruals is lower than last year's reported earrings, discretionary accruals will be positive and (2) if the current year's income before discretionary accruals is already higher than last year's reported earrings, discretionary accruals will be negative. They conclude as follows:

We suggest that smoothing income around the managers' assessment of the firm's permanent earnings enhances the market's perception of the firm whose earnings are being managed. When firms consistently manage earnings to present a smooth pattern of profits to market participants, they avoid t he dips in earnings (and related reputation effects) that may follow periods of over-reported earnings. We hypothesize and present evidence that earnings response coefficients, which reflect the relation between unexpected earnings and market returns, as well as the perceived reliability of reported earnings, are higher for firms that engage consistently in income smoothing.[86]

Finally, Chaney and Lewis[87] investigated income smoothing and underperformance in initial public offerings. They found a positive association between a proxy for income smoothing and firm performance, in the sense that (1) firms that perform well tend to report earnings with less variability relative to cash from operations compared to other firms and (2) the earnings response coefficient is greater for firms that are able to smooth earnings relative to cash flows. The result is interpreted as being totally consistent with the hypothesis that the market is better able to assess the information content of earnings for firms with smoother earnings.

NOTES

1. A. Belkaoui, *Accounting and Public Policy* (Westport, CT: Quorum Books, 1995).

2. A. Christie, "Aggregation of Test Statistics: On Evaluation of the Evidence as Contracting and Size Hypotheses," *Journal of Accounting and Economics* 12 (1990).

3. S. Lilien, M. Mellman, and V. Pastena, "Accounting Changes: Successful or Unsuccessful Firms," *The Accounting Review* (October 1988), pp.642-651.

4. A. Belkaoui, "The Effect of Bond Ratings on Accounting Changes," Working Paper, University of Illinois at Chicago, 2002.

5. "SEC Chairman Discusses Earnings Management," *Deliotte & Touche Review* (October 12, 1998), p.1.

6. S.R. Heyworth, "Smoothing Periodic Income," *The Accounting Review* (January 1953), p.32.

7. R.J. Monsen and A. Downs, "A Theory of Large Managerial Firms," *The Journal of Political Economy* (June 1965).

8. M.J. Gordon, "Postulates, Principles, and Research in Accounting," *The Accounting Review* (April 1964), pp.251-263.

9. Ibid., pp.261-262.

10. C.R. Beidleman, "Income Smoothing: The Role of Management," *The Accounting Review* (October 1973), p.653.

11. M.J. Gordon, B.M. Horwitz, and P.T. Meyers, "Accounting Measurement and Normal Growth of the Firm," in R. Jaedicke, Y. Ijiri, and O. Nielsen (eds.), *Research in Accounting Measurement* (Evanston, IL: American Accounting Association, 1966), pp.221-231.

12. Hepworth, "Smoothing Periodic Income," pp.32-39.

13. G. White, "Discretionary Accounting Disclosures and Income Normalization," *Journal of Accounting Research* (Autumn 1970), pp.260-273.

14. D. Buckmaster, "Income Smoothing in Accounting and Business Literature Prior to 1954," *The Accounting Historian's Journal* (December 1992), pp.147-173.

15. Ibid., p.155.

16. E. Matheson, *The Depreciation of Factories, Mines and Industrial Undertaking and Their Valuation* (London: E. and F.N. Spon, 1910; reprint, New York: Arno Press, 1976), p.44.

17. J.P. Joplin, "Secret Reserves," *Journal of Accountancy* (December 1910), pp.407-417.

18. A.B. Grunder and D.R. Becker, "The Straight-Line Depreciation Accounting Practice of Telephone Companies in the United States," in *International Congress*

on Accounting (New York: International Congress, 1930), pp.351-403.

19. L.R. Dicksee, *Depreciation, Reserves, and Reserve Funds* (London: Gee & Co., 1903).

20. J.F. Johnson and E.S. Meade, "Editorial: Maintenance Expenses and Concealment of Earnings," *Journal of Accountancy* (March 1906), pp.410-412.

21. Ibid.

22. Joplin, "Secret Reserves."

23. H.T. Warshaw, "Inventory Valuation and the Business Cycle," *Harvard Business Review* (October 1924), pp.27-34.

24. A.R. Davis, "Inventory Valuation and Business Profits: The Case for a Cost or Market Basis," *N.A.C.A. Bulletin* (December 1973), pp.400-409.

25. A. Cotter, *Fool's Profits* (New York: Barwin's Publishing, 1940).

26. Ibid.

27. Heyworth, "Smoothing Periodic Income," p.34.

28. Gordon, "Postulates, Principles, and Research in Accounting," pp.251-263.

29. Ibid.

30. Beidleman, "Income Smoothing," pp.658-667.

31. Ibid., p.654.

32. Ibid.

33. R.M. Cyert and L.G. March, *A Behavioral Theory of the Firm* (Englewood Cliffs, NJ: Prentice-Hall, 1963).

34. M. Schiff and A.Y. Levin, "Where Traditional Budgeting Fails," *Financial Executive* (May 1968), pp.57-62.

35. J.D. Thompson, *Organizations in Action* (New York: McGraw-hill, 1967).

36. J.Y. Kamin and J. Ronen, "The Smoothing of Income Numbers: Some Empirical Evidence in Systematic Differences among Management-Controlled and Owner-Controlled Firms," *Accounting, Organizations and Society* 3, 2 (1978), pp.141-153.

37. A. Barnea, J. Ronen, and S. Sadan, "Classificatory Smoothing of Income with Extraordinary Items," *The Accounting Review* (January 1976), pp.110-122.

38. A. Belkaoui, *Behavioral Accounting* (Westport, CT: Greenwood Press, 1989).

39. R. Copeland, "Income Smoothing," *Empirical Research in Accounting: Selected Studies*, suppl. to *Journal of Accounting Research* 6 (1968), p.101.

40. D. Fudenberg and J. Tirole, "A Theory of Income and Dividend Smoothing Based on Incumbency Rents," *Journal of Political Economy* 1 (1995), pp.75-93.

41. N. Eckel, "The Income Smoothing Hypothesis Revisited," *Abacus* 17 (June 1981), pp.28-40.

42. Ibid., p.28.

43. Ibid., p.29.

44. R.A. Lamber, "Income Smoothing as Rational Equilibrium Behavior," *The Accounting Review* 59 (October 1984), p.606.

45. P.E. Dascher and R.E. Malcolm, "A Note on Income Smoothing in the Chemical Industry," *Journal of Accounting Research* (Autumn 1970), pp.253-254.

46. M.J. Gordon, "Discussions of the Effects of Alternative Accounting Rules for Nonsubsidiary Investments," *Empirical Research in Accounting: Selected Studies*, suppl. to *Journal of Accounting Research* 4 (1966), p.223.

47. Copeland, "Income Smoothing," 6, p.101.

48. Barnea, Ronen, and Sadan, "Classificatory Smoothing of Income with Extraordinary Items," p.111.

49. Copeland, "Income Smoothing," p.102.

50. Beidleman, "Income Smoothing," p.658.

51. T.R. Archibald, "The Return to Straight-Line Depreciation: An Analysis of a Change in Accounting Method," *Empirical Research in Accounting: Selected Studies*, suppl. to *Journal of Accounting Research* 5 (1967), pp.164-180.

52. R.M. Barefield, and E.E. Comiskey, "The Smoothing Hypothesis: An Alternative Test," *The Accounting Review* (April 1972), pp.291-298.

53. Beidleman, "Income Smoothing," pp.653-667.

54. Copeland, "Income Smoothing," p.101-116.

55. N. Dopuch and D. Drake, "The Effect of Alternative Accounting Rules for Nonsubsidiary Investments," *Empirical Research in Accounting: Selected Studies* (1966), pp.192-219.

56. Gordon, Horwitz, and Meyers, "Accounting Measurement and Normal Growth of the Firm," pp.220-223.

57. Kamin and Ronen, "The Smoothing of Income Numbers," pp.141-153.

58. A. Belkaoui and R.D. Picur, "The Smoothing of Income Numbers: Some Empirical Evidence on the Systematic Differences between Core and Periphery Industrial Sectors," *Journal of Business Finance & Accounting*, 11, 4 (Winter 1984), pp.527-545.

59. W.D. Albrecht, and F.M. Richardson, "Income Smoothing by Economic Sector," *Journal of Business Finance & Accounting* 17, 5 (Winter 1990), pp. 713-730.

60. G. Breton and Jean Piere Chenail, "Une Etude Emperique du Lissage des Benefices dansles Enterprises

Canadiennes," *Comptabilite, Controle, Audit* (March 1997), pp.53-68.

61. J. Kinnunen, E. Kasanen, and J. Nisleanen, "Earnings Management and the Economy Sector Hypothesis: Empirical Evidence on a Converse Relationship in the Finnish Case," *Journal of Business Finance and Accounting* (June 1995), pp.497-520.

62. Ibid., p.498.

63. H. Genay, "Assessing the Condition of Japanese Banks: How Informative Are Accounting Earnings?" *Economic Perspectives* 22, 4 (1998), pp.12-34; M. Sheikkoleslami, "The Impact of Foreign Stock Exchange Listing on Income Smoothing: Evidence from Japanese Firms," *International Journal of Management* 11,2 (1994), pp.737-742.

64. R.E. Bragshaw and A.E.K. Elchni, "The Smoothing Hypothesis and the Role of Exchange Differences," *Journal of Business Finance and Accounting* 16, 5 (1989), pp.621-633; V. Beattie, S. Brown, D. Ewers, B. John, S. Manson, S. Thomas, and M. Turner, "Extraordinary Items and Income Smoothing: A Positive Accounting Approach," *Journal of Business Finance and Accounting* 21, 6 (1994), pp.791-811.

65. S.M. Saudagaran and J.F. Sepe, "Replication of Moses Income Smoothing Tests with Canadian and U.K. Data, A Note," *Journal of Business Finance and Accounting* 23, 8

(1996), pp.1219-1222; Breton and Chenail, "Une Etude Empirique," p.54.

66. S. Chalayer, "Le Lissage des Resultats: Elements Enqlicatifs Avances des Ia Literature," *Comptailite, Controle, Audit*, 2, 1 (1995), pp.89-104.

67. N. Ashani, H.C. Koh, S.L. Tan, and W.H. Wang, "Factors Affecting Income Smoothing among Listed Companies in Singapore," *Accounting and Business Research*, 24, 96 (1994), pp.291-301.

68. K. Fudenberg and J. Tirole, "A Theory of Income and Dividend Smoothing Based on Incumbency Results," *Journal of Political Economy*, 103 (1995), pp.75-93.

69. M.L. DeFond and C.W. Park, "Smoothing Income in Anticipation of Future Earnings," *Journal of Accounting and Economics* 23 (1997), p.1116.

70. Ibid., pp.115-139.

71. A.S. Ahmed, G.J. Lobo, and J. Zhou, "Job Security and Income Smoothing: An Empirical Test of the Fudenberg and Tirole (1995) Model," Working Paper, Syracuse University, October 2000.

72. P.T. Elgers, R.J. Pfeiffer Jr., and S.L. Porter, "Anticipatory Income Smoothing: A Re-Examination," Working Paper, University of Massachusetts, February 2000.

73. Gordon, "Postulatres, Principles and Research in Accounting," p.262.

74. Beidleman, "Income Smoothing," p.655.

75. B. Lev and S. Kunitzky, "On the Association between Smoothing Measures and the Risk of Common Stock," *The Accounting Review* (April 1974), p.268.

76. O.D. Moses, "Income Smoothing and Incentives: Empirical Tests Using Accounting Changes," *The Accounting Review* (April 1987), p.366.

77. J.S. Demski, J.M. Patell, and M.A. Wolfson, "Decentralized Choice of Monitoring Systems," *The Accounting Review* 59 (1984), pp.16-34.

78. B. Trueman and S. Titman, "An Explanation for Accounting Income Smoothing," *Journal of Accounting Research* (Supplement, 1988), pp.127-139.

79. Beattie et al., "Extraordinary Items and Income Smoothing," pp.791-811.

80. G.G. Booth, J. Kallanki, and T. Martikainem, "Post Announcement Drift and Income Smoothing; Finnish Evidence," *Journal of Business Finance and Accounting* 23 (1996), pp.1197-1211.

81. S.G. Badrinath, D. Gay, and J.P. Kale, "Patterns of Institutional Investment, Prudence and the Managerial 'Safety Net' Hypothesis," *Journal of Risk and Insurance* 56 (1989), pp.605-629.

82. S.E. Nichelson, J. Jordan-Wagner, and C.W. Wroton, "A Market Based Analysis of Income Smoothing,"

Journal of Business Finance and Accounting 22, 8 (1995), pp.1179-1193.

83. Z. Wang and T.H. Williams, "Accounting Income Smoothing and Stockholder Wealth," *Journal of Applied Business Research* 10, 3 (1994), pp.96-104.

84. Ibid., p.102.

85. P.K. Chaney, D.C. Jeter, and C.M. Lewis, "The Use of Accruals in Income Smoothing: A Permanent Earnings Hypothesis," *Advances in Quantitative Analysis of Finance and Accounting* 6 (1998), pp.103-135.

86. Ibid., p.131.

87. P.K. Chaney and C.M. Lewis, "Income Smoothing and Underperformance in Initial Public Offerings," *Journal of Corporate Finance* 4 (1998), pp.1-29.

SELECTED REFERENCES

Albrecht, W.D., and F.M. Richardson. "Income Smoothing by Economic Sector." *Journal of Business Finance & Accounting* 17, 5 (Winter 1990), pp.713-730.

American Institute of Certified Public Accountants (AICPA). *Report of the Study Group on the Objectives of Financial Statements*. New York: AICPA, October 1973.

Amihud, Y., J. Kamin, and J. Ronen. "Managerialism and Ownerism in Risk-Return Preferences." Ross Institute of Accounting Research (R.I.A.R.) Working Paper 95-4, New York University, 1975.

Archibald, T.R. "The Return to Straight-Line Depreciation: An Analysis of a Change in Accounting Method." *Empirical Research in Accounting: Selected Studies,* suppl. to *Journal of Accounting Research* 5 (1967), pp.161-180.

Barefield, R.M., and E.E. Comiskey. "The Smoothing Hypothesis: An Alternative Test." *The Accounting Review* (April 1972), pp.291-298.

Barnes, A., J. Ronen, and S. Sadan. "Classificatory Smoothing of Income with Extraordinary Items." *The Accounting Review* (January 1976), pp.110-122.

_____. "The Implementation of Accounting Objectives—An Application to Extraordinary Items." *The Accounting Review* (January 1975), pp.58-68.

Baumol, W.J. *Business Behavior, Value and Growth.* New York: Macmillan, 1959.

Beidleman, C.R. "Income Smoothing: The Role of Management." *The Accounting Review* (October 1973), pp.653-667.

Belkaoui, A., and R.D. Picur. "The Smoothing of Income Numbers: Some Empirical Evidence on the Systematic Differences between Core and Periphery Industrial Sectors." *Journal of Business Finance & Accounting* 11, 4 (Winter 1984), pp.527-545.

Bernard, V.L., and R.S. Stober. "The Nature and Amount of Information Reflected in Cash Flows and Accruals." *The Accounting Review* (October 1989), pp.624-652.

Copeland, R., "Income Smoothing." *Empirical Research in Accounting: Selected Studies,* supple. to *Journal of Accounting Research* 6 (1968), pp.101-116.

Copeland, R., and R. Licastro. "A Note on Income Smoothing." *The Accounting Review* (July 1968), pp.540-545.

Copeland, R., and J. Wojdak. "Income Manipulation and the Purchase Pooling Choice." *Journal of Accounting Research* (Autumn 1969), pp.188-195.

Cushing, B.E. "An Empirical Study of Changes in Accounting Policy." *Journal of Accounting Research* (Autumn 1969), pp.196-203.

Cyert, R.M., and J.G. March *A Behavioral Theory of the Firm.* Englewood Cliffs, NJ: Prentice-Hall, 1963.

Dascher, P.E., and R.E. Malcolm. "A Note on Income Smoothing in the Chemical Industry." *Journal of Accounting Research* (Autumn 1970), pp.253-259.

Eckel, N. "The Income Smoothing Hypothesis Revisited." *Abacus* 17 (June 1981), pp.28-40.

Gordon, M.J. "Postulates, Principles and Research in Accounting." *The Accounting Review* (April 1964), pp.251-263.

Gordon, M.J., B.M. Horwitz, and P.T. Meyers. "Accounting Measurement and Normal Growth of the Firm." In R. Jaedicke, Y. Ijiri, and O. Nielsen (eds.), *Research in Accounting Measurement.* Evanston, IL: American Accounting Association, 1966, pp.221-231.

Hepworth, S.R. "Smoothing Periodic Income." *The Accounting Review* (January 1953), pp.32-39.

Horwitz, B.N. "Comments on Income Smoothing: A Review by J. Ronen, S. Sadan and C. Snow." *Accounting Journal* (Spring 1977), pp.27-29.

Imhoff, E.A., Jr. "Income Smoothing—A Case for Doubt." *Accounting Journal* (Spring 1977), pp.85-101.

_____. "Income Smoothing: An Analysis of Critical Issues." *Quarterly Review of Economics and Business* (Autumn 1981), pp.23-42.

Jeter, D.C., and P.K. Chancy. "An Empirical Investigation of Factors Affecting the Earnings Association Coefficient." *Journal of Business Finance & Accounting* 19, 6 (November 1992), pp.839-863.

Jordan-Wagner, J., and C.W. Wootton. "An Analysis of Earnings in Oil Related Industries." *Petroleum Accounting and Financial Management Journal* (Spring 1993), pp.110-123.

Lamber, R.A. "Income Smoothing as Rational Equilibrium Behavior." *The Accounting Review* 59 (October 1984), pp.604-618.

Lev, B., and S. Kunitzky. "On the Association between Smoothing Measures and the Risk of Common Stock." *The Accounting Review* (April 1974), pp.259-270.

Mason, R.D., and D.A. Lind. *Statistical Techniques in Business and Economics,* 8th ed. Homewood, IL: Irwin, 1993, pp.136-137.

Moses, O.D. "Income Smoothing and Incentives: Empirical Tests Using Accounting Changes." *The Accounting Review* (April 1987), pp.358-377.

O'Hanlon, J. "The Relationship in Time between Annual Accounting Returns and Annual Stock Market Returns in the UK." *Journal of Business Finance & Accounting* 18, 3 (April 1991), pp.305-314.

Ronen, J., and S. Sadan. "Classificatory Smoothing: Alternative Income Models." *Journal of Accounting Research* (Spring 1975), pp.133-149.

_____. *Smoothing Income Numbers, Objectives, Means, and Implications.* Reading, MA: Addison Wesley, 1981.

Strong, N. "Modelling Abnormal Returns: A Review Article." *Journal of Business Finance & Accounting* 19, 4 (June 1992), pp.531-553.

Thorne, D. "The Information Content of the Trend between Historic Cost Earnings and Current Cost Earnings (United States of America)." *Journal of Business Finance & Accounting* 18, 3 (April 1991), pp.289-303.

Trueman, B., and S. Titman. "An Explanation for Accounting Income Smoothing." *Journal of Accounting Research* (Supplement, 1988), pp.127-139.

Zmijewski, M.E., and R.L. Hagerman. "An Income Strategy Approach to the Positive Theory of Accounting Standard Setting/Choice." *Journal of Accounting and Economics* (August 1981), pp.129-149.

Chapter 5:
EARNINGS MANAGEMENT

INTRODUCTION

Managers have the flexibility of choosing between the alternative ways to account for transactions as well as choosing between options within the same accounting treatment. This flexibility, which is intended to allow managers to adapt to economic circumstances and portray the correct economic consequences or transactions, can also be used to affect the level of earnings at any particular time with the objective of securing gains for management and the stakeholders. This is the essence of earnings management, which is the ability to "manipulate" the choices available and make the right choices that can achieve a desired level of income. It is another flagrant example of designed accounting, which is the object of this chapter.

NATURE OF EARNINGS MANAGEMENT

Conceptual Definitions of Earnings Management

Various definitions have been offered to explain earnings management as a special form of "designed" rather than "principled" accounting. Schipper sees earnings management as a purposeful intervention in the external reporting process with the intent of obtaining some private gain.[1] This is assumed to be possible through either a selection of accounting methods within Generally Accepted Accounting Principles (GAAP) or application of given methods in particular ways.[2] Schipper also views earnings management from either an economic (or true) income perspective or an informational perspective. The true income perspective assumes (1) the existence of a true economic income that is distributed by a deliberate earnings management and/or by measurement errors embedded in accounting rules and (2) noisy unmanaged earnings acquire through earnings management new properties in terms of amount, bias, or variance. The informational perspective assumes (1) that earnings are one of the signals used for decisions and judgments and (2) that managers have private information that they can use when they choose elements within GAAP under different sets of contracts that determine their conversation and behavior.[3]

The information perspective in better explicated in the following definitions:

Earnings management occurs when mangers use judgment in financial reporting and in structuring transactions to alter financial reports to either mislead some stakeholders about the underlying economic performance of the company or to influence contractual outcomes that depend on reported accounting numbers.[4]

This definition of Healy and Wahlen focuses on the exercise of judgment in financial reports to (1) either mislead the stakeholders who do not or cannot do earrings management and (2) make financial reports more informative to users. There is therefore a good and bad side to earnings management; the bad side is the cost created by the misallocation of resources, and the good side is made up of the potential improvements in management's credible communication of private information to external stakeholders, improving resource allocation decisions.[5]

Earnings Management as Accrual Management

Basically, the operational definition of earnings management is the potential use of accrual management with the intent of obtaining some private gain. The following relationships are central to an understanding of earnings management as accrual management.

1. Total accruals = Reported net income – Cash flows from operations

2. Total accruals = Nondiscretionary accruals + Discretionary accruals

The general approach for estimating discretionary accruals is to regress total accruals on variables that are proxies for normal accruals. Unexpected accruals or discretionary accruals are considered to be the unexplained (the residual) components of total accruals.

In addition to the use of unexpected accruals and discretionary accruals as a proxy for earnings management, many studies provided evidence on which specific accruals or accounting methods are used for earnings management. Examples of specific accruals proven to be used for earnings management include:

1. Depreciation estimates and bad debt provisions surrounding initial public offers[6]

2. Loan loss reserves of banks[7] and claim loss reserves of insurers[8]

3. Deferred tax valuation allowances[9]

ACCRUALS MODELS

Discretionary accruals models involve first the computation of total accruals. Therefore, total accruals models are presented first, followed by discretionary accruals models.

Total Accruals Models

Two models are generally used for the computation of accruals: the balance sheet approach and the cash-flow approach.

The balance sheet approach for the computation of total accruals (TA) is as follows:

$$TA_t = \Delta CA_t - \Delta Cash_t - \Delta CL_t + \Delta DCL_t - DEP_t$$

where ΔCA_t is the change in the current assets in year t (Compustat No.4); $\Delta Cash_t$ is the change in cash and cash equivalent in year t (Compustat No.1); ΔCL_t is the change in current liabilities in the year t (Compustat No.5); ΔDCL_t is the change in debt included in current liabilities in the year t (Compustat No.34); and DEP_t is the depreciation and amortization expense in year t (Compustat No.14). Based on the findings that studies relying on the traditional balance sheet approach to the measurement of total accruals suffer from potential contamination from measurement of total accruals, Collins and Hribar[10] suggested a straightforward approach that computes total accruals as the difference between net income and operating cash-flow (taken from the cash-flow statement).

Discretionary Accruals Models

Six competing discretionary accruals models are considered in the literature. They are as follows:

The DeAngelo Model

The discretionary portion of accruals in the DeAugelo model[11] is the difference between total accruals in the event year t scaled by total assets (A_{t-1}) and nondiscretionary accruals (NDA_t). The measure of nondiscretionary accruals (NDA_t) rests on last period's total accruals (TA_{t-1}) scaled by lagged total assets (A_{t-2}). In other words:

$$NDA_t = TA_{t-1} / A_{t-2}$$

The Healy Model

In the Healy model[12] the nondiscretionary accruals (NDA_t). are the mean of total accruals TA_t scaled by lagged total assets (A_{t-1}) from the estimation period. In other words:

$$NDA_t = 1/n\Sigma_y (TA_y / A_{y-1})$$

where NDA_t is nondiscretionary accruals in the year t scaled by lagged total assets; n is the number of years in the estimation period; and γ is a year subscript for years (t-n, t-n+1,... t-1) included in the estimation period. The discretionary portion is the difference between the total accruals in the event year scaled by A_{t-1} and NDA_t. The main difference between the DeAngelo model and the Healy model is that NDA follows a random walk process in the DeAngelo model and a mean reverting process in the Healy model.

The Jones Model[13]

The main objective of the Jones model is to control for the effect of changes in the firm's circumstances on nondiscretionary accruals. The nondiscretionary accruals in the event year are expressed as follows:

$$NDA_t = \alpha_1 (1 / A_{t-1}) + \alpha_2 (\Delta REV_t / A_{t-1}) + \alpha_3 (PPE_t / A_{t-1})$$

where NDA_t is the nondiscretionary accruals in the year t scaled by lagged total assets; ΔREV_t is the revenue in the year t less revenues in year t-1; PPE_t is gross property plant and equipment at the end of the year t; A_{t-1} is total assets at the end of the year t-1; and α_1, α_2, α_3 are the firm-specific parameters.

The estimate of the firm-specific parameters is obtained by using the following model in the estimation period:

$$TA_t / A_{t-1} = \alpha_1(1/A_{t-1}) + \alpha_2(\Delta REV_t / A_{t-1}) + \alpha_3(PPE_t / A_{t-1}) + E_t$$

where α_1, α_2, and α_3 represent the OLS estimates of α_1, α_2, and α_3. The residual E_t represents firm-specific discretionary portion of the total accruals.

The variations of the Jones model include:

1. A model that expands the Jones model by adding lagged total accruals and lagged stock returns as two additional explanatory variables.[14]

2. A model that replaces "changes in sales" in the Jones model by "change in cash sales."[15]

The Modified Jones Model

In order to eliminate the conjectured tending of the Jones model to measure discretionary accruals with error when discretion is exercised over revenue recognition, the modified model estimates nondiscretionary accruals during the event period (i.e., during periods in which earnings management is hypothesized) as follows:

$$NDA_t = \alpha_1(1/A_{t-1}) + \alpha_2[(\Delta REV_t - \Delta REC_t)/A_{t-1}] + \alpha_3(PPE_t / A_{t-1})$$

where ΔREC_t is net receivables in year t less net receivables in year $t-1$, and other variables are as in the previous equation.

The estimates of α_1, α_2, and α_3 and nondiscretionary accruals are obtained from the original Jones model, not from the modified model, during the estimation period (in which no systematic earnings management is hypothesized). The difference between the two models is explicated as follows:

Revenues are adjusted for the change in receivables in the event period. The original Jones model implicitly assumes that discretion is not exercised over revenue in either the estimation period or the event period. The modified version of the Jones model implicitly assumes that all changes in the credit sales in the event period result from earnings management. This is based on the reasoning that it is easier to manage earnings by exercising discretion over the recognition of revenue on credit sales than to manage earnings by exercising discretion over the recognition of revenue on cash sales. If this modification is successful, then the estimate of earnings management has taken place through the management of revenues.[16]

The Industry Model

The industry model relaxes the assumption that nondiscretionary accruals are constant over time. Rather than attempting a modeling of the determinants of nondiscretionary accruals directly, the industry model assumes that the variations in the determinants of nondiscretionary accruals are common across firms in the same industry. The model is expressed as follows:

$$NDA_t = \beta_1 + \beta_2 median; (TA_t / A_{t-1})$$

where NDA_t is measured by the Jones model and median; TA_t/A_{t-1} is the median value of total accruals in year t scaled by lagged total assets for all nonsample firms in the same two-digit standard industrial classification (SIC) industry (industry j). The firm-specific parameters B_1 and B_2 are obtained from an ordinary least squires regression in the observation in the estimation period. The ability of the industry model to mitigate measurement error in discretionary accruals hinges critically on the following two factors:

First, the industry removes variation in nondiscretionary accruals that is common across firms in the same industry. If changes in nondiscretionary accruals largely reflect responses to changes in firm-specific circumstances, then the industry model will not extract all nondiscretionary accruals from the discretionary accrual proxy. Second, the industry removes variation in discretionary accruals that is this problem depends on the extent to which the earnings management stimulus is correlated across firms in the same industry.[17]

The Kang and Sivaramakrishnan Model

The Kang and Sivaramakrishnan model[18] relies on an alternative approach that (1) estimates managed accruals using the level rather than change of current assets and current liabilities, (2) includes cost of goods sold as well as other expenses, and (3) does not require the regression to be uncontaminated. The model is expressed as follows:

$$AB_{i,t} = \Phi_0 + \Phi_1[\delta_{1,i}REV_{i,t}] + \Phi_2[\delta_{2,i}EXP_{i,t}] + \Phi_3[\delta_{3,i}GPPE_{i,t}] + u_{i,t}$$

where

$AB_{i,t}$ = accrual balance

= $AR_{i,t} + INV_{i,t} + OCA_{i,t} - CL_{i,t} - DEP_{i,t}$

$AR_{i,t}$ = receivables, excluding tax refunds

$INV_{i,t}$ = inventory

$OCA_{i,t}$ = current assets other than cash, receivables, and inventory

$CL_{i,t}$ = current liabilities excluding taxes and current maturities of long-term debt

$DEP_{i,t}$ = depreciation and amortization

$REV_{i,t}$ = net sales revenues

$EXP_{i,t}$ = operating expenses (cost of goods sold, selling, and administrative expenses before depreciation)

$GPPE_{i,t}$ = gross property plant and equipment

$NTA_{i,t}$ = net total assets

$$\delta_{1,i} = \frac{AR_{i,t} - 1}{REV_{i,t} - 1}$$

$$\delta_{2,i} = \frac{NV_{i,t-1} + OCA_{i,t-1} - CL_{i,t-1}}{EXP_{i,t-1}}$$

$$\delta_{3,i} = \frac{DEP_{i,t} - 1}{GPPE_{i,t-1}}$$

The parameters and δ_1, δ_2 and δ_3 are turnover ratios that accommodate firm-specificity and compensate for the fact that the equation is estimated from a pooled sample.

DETECTION OF EARNINGS MANAGEMENT

Financial reporting allows a distinction between best performing firms and poorly performing firms and better and more efficient resource allocation and financial analysis by stakeholders. The U.S. accounting standards permit managers to exercise judgment in financial reporting, allowing them to provide not only timely and credible information but also relevant information under alternative standards. The situation creates opportunities, however, for "earnings management," in which managers select reporting methods and estimates that do not reflect the firm's true economic picture. This led the chairman of the Securities and Exchange Commission (SEC), Arthur Levitt, to warn about the threat to the credibility of financial reporting created by abuses of "big bath" restructuring charges, premature revenue recognition, "cookie jar" reserves, and write-offs of purchases in process R&D.[19] A good definition of earnings management follows:

Earnings Management occurs when managers use judgment in financial reporting and in structuring transactions to alter financial reports to either mislead some stakeholders about the underlying economic performance of the company or to influence contractual outcomes that depend on reporting accounting numbers.[20]

The detection of earnings management can be accomplished by:[21]

1. The use of simple analytical procedures that can reveal unusual relationships and significant changes in financial statement item relationships.

2. The use of sophisticated models to assess the risk of earnings manipulation such as the use of artificial neural network technology to assess fraud.[22]

3. The use of a profit model that can yield an earnings manipulation index as a linear combination of financial variables to be converted to a "profitability manipulation."

The third technique is of interest to international accounting and can best be illustrated by the Beneish profit model.[23] With the objective of differentiating between GAAP violators and control firms, Beneish uses a number of variables to proxy for (1) the *probability of detection* of the violation by the market through distortions in the financial statements and (2) *incentive/ability* to violate GAAP.

The six financial statement variables designed to capture distortions in financial statement data to assess the probability of detection are:[24]

1. Day's sales in receivables index—measuring whether changes in receivables are in time with changes in sales.

2. Gross margin index—assessing whether gross margins have deteriorated, a negative signal about a firm's prospects.

3. Asset quality index—measuring changes in the risk of assets realization, with an increase to be interpreted as indicating an increased propensity to capitalize and therefore defer costs.

4. Depreciation index—measuring the change in the rate of depreciation.

5. SG&A index—measuring sales general and administrative expense (SG&A) relative to sales with a disproportionate increase in SG&A relative to sales to be considered as a negative signal suggesting loss of managerial cost control or unusual sales effort.

6. Total accruals to total assets—measuring the extent to which earnings are cash-based, with high increases in noncash working capital to reflect possible manipulation.

These variables are defined in Figure 5.1.

The five variables intended to measure a firm's incentives/ability to violate GAAP are:[25]

1. Capital structure, as the incentives to violate GAAP increase with leverage.

2. Prior market performance, as the incentives to violate GAAP increase with declining stock prices.

3. Time listed, as firms may violate GAAP and manipulate earnings at the time of initially going public or shortly thereafter.

4. Sales growth, as high-growth firms may have an incentive to dispel the impression that their growth is decelerating following a stock price drop at the release of bad news.

5. Prior positive accruals decisions, as incentives to violate GAAP may increase if managers attempt to avoid accrual reversals or cannot increase earnings.

The five proxies are operationalized by six variables: leverage, abnormal return, time listed, sales growth index, declining cash sales dummy, and positive accruals dummy. They are defined in Figure 5.1.

The earnings manipulation index, proposed by Beneish probit analysis, is expressed as the following linear combination:

Manipulation Index = - 2.224 + 0.221* (Day's Sales in Receivables Index)

+ 0.102* (Gross Margin Index) + 0.007* (Assets Quality Index)

+ 0.062* (Depreciation Index) + 0.198* (SG&A Index)

- 2.415* (Total Accruals to Total Assets) + 0.040* (Sales Growth Index)

- 0.684* (Abnormal Return) - 0.001* (Time Listed)

+ 0.587* (Leverage Index) + 0.421* (Positive Accrual Dummy)

- 0.413* (Declining Cash Sales Dummy)

The probability of manipulation is then computed by looking up the manipulation index in a standard normal distribution table, where F(x) is the cumulative area under the standard normal distribution. That is:

Probability of earnings manipulation = F (Manipulation Index).

Figure 5.1 Variables Used in the Beneish (1997) Probit Model

Variable	Definition	Hypothesized Relationship with Dependent Variable
Days Sales in Receivables Index	$\dfrac{\dfrac{Receivables_t[2]}{Sales_t[12]}}{\dfrac{Receivables_{t-1}[2]}{Sales_{t-1}[12]}}$	+
Gross Margin Index	$\dfrac{\dfrac{Sales_{t-1}[12] - COGS_{t-1}[41]}{Sales_{t-1}[12]}}{\dfrac{Sales_{t-1}[12] - COGS_{t-1}[41]}{Sales_{t-1}[12]}}$	+
Asset Quality Index	$\dfrac{(1 - \dfrac{CurrentAssets_t[4] + PPE_t[8]}{TotalAssets_t[6]})}{(1 - \dfrac{CurrentAssets_{t-1}[4] + PPE_{t-1}[8]}{TotalAssets_{t-1}[6]})}$	+
Depreciation Index	$\dfrac{\dfrac{Depreciation_{t-1}[14 - 65]}{Depreciation_{t-1}[14 - 65 + PPE_{t-1}[8]}}{\dfrac{Depreciation_t[14 - 65]}{Depreciation_t[14 - 65 + PPE_t[8]}}$	+
SG&A Index	$\dfrac{\dfrac{SG \& AExpense_t[189]}{Sales_t[2]}}{\dfrac{SG \& AExpense_{t-1}[189]}{Sales_{t-1}[2]}}$	+

Figure 5.1 (continued)

Variable	Definition	Hypothesized Relationship with Dependent Variable
Total Accruals to Total Assets		

$$\begin{bmatrix} (\Delta CurrentAss_t[4] - \Delta Cash_t[1] \\ (\Delta CurrentLiab._t[5] - \Delta Short-termdebt_t[34] - \\ Deprec.\& Amort_t[14] - DefferedtaxonEarnings[50] + \\ EquityinEarnings[55] \end{bmatrix}$$?

| Sales Growth Index | Salest[12]/Salest-1[12] | + |

Abnormal Return — Size-adjusted return for a 12-month period ending on the month prior to release of the financial statements. Computed by subtracting from the firm's buy-and-hold return the buy-and-hold return on size-matched, value-weighted portfolio of the firms.

Time Listed — Distance in months between the fiscal year- end and the date the company was first listed on either the New York, American, or NASDAQ exchange.

Leverage

$$\frac{LTD_{t-1}[9] + CurrentLiabilities_{t-1}[5]}{TotalAssets_{t-1}[6]}$$

  –
  +

Positive Accruals   1 if total accruals were positive in the current and prior year; 0 otherwise.

Dummy   +

Declining Sales 1 if cash sales in the current year were lower   –

Dummy   than in the previous year; 0 otherwise.   ?

$CashSales_t = Sales_t - (\Delta\ Receivables_t)$

Annual Compustat data items are provided in brackets.

Δ means the change in the account from previous year.

t refers to the year of interest.

Beneish derives cutoff values based on different relative costs of Type I versus Type II errors. A Type I error occurs when a GAAP violator is incorrectly classified as a control firm. Conversely, a Type II error occurs when a control firm is incorrectly classified as a GAAP violator.

The Beneish model relies on various cutoff values that can delineate different levels of risk of earnings manipulation. A cutoff value of 11.72 percent results in only 45 percent of GAAP violators being correctly classified as violators and only 3.6 percent of the control firms being correctly classified as violators. A cutoff value of 5.99 percent results in 67 percent of GAAP violators being correctly classified and 13.5 percent of control firms being incorrectly classified as violators. A cutoff value of 4.3 percent results in 76 percent of GAAP violators being correctly classified and 20.4 percent of control firms being incorrectly classified as violators. Finally, a cutoff value of 2.94 percent results in 83 percent of GAAP violators being correctly classified as violators and 28.6 percent of control firms being incorrectly classified as violators. Selection of the appropriate cutoff depends on different decision makers and different levels of risk.

THE MISPRICING OF DISCRETIONARY ACCRUALS

There is sufficient evidence showing that investors do correctly use available information in forecasting future earnings performance.[26] It reflects investors' naïve fixation on reported earnings, rather than earnings ability to summarize value-relevant information. Most analysts would argue that since investors tend to "fixate" on reported earnings, examining the accrual and the cash-flow components of current earnings can be used to detect mispriced securities. The reasoning is that accrual and cash-flow components of earnings have different implications for the assessment of future earnings. Accordingly, Sloan[27] investigated whether stock prices reflect information about future earnings contained in the accrual and cash-flow components of current earnings. The persistence of earnings performance was found to depend on the relative magnitudes of the cash and accrual components of earnings.

However, stock prices acted as if investors failed to identify correctly the different properties of the two components of earnings. The market erroneously overestimates the persistence of the accruals component of accrual earnings while underestimating the persistence of the cash-flow component. Accruals also exhibit negative serial correlation or mean reversion tendencies. The end result is that the market responds as if surprised when seemingly predictable earnings reversal occurs in the following year. Similarly, Subramanyam[28] finds that abnormal accruals are positively related to future profitability. Xie[29] provides more evidence on the issue, estimating abnormal accruals after controlling for major unusual accruals and nonarticulation events (i.e., mergers, acquisitions, and divestitures), and found that this refined measure of abnormal accruals, which isolates managerial discretion, is still overpriced. These results are consistent with DeFond and Park's[30] conclusion that the market overprices abnormal accruals because investors underanticipate the future reversal of these accruals.

ISSUES IN EARNINGS MANAGEMENT

1. It is very easy to suspect that earnings management is intended to meet expectations of financial analysts or management (represented by public forecasts of earnings). In fact, there is evidence of (1) managers' taking actions to manage earnings upward to avoid reporting earnings lower than an analyst's forecast,[31] (2) financial analysts' stock recommendation (e.g., buy, hold, and sell) as a good predictor of earnings management,[32] (3) firms in danger of falling short of a management earnings forecast using unexpected accruals to manage earnings upward,[33] and (4) firms with a high percentage of institutional ownership typically not cutting research and development spending to avoid a decline in reported earnings.[34]

2. There are good reasons to suspect that earnings management is intended to influence short-term price performance in various ways.

    1. There is evidence of negative unexpected accruals (income-decreasing) prior to management buyout.[35]

    2. There is evidence of positive (income-increasing) unexpected accruals prior to seasoned equity offering,[36] initial public offers,[37] and

359

stock-financed acquisitions.[38] A reversal of unexpected accruals seems to follow initial public offers and stock-financed acquisitions.

3. Earnings management is due and can persist because of asymmetric information, a condition caused by management's knowing information that they are not willing to disclose. The persistence is due to blocked communication where managers cannot communicate all their private information unless the principal contractually precommits not to use the information against the managers. Incentives for managers to reveal their private information truthfully, created by blocked communication, becomes a key for earnings management.

4. Earnings management takes place in the context of a feasible reporting set and a given set of contracts that determine sharing rules among stakeholders. Both contract sets are endogenous to the earnings management question. As the environment conditions change, both the reporting and contractual sets change, also leading to different forms of earnings management over time. For example, in environmental conditions where accounting data are used in compensation contracts, there is a strong incentive for managers to manage the data used in contracts. As a result the contracting use leads to an internal or stewardship incentive for earnings management.[39]

5. Corporate strategies for earnings management follow one or more of three approaches: (1) choosing

from the flexible options available within GAAP, (2) relying on the subjective estimates and application choices available within the options, and (3) using asset acquisitions and dispositions and the timing for reporting them.[40] Note here that the choices made within GAAP constitute earnings management, while choices made outside GAAP constitute fraud. The court may be the one to decide in some cases whether some management reporting actions that are taken outside the bounds of GAAP are fraud or earnings management.[41]

6. The earnings game—or, more precisely, the quarterly earnings report game—may be a major reason for earnings management.[42] Management is tempted to issue an earnings report that satisfies Wall Street's expectations more than it reflects financial reality. DeGeorge et al.[43] found that quarterly earnings reports that meet analysts' expectations exactly or exceed them by just a penny per share happen more frequently than would be likely in a random statistical distribution, while reports that miss by just a penny occur far less frequently.

7. Earnings management is a result of attempts to exceed thresholds.[44] The three thresholds of importance to executives are:

   1. "to report positive profits, that is, report earnings that are above zero;

2. to sustain recent performance, that is, make at least last year's earnings; and

3. to meet analysts' expectations, particularly the analysts' consumer earnings forecast."[45]

Empirical explorations identified earnings management to exceed each of the three thresholds, with the positive profit threshold predominating.[46]

8. Earnings management may originate as a result of meeting covenants of implicit compensation contracts. Evidence for this thesis takes the following forms:

   1. Divisional managers for a large multinational firm are likely to defer income when the earnings target in their bonus plan will not be met and when they are entitled to the maximum bonuses permitted under the plan.[47]

   2. Firms with caps on bonuses are more likely to report accruals that defer income when that cap is reached than firms that have comparable performance but no bonus cap.[48]

   3. During a proxy contest, incumbent managers exercised accounting discretion to improve reported earnings.[49]

   4. Chief executive officers (CEOs) in their final years in office reduced R&D spending, presumably to increase reported earnings.[50]

9. Earnings management arises from the threat of two forms of regulation: industry-specific regulation and antitrust regulation. The banking and insurance industries are good examples of the existence of regulatory monitoring that is tied to accounting data. As stated by Healy and Wahlen:

> Banking regulations require that banks satisfy certain capital adequacy requirements that are written in terms of accounting numbers. Insurance regulations require that insurers meet conditions for minimum financial health. Utilities have historically been rate-regulated and permitted to earn only a normal return in their invested assets. It is frequently asserted that such regulations create incentives to manage the income statement and the balance sheet variables of interest to regulators.[51]

There is, in fact, a lot of evidence supporting the above hypothesis. For example:

1. Banks that are close to minimum capital requirements tend to overstate loan loss provisions, understate loan write-offs, and recognize abnormal gains on securities portfolios.[52]

2. Financially weak property casualty insurers that risk regulatory attention tend to understate claim loss reserves[53] and engage in reinsurance transactions.[54]

10. Because of the need for government subsidies or protection as well as the fear of antitrust investigations or other political consequences, managers may resort to earnings management. A lot of evidence supports this hypothesis. For example:

1. Firms under investigation for antitrust violations reported income-decreasing abnormal accruals in the investigation years.[55]

2. Firms in industries seeking import-relief tend to defer income in the year of application.[56]

3. Firms in the cable television industry tend to defer earnings during the period of congressional scrutiny.[57]

4. Firms subject to price controls will adjust their discretionary accounting accruals downward to reduce net income and to increase the likelihood of approval of the requested price increase.[58]

5. The magnitude of the discretionary component of the postretirement obligation is negatively associated with the extent of the external regulations and auditor quality.[59]

6. More unionized firms are more likely to use immediate recognition of Statement of Financial Accounting Standards No. 106 on Employer's Accounting for Postretirement Benefits Other than Pensions, which is consistent with incentives to reduce labor negotiation costs.[60]

11. Firm valuation is generally assumed to be one of the targets of earnings management. Various analytical models have tried to explicate that relationship. Gigler[61] considers the case of the firm whose trade-off, when determining which income figure to disclose, is between the cost of acquiring new capital and the cost of competition. An overstatement of disclosed income will occur if the reduced cost of capital were higher than the increased cost of competition. The credibility of the disclosed income is possible because the firm incurs a proprietary cost by misrepresenting income. Chaney and Lewis[62] are concerned with an explanation for why corporate offices manage the disclosure of accounting information. They show that earnings management affects firm value when value-maximizing managers and investors are asymmetrically informed. Eilifsen et al.[63] add to the previous two models by showing that if taxable income were linked to accounting income, there will exist an automatic safeguard against manipulation of earnings, a claim also made by Johansson and Ostman.[64]

CONCLUSION

Earnings management is a deliberate choice of specific accounting techniques or options intended to secure a given level of earnings and some private gains. This chapter explicated the nature of earnings management from both a conceptual and operational viewpoint, described the different accruals models used in the literature to estimate discretionary or unexpected accruals, presented a model for the detection of earnings management, and discussed various issues, theoretical and empirical, on the form of designed accounting.

NOTES

1. K. Schipper, "Earnings Management," Accounting Horizons (December 1989), p.92.

2. Ibid., p.93.

3. Ibid.

4. P.N. Healy and J.N. Wahlen, "A Review of the Earnings Management Literature and Its Implications for Standard Setting," *Accounting Horizons* 4 (1999), p.368.

5. Ibid, p.369.

6. S.H. Toeh, T.J. Wong, and G. Rao, "All Accruals during Initial Public Offerings Opportunistic?" *Review of Accounting Studies* 3 (1998), pp.173-208.

7. C. Liu, S. Ryan, and J. Wahlen, "Differential Valuation Implications of Loan Across Banks and Fiscal Quarters," *The Accounting Review* (January 1997), pp.133-156.

8. K.R. Petroni, "Optimistic Reporting in the Property Casualty Insurance Industry," *Journal of Accounting and Economics* 18 (1994), pp.157-179.

9. G. Visvanathan, "Deferred Tax Valuation Allowances and Earnings Management," *Accrual of Financial Statement Analysis* 3 (1998), pp.6-15.

10. D.W. Collins and S.P. Hibar, "Errors in Estimating Accruals; Implications for Empirical Research," Working paper, University of Iowa, 1999.

11. L. DeAngelo, "Accounting Numbers as Market Valuation Substitutes: A Study of Management Buyouts of Public Shareholders," *The Accounting Review* 62, 3, pp.431-453.

12. P.M. Healey. "The Effects of Bonus Schemes in Accounting Decisions," *Journal of Accounting and Economics* 7 (1989), pp.85-107.

13. J. Jones, "Earnings Management during Import Relief Investigations," *Journal of Accounting Research* 29 (1991), pp.193-228.

14. R.D. Beneish, "Detecting GAAP Violations: Implications for Assessing Earnings Management among Firms with Extreme Financial Performance," *Journal of Accounting and Public Policy* 16 (1997), pp.271-309.

15. R.D. Beneish, "Discussion of All Accruals during the Initial Public Offerings Opportunistic?" *Review of Accounting Studies* 3 (1998), pp.209-221.

16. P.M. Dechow, R.G. Sloan, and A.P. Sweeney, "Detecting Earnings Management," *The Accounting Review* 70 (1995), p.199.

17. Ibid., p.42.

18. S.-H. Kang and K. Sivaramakrishnan, "Issues in Testing Earnings Management and an Instrumental Variable Approach," *Journal of Accounting Research* 33 (1995), pp.353-366.

19. From Chairman Levitt's remarks in speech entitled "The Numbers Game," delivered at New York University on September 28, 1998.

20. Healy and Wahlen, "A Review of Earnings Management Literature," p.368.

21. C.I. Wiedman, "Instructional Case: Detecting Earnings Manipulation," *issues in Accounting Education* 14, 1 (February 1999), pp.157-158.

22. B.P. Green and J.H. Choi, "Assessing the Risk of Management Fraud through Neural Network Technology," *Auditing: A Journal of Practice and Theory* 16 (1997), pp.14-28.

23. Beneish, "Detecting GAAP Violations," pp.271-309.

24. Wiedman, "Instructional Case: Detecting Earnings Manipulation," p.160.

25. Ibid., p.161.

26. J. On and S. Penman, "Financial Statement Analysis and the Prediction of Stock Returns," *Journal of Accounting and Economics* 11 (1998), pp.159-330; V. Bernard and J. Thomas, "Evidence That Stock Prices Do Not Fully Reflect the Implications of Current Earnings for Future Earnings," *Journal of Accounting and Economics* 13 (1990), pp.305-340; L.A. Maines and J.R. Hand, "Individuals' Perceptions and Misperceptions of the Time Series Properties of Quarterly Earnings," *The Accounting Review* (July 1996), pp.317-336.

27. R.G. Sloan, "The Stock Prices Fully Reflect Information in Accruals and Cash Flows about Future Earnings," *The Accounting Review* 3 (1996), pp.289-315.

28. K.R. Subramanyam, "The Pricing of Discretionary Accruals," *Journal of Accounting and Economics* 12 (1996), pp.149-282.

29. H. Xie, "The Mispricing of Abnormal Accruals," *The Accounting Review* 76 (2001), pp.357-373.

30. M.L. DeFond and C.W. Park, "The Reversal of Abnormal Accruals and the Market Valuation of Earnings Surprises," *The Accounting Review* (July 2001), pp.145-176.

31. D., Burgstahler and M. Eames, "Management of Earnings and Analyst Forecasts," Working paper, University of Washington, 1998.

32. J. Abarbanell and R. Lehavy, "Can Stock Recommendations Predict Earnings Management and Analyst's Earnings Forecast Errors?" Working paper, University of California at Berkeley, 1998.

33. R. Kaznik, "On the Association between Voluntary Disclosure and Earnings Management," *Journal of Accounting Research* 37 (1999), pp.57-82.

34. B. Bushee, "The Influence of Institutional Investors on Myopic R&D Investment Behavior," *The Accounting Review* 3 (1998), pp.305-333.

35. S. Perry and T. Williams, "Earnings Management Preceding Management Buyout Offers," *Journal of Accounting and Economics* 15 (1992), pp.157-179.

36. S.H. Teoh, I. Welch, and T.J. Wong, "Earnings Management and the Long-Term Market Performance of Initial Public Offerings," *Journal of Finance* (December 1998), pp.1935-1974.

37. S.H. Teoh, I. Welch, and T.J. Wong, "Earnings Management and the Post Issue Performance of Seasoned Equity Offerings," *Journal of Financial Economics* (October 1998), pp.63-99; S.H. Teoh, I. Welch, T.J. Wong, and G. Rao, "Are Accruals during Initial Public Offerings Opportunistic?" *Review of Accounting Studies* 3 (2000), pp.175-208.

38. M. Erickson and S.W. Wang, "Earnings Management by Acquiring Firms in Stock for Stock Mergers," *Journal of Accounting and Economics* 97 (April 1999), pp.149-176.

39. R. Dye, "Earnings Management in an Overlapping Generations Model," *Journal of Accounting Research* 26 (1998), pp. 195-235.

40. P.R. Brown, "Earnings Management: A Subtle (and Troublesome) Twist to Earnings Quality," *The Journal of Financial Statement and Analysis* (Winter 1999), p.62.

41. Ibid.

42. H. Collingwood, "The Earnings Game," *Harvard Business Review* (June 2001), pp.65-74.

43. F. DeGeorge, J. Patel, and R. Zeckhauser, "Earnings Management to Exceed Thresholds," *Journal of Business* 72 (1999), pp.1-33.

44. Ibid.

45. Ibid.

46. Ibid.

47. F.A. Guidry, A. Leone, and S. Rock, "Earnings-based Bonus Plans and Earnings Management by Business Unit Managers," *Journal of Accounting and Economics* 26 (1999), pp.113-142.

48. R. Holhausen, D. Larker, and R. Sloan, "Annual Bonus Schemes and the Manipulation of Earnings," *Journal of Accounting and Economics* 19 (1995), pp.29-74.

49. L.E. DeAngelo, "Managerial Competition, Information Costs, and Corporate Governance: The Use of Accounting Performance Measures in Proxy Contests," *Journal of Accounting and Economics* 10 (1988), pp.3-36.

50. P. Dechow and R.G. Sloan, "Executive Incentives and the Horizon Problem: An Empirical Investigation," *Journal of Accounting and Economics* 14 (1991), pp.51-89.

51. P.M. Healy and J.M. Wahlen, "A Review of the Earnings Management Literature and Its Implications for Standard Setting," *Accounting Horizons* 4 (1999), pp.365-383.

52. S. Moyer, "Capital Adequacy Ratio Regulations and Accounting Choices in Commercial Banks," *Journal of*

Accounting and Economics 12 (1990), pp.123-154; M. Scholes, G.P. Wilson, and M. Wolfson, "Tax Planning, Regulatory Capital Planning, and Financial Reporting Strategy for Commercial Banks," *Review of Financial Studies* 3 (1990), pp.625-650; A. Beatty, S. Chamberlain, and J. Magliolo, "Managing Financial Reports of Commercial Banks: The Influence of Taxes, Regulatory Capital and Earnings," *Journal of Accounting Research* 33 (1995), pp.231-261; J. Collins, D. Shackelford, and J. Wahlen, "Bank Differences in the Coordination of Regulatory Capital, Earnings and Taxes," *Journal of Accounting Research* 2 (1995), pp.263-291.

53. K.R. Petroni, "Optimistic Reporting in the Property Casualty Insurance Industry," *Journal of Accounting and Economics* 15 (1992), pp.485-508.

54. R. Adiel, "Reinsurance and the Management of Regulatory Ratios and Taxes in the Property-Casualty Insurance Industry," *Journal of Accounting and Economics* 22, 1-3 (1996), pp.207-240.

55. S. Cahan, "The Effect of Anti-Trust Investigations on Discretionary Accruals: A Refined Test of the Political Cost Hypothesis," *The Accounting Review* 67 (1992), pp.77-95; S. Makar and P. Alam, "Earnings Management and Antitrust Investigations: Political Costs over Business Cycles," *Journal of Business Finance and Accounting* 5 (1998), pp.701-720.

56. J.J. Jones, "Earnings Management during Import Relief Investigations," *Journal of Accounting Research* 29 (1991), pp.193-228.

57. K.G. Key, "Political Cost Incentives for Earnings Management in the Cable Television Industry," *Journal of Accounting and Economics* 3 (1997), pp.309-337.

58. S. Lim and Z. Matolcsy, "Earnings Management of Firms Subject to Produce Price Controls," *Accounting and Finance* 39 (1999), pp.131-150.

59. S. Asthana, "The Impact of Regulatory and Audit Environment on Managers' Discretionary Accounting Choices: The Case of SFAS No. 196," *Accounting for the Public Interest* 1 (2001), pp.23-96.

60. J. D'Souza, J. Jacob, and K. Ramesh, "The Use of Accounting Flexibility to Reduce Labor Renegotiation Costs and Manage Earnings," *Journal of Accounting and Economics* 30 (2001), pp.187-208.

61. F. Gigler, "Self-Enforcing Voluntary Disclosures," *Journal of Accounting Research* 32 (1994), pp.24-40.

62. P.K. Chaney and C.M. Lewis, "Earnings Management and Firm Valuation under Asymmetric Information," *Journal of Corporate Finance* 1 (1995), pp.319-345.

63. A. Eilifsen, K.H. Knivsfla, and F. Saettem, "Earnings Manipulation: Cost of Capital versus Tax," *The European Accounting Review* 8 (1999), pp.481-491.

64. S.E. Johansson and L. Ostman, *Accounting Theory—Integrating Behavior and Measurement* (London: Pitman, 1995), p.201.

SELECTED REFERENCES

Adiel, R. "Reinsurance and the Management of Regulatory Ratios and Taxes in the Property-Casualty Insurance Industry." *Journal of Accounting and Economics* 22, 1-3 (1996), pp.207-240.

Ayers, B.C. "Deferred Tax Accounting under SFAS No. 109: An Empirical Investigation of Its Incremental Value-Relevance Relative to APB No.11." *The Accounting Review* 73, 2 (1998), pp.195-212.

Beatty, A., S. Chamberlain, and J. Magliolo. "Managing Financial Reports of Commercial Banks: The Influence of Taxes, Regulatory Capital and Earnings." *Journal of Accounting Research* 33, 2 (1995), pp.231-261.

Beaver, W., C. Eger, S. Ryan, and M. Wolfson. "Financial Reporting, Supplemental Disclosures and Bank Share Prices." *Journal of Accounting Research* (Autumn 1989), pp.157-178.

Beneish, M.D. "Detecting GAAP Violation: Implications for Assessing Earnings Management among Firms with Extreme Financial Performance." *Journal of Accounting and Public Policy* 16 (1997), pp.271-309.

_____. "Discussion of: Are Accruals during Initial Public Offerings Opportunistic?" *Review of Accounting Studies* 3 (1998), pp.209-221.

Burgstahler, D., and I. Dichev. "Earnings Management to Avoid Earnings Decreases and Losses." *Journal of Accounting and Economics* 24 (1997), pp.99-126.

_____. "Incentives to Manage Earnings to Avoid Earnings Decreases and Losses: Evidence from Quarterly Earnings." Working paper, University of Washington, 1998.

Burgstahler, D., and M. Eames. "Management of Earnings and Analysts' Forecasts." Working paper, University of Washington, 1998.

Bushee, B. "The Influence of Institutional investors on Myopic R&D Investment Behavior." *The Accounting Review* 73, 3 (1998), pp.305-333.

Cahan, S. "The Effect of Antitrust Investigations on Discretionary Accruals: A Refined Test of the Political Cost Hypothesis." *The Accounting Review* 67 (1992), pp.77-95.

Collins, J., D. Shackelford, and J. Wahlen. "Bank Differences in the Coordination of Regulatory Capital, Earnings and Taxes." *Journal of Accounting Research* 33, 2 (1995), pp.263-291.

DeAngelo, L.E. "Managerial Competition, Information Costs, and Corporate Governance: The Use of Accounting Performance Measures in Proxy Contests." *Journal of Accounting and Economics* 10 (1988), pp.3-36.

DeAngelo, L.E., H. DeAngelo, and D. Skinner. "Accounting Choices of Troubled Companies." *Journal of Accounting and Economics* 17 (January 1994), pp.113-143.

Dechow, P. "Accounting Earnings and Cash Flows as Measure of Firm Performance: The Role of Accounting Accruals." *Journal of Accounting and Economics* 18, 1 (1994), pp.3-40.

Dechow, P., and R.G. Sloan. "Executive Incentives and the Horizon Problem: An Empirical Investigation." *Journal of Accounting and Economics* 14 (1991), pp.51-89.

Dechow, P., R.G. Sloan, and A.P. Sweeney. "Causes and Consequences of Earrings Manipulation: An Analysis of Firms Subject to Enforcement Actions by the SEC." *Contemporary Accounting Research* 13, 1 (1996), pp.1-36.

Defeo, V., R. Lamber, and D. Larcker. "The Executive Compensation Effects of Equity-for-Debt Swaps." *The Accounting Review* 54 (1989), pp.201-227.

Defond, M.L., and J. Jiambalvo. "Debt Covenant Effects and the Manipulation of Accruals." *Journal of Accounting and Economics* 17 (January), pp.145-176.

Degeorge, F., J. Patel, and R. Zeckhauser. "Earnings Management to Exceed Thresholds." Working paper, Boston University, 1998.

Dye, R. "Earnings Management in an Overlapping Generations Model." *Journal of Accounting Research* 6 (1988), pp.195-235.

Erickson, M., and S-W. Wang. "Earnings Management by Acquiring Firms in Stock for Stock Mergers." *Journal of Accounting and Economics* 27 (April 1999), pp.149-176.

Foster, G. "Briloff and the Capital Market." *Journal of Accounting Research* 17 (Spring), pp.262-274.

Gaver, J., K. Gaver, and J. Austin. "Additional Evidence on Bonus Plans and Income Management." *Journal of Accounting and Economics* 18 (1995), pp.3-28.

Guay, W.A., S.P. Kothari, and R.L. Watts. "A Market-Based Evaluation of Discretionary Accrual Models." *Journal of Accounting Research* 34 (Supplement, 1996), pp.83-105.

Healy, P.M. and E. Engel. "Discretionary Behavior with Respect to Allowances for Loan Losses and the Behavior of Security Prices." *Journal of Accounting and Economics* 22 (1996), pp.177-206.

Healy, P.M., and M. McNichols. "The Characteristics and Valuation of Loss Reserves of Property-Casualty Insurers." Working paper, Stanford University, 1998.

Healy, P.M., and J.M. Wahlen, "A Review of the Earnings Management Literature and Its Implications for Standard Setting." *Accounting Horizons* 4 (1999), pp.365-384.

About the Au1thor

Ahmed Riahi-Belkaoui is an Emeritus Professor at the University of Illinois at Chicago. Previously, he was named University Scholar at UIC (2000-2003), CBA Distinguished professor (1996-2001), 2000 AAA outstanding International Educator, and founding editor of the Review of Accounting and Finance (2001-2007). His research interests embrace socio-economic accounting, behavioral accounting, and social and political issues. He has published over 76 books, including Social Status Matters, and Qaddafi: The man and His Policies, and more than one hundred eighty articles and reviews in major journals.

PUBLICATIONS

Books by Professor Ahmed Riahi-Belkaoui

1. FINANCIAL ACCOUNTING: THEORY AND ANALYSIS:

   1. **Elements de Theorie Comptable** (Universite d'Ottawa, Departement de Commerce, 1974), pp.168

   2. **Corporate Financial Disclosure in Canada,** Canadian Certified General Accountants Association,

Monograph #1 (Vancouver, British Columbia, 1978), pp.63. (Co-author: Alfred Kahl).

3. **Theorie Comptable,** (Presses de L' Universite du Quebec, Quebec, 1984). 2nd Edition, pp. 416.

4. **Accounting Theory,** (International Thomson Publishing, 2004) 5th Edition.(Translated in Chinese, Habasa Indonesian, and Korean) pp.598

5. **Industrial Bond Ratings and the Rating Process** (Greenwood Publishing Group, 1983): 198.

6. **Inquiry and Accounting: Alternative Methods and Research Perspectives** (Greenwood Publishing Group, 1987): 355.

7. **Determinants of Executive Compensation: Ownership, Performance, Firm Size and Corporate Diversification** (Greenwood Publishing Group, 1991): 163. Co-author: Ellen Pavlik.

8. **Accounting in the Dual Economy** (Greenwood Publishing Group, 1991): 159.

9. **Accounting: A Multiple Paradigm Science** (Greenwood Publishing Group, 1996)

10. **Accounting Theory: The Australian** Edition (Harcourt, 3rd Edition, 2005)

11. **Critical Financial Accounting Problems: Issues and Solutions** (Greenwood Publishing Group, 1998)

12. **Research Perspectives in Accounting** (Greenwood Publishing Group, 1997)

13. **Financial Analysis and the Predictability of Important Economic Events** (Greenwood Publishing Group, 1998)

14. **Capital Structure: Determination, Evaluation and Accounting** (Greenwood Publishing Group, 1999)

15. **Earnings Measurement, Determination, Management and Usefulness** (Greenwood Publishing, 1999)

16. **Accounting and the Investment Opportunity Set** (Greenwood Publishing Group, 2000).

17. **Financial Statements: Present and Future Scope** (Greenwood Publishing Group, 2001).

18. **Accounting: Principled or Designed** (Greenwood Publishing, 2003)

19. **Wealth and Value Added** (Booksurge, 2010)

2. PUBLIC POLICY AND PUBLIC INTEREST ACCOUNTING.

1. **Socio-Economic Accounting** (Greenwood Publishing Group, 1984).

2. **Public Policy and the Problems and Practices of Accounting** (Greenwood Publishing, 1985): 204.

3. **The Coming Crisis in Accounting** (Greenwood Publishing Group, 1989).

4. **Accounting for Corporate Reputation** (Greenwood Publishing Group, 1992). Co-author: Ellen Pavlik.

5. **Morality in Accounting** (Greenwood Publishing Group, 1992).

6. **Human Resource Valuation** (Greenwood Publishing Group, 1995). Co-author: Janice Monti-Belkaoui.

7. **Fairness in Accounting** (Greenwood Publishing Group, 1996) Co-author: Janice Monti-Belkaoui.

8. **Corporate Social Awareness and Financial Outcomes** (Greenwood Publishing Group, 1999).

9. **Wealth and Value Added: Reporting, Analysis and Taxation** (Book surge, 2010)

3. MANAGEMENT ACCOUNTING.

1. **The Conceptual Foundations of Management Accounting** (Addison Wesley, 1980).

2. **Cost Accounting : A Multidimensional Emphasis** (Dryden Press, 1983): 636.

3. **The Learning Curve: A Management Tool** (Greenwood Publishing Group, 1986): 245.

4. **Handbook of Management Control Systems** (Greenwood Publishing Group, 1986): 355.

5. **Quantitative Models in Accounting: A Guide to Practitioners** (Greenwood Publishing, 1987): 355.

6. **Handbook of Cost Accounting: Theory and Techniques** (Greenwood Publishing Group, 1991): 381.

7. **The New Foundations of Management Accounting** (Greenwood Publishing Group, 1992).

8. **Quality and Control: An Accounting Perspective** (Greenwood Publishing Group, 1992).

9. **Organizational and Budgetary Slack** (Greenwood Publishing Group, 1994)

10. **The Nature and Consequences of the Multidivisional Structure** (Greenwood Publishing, 1995)

11. **Long term Leasing: Accounting, Evaluation and Consequences** (Greenwood Publishing, 1998)

12. **Advanced Management Accounting** (Greenwood Publishing, 2001)

13. **Evaluating Capital Projects** (Greenwood Publishing 2001)

4. INTERNATIONAL ACCOUNTING

1. **International Accounting** (Greenwood Publishing Group, 1985).

2. The New Environment in International Accounting: Issues and Practices (Greenwood Publishing Group, 1987): 220.

3. **Judgement in International Accounting** (Greenwood Publishing Group, 1990).

4. **Multinational Management Accounting** (Greenwood Publishing Group, 1991).

5. **Multinational Financial Accounting** (Greenwood Publishing Group, 1991).

6. **Value Added Reporting: The Lessons for the U.S.** (Greenwood Publishing Group, 1992): 165.

7. **Accounting for the Developing Countries** (Greenwood Publishing Group, 1994)

8. **International and Multinational Accounting** (Dryden Press, 1994).

9. **The Cultural Shaping of Accounting** (Greenwood Press, 1995).

10. **The Linguistic Shaping of Accounting** (Greenwood Press, 1995).

11. **Performance Results in Value Added Reporting** (Greenwood Publishing Group, 1996).

12. **Multinationality and Financial Performance** (Greenwood Publishing Group, 1996).

13. **Disclosure Adequacy: Nature and Determinants** (Greenwood Publishing Group, 1997).

14. **Significant Current Issues in International Taxation** (Greenwood Publishing Group, 1998).

15. **The Nature, Estimation and Management of Political Risk** (Greenwood Publishing Group, 1998).

16. **Performance Results of Multinationality** (Greenwood Publishing Group, 1999).

17. **Value Added Reporting and Research** (Greenwood Publishing Group, 1999).

18. **The Role of Corporate Reputation for Multinational Firms: Accounting, Organizational and Market Considerations** (Greenwood Publishing Group, 2001)

19. **International Financial and Managerial Accounting** (Greenwood Publishing Group, 2002)

20. **Multinationality: Earnings, Efficiency and Market Considerations** (Greenwood Publishing Group, 2002).

21. **International Accounting and Economic Development: The Interactions of Economic and Social Indicators** (Greenwood Publishing, 2002)

5. BEHAVIORAL ACCOUNTING

    1. **Behavioral Accounting** (Greenwood Publishing Group, 1989).

    2. **Human Information Processing** (Greenwood Publishing Group, 1989).

    3. **Behavioral Management Accounting** (Greenwood Publishing Group, 2002).

6. SOCIOLOGY

    1. **Social Status Matters** (Booksurge, 2009).

7. FICTION, NONFICTION AND OTHER BOOKS

    1. **Sherazade and Her Two Lovers** (Catskill, NY: Press-Tige Publishing Inc 1996)

    2. **Like a Firm Knot in a Rope** (Chicago; A.D. Press, 2001) also published as .**The Baraka** (Catskill, NY: Press-Tige Publishing Inc 1997)

    3. **Qaddafi: The Man and His Policies** (Gower House, Ashgate Publishing, Avebury, 1996)

    4. **So You Want to Be Sophisticated** (Catskill, NY: Press-Tige Publishing Inc 1997)

5. **Conjugal Blues** .(Catskill, NY; Press-Tige Press, 1999)

6. **Shame** (Huntington, WV: Aegina Press, 1998)

7. **Written (Mektoub)** (Thomaston, ME: Century Press, 2000).

8. **Putting on the Dog: Guide to American Sophistication** (American Literary Press, 2004)

9. **Love and Obsession in Chicago** (Booksurge. 2009)

10. **On The Wrong Side of Chicago Beds: A Tale of Lust, Art and Politics** (Booksurge. 2009)

11. **How to Become Sophisticated** (Booksurge. 2009)